DEAR ONES AT HOME

DEAR ONES AT HOME

Letters from Contraband Camps

selected and edited by

HENRY L. SWINT

Vanderbilt University Press   Nashville   1966

INTRODUCTION

*T*o many members of the Federal armies of invasion during the Civil War, the plight of the freedmen seemed hardly less distressing than that of the slave. Ignorant, homeless, ragged, and hungry, the Negroes by thousands flocked to the Union camps, creating grave problems of supply and sanitation and even hampering military movements. General Benjamin F. Butler, who first "confiscated" the escaping slaves as "contraband of war," not only employed the Negroes as laborers but also established relief stations and schools for them. A similar problem confronted General Ulysses S. Grant in the Mississippi Valley, where "hordes" of Negroes threatened to swamp his armies and delay his advance. In an effort to cope with the situation, Grant appointed John Eaton Superintendent of Freedmen in that area.[1] When General Thomas W. Sherman and Admiral Samuel F. DuPont took the Sea Islands in November 1861, they assumed control over and responsibility for almost 10,000 Negroes. Sherman proposed that labor superintendents and teachers be sent to the Islands to deal with the situation. Because the Sea Island cotton was especially valuable in international trade, the control of the plantations and their cotton had been placed in the hands of Secretary of the Treasury Salmon P. Chase. With a long history of service in the abolitionist cause, Chase was sympathetic and understanding. With the approval of President Lincoln, he sent Edward L. Pierce, who already had worked with Butler's contrabands at Fortress Monroe, to the Sea Islands. Pierce's calls to his Boston friends for help in the tremendous task which he found there brought about

1. Benjamin F. Butler, *Autobiography and Personal Reminiscences of Major-General Benj. F. Butler: Butler's Book,* pp. 256–263; Benjamin F. Butler, *Private and Official Correspondence of General Benjamin F. Butler,* I, 102–103, 104–108, 112–114; V, 610 ff.; John Eaton, *Grant, Lincoln, and the Freedmen,* pp. 11–12. See also Robert S. Holzman, *Stormy Ben Butler.*

the organization of the Boston Educational Commission, which developed into the New England Freedmen's Aid Society.[2]

Stories of the degradation, misery, and want in which the freedmen lived touched the hearts of thousands of men and women throughout the North, and "freedmen's aid societies" were hastily organized in many towns and cities, especially in New England, where many "branch societies" affiliated with the New England Freedmen's Aid Society. Similar organizations were operating in New York, Philadelphia, Cincinnati, Baltimore, and other cities before 1863, in addition to such older organizations as the American Missionary Association, a veteran in the field of abolition, and the relatively new Freedmen's Aid Society of the Methodist Church. These societies were responsible for extensive work among the freedmen. Thousands of boxes, bales, and barrels of clothing, tools, seed, utensils, and other necessities were sent South, and Lyman Abbott, secretary of the American Union Commission, estimated in 1867 that over five million dollars already had been contributed for the relief and education of the freedmen.[3]

By the end of Reconstruction several thousand teachers were working in schools in every part of the South, closely cooperating with the Freedmen's Bureau in educating the Negroes and caring for their immediate physical wants. Teachers were selected and their salaries were paid by the societies; their transportation was supplied by the Bureau, and often the schools in which they worked were rented by the Bureau or built by Bureau funds. There was a Superintendent of Education in each state, responsible both to the Assistant Commissioner of the Bureau for the state and to John Watson

2. [Edward L. Pierce], "The Contrabands at Fortress Monroe," *Atlantic Monthly*, VIII (November 1861), 626-640; [Pierce], "The Freedmen at Port Royal," *Ibid*, XII (September 1863), 291–315. See also Port Royal Correspondence, The National Archives, and Guion G. Johnson, *A Social History of the Sea Islands with Special Reference to St. Helena Island, South Carolina*. For a detailed and accurate description of this venture see Willie Lee Rose, *Rehearsal for Reconstruction: The Port Royal Experiment*.

3. J. H. Parmelee, "The Freedmen's Aid Societies," United States Department of the Interior, Bureau of Education, *Bulletin*, No. 38 (1916), I, 296. See also Richard B. Drake, "The American Missionary Association and the Southern Negro" (Unpublished Ph.D. Dissertation, Emory University, 1957).

Alvord, Superintendent of Education of the Bureau. Teachers reported regularly to the state officials and to Superintendent Alvord; their reports comprise a rich and relatively unused source for the study of the history of the period. In addition to these reports, many teachers agreed to write regularly to the society which sponsored them, giving an account of their experiences. Undoubtedly many teachers frequently wrote to members of their families, also, so that there are three manuscript sources for the study of the work and experiences of the teachers—the manuscripts of the Bureau of Refugees, Freedmen, and Abandoned Lands; letters to sponsoring societies; and private family letters. Unfortunately, few large collections of family letters have been published. Such collections as the *Letters and Diary of Laura M. Towne: Written from the Sea Islands of South Carolina; Letters from Port Royal: Written at the Time of the Civil War;* and *The Journal of Charlotte L. Forten* are rare but revealing documents.[4]

Not all the friends of the freedmen considered the work of relief and education to be merely humanitarian effort, for to them the Civil War was the culmination of a righteous crusade, a grand step toward the complete nationalization of the country. The Negro must be freed, the slave oligarchy crushed, King Cotton dethroned, and the "face of Southern society" changed. When the Federal armies had triumphed, barbarism would be cleansed from the land and "one common civilization" would "cover the land as waters cover the sea."[5] The complete regeneration of the South, its full integration into the nation, would not be accomplished by armed force alone.

4. *Letters and Diary of Laura M. Towne: Written from the Sea Islands of South Carolina,* ed. Rupert S. Holland; Elizabeth Ware Pearson (ed.), *Letters from Port Royal Written at the Time of the Civil War; Journal of Charlotte L. Forten,* ed. Ray A. Billington. See also W. H. Pease, "Three Years Among the Freedmen: William C. Gannett and the Port Royal Experiment," *Journal of Negro History,* XLII (April 1957), 98–117; Richard L. Morton (ed.), " 'Contrabands' and Quakers in the Virginia Peninsula, 1862–1869," *The Virginia Magazine of History and Biography,* LXI (October 1953), 419–429; Morton (ed.), "Life in Virginia, by a 'Yankee Teacher,' Margaret Newbold Thorpe," *ibid.,* LXIV (April 1956), 180–207; Morton (ed.), "A 'Yankee Teacher' in North Carolina, by Margaret Newbold Thorpe," *The North Carolina Historical Review,* XXX (October 1953), 564–582; and Mary Ames, *From a New England Woman's Diary in Dixie in 1865.*

5. *Independent,* October 22, 1868.

The prejudice of the Southern white man and the ignorance of both white and Negro would keep the Negro in slavery and the South out of its proper relationship to the rest of the nation. The Negro must be given the suffrage and protected in its use; he must be taught to vote correctly and thus to assist in the moral, as well as the social and political, regeneration of the South.

The extreme Radicals in Congress hoped to use the Freedmen's Bureau as the instrument for a thoroughgoing social and economic revolution. Others, with that reliance upon education which has characterized American thought since early in the nineteenth century, considered the school the proper instrument of social and moral regeneration. Only through the school could the North hope to "redeem and regenerate the South"; only through the school could the South be induced to accept the moral code of the North. There were enough teachers in New England to "make a New England out of the South." The schoolroom must supplant the fort, the primer and the Bible, the rifle and the sword. "Schools and the Gospel" were to be the new "munitions of war," munitions more effective than "Congressmen, President, Supreme Court, or U.S. Army." [6]

But it was accounts of the conditions in which the freedmen in Virginia lived, rather than any militant concept of reform or renovation, which so stirred two intelligent and highly educated Friends of Worcester, Massachusetts, Lucy and Sarah Chase, that they determined to work among the freedmen. Their father, Anthony Chase, was a successful and highly respected businessman, treasurer of Worcester County for thirty-five years; their mother was a daughter of Pliny Earle, who developed the manufacture of machine-card cloth in the United States. Anthony Chase was a man of varied interests. He and his brother-in-law, John M. Earle, were merchants; Chase was part-owner of the *Massachusetts Spy*, a newspaper

6. George R. Bentley, *A History of the Freedmen's Bureau; Nation*, August 24, 1865, p. 225; *Freedmen's Journal*, January 1, 1865, p. 3, quoted in Luther P. Jackson, "The Educational Efforts of the Freedmen's Bureau and Freedmen's Aid Societies in South Carolina, 1862–1872," *The Journal of Negro History*, VIII (January 1923), 28; *Independent*, September 24, 1868; *Congregationalist*, April 9, 1868; *American Missionary*, X (July 1866), 145–146.

published in Worcester; he was agent of the Worcester and Providence Boating Company, an official in a Worcester insurance company and in various banks, and one of the founders of the Worcester Lyceum.[7]

Lucy and Sarah shared with several brothers and sisters the intellectually stimulating life of a prosperous Quaker family in a New England town of many educational and cultural advantages. To the reforming fervor of New England in the period 1830–1860, they added the humanitarian interest and the sacrificial spirit of Quaker abolitionists. The echoes of the opening guns of the Civil War carried to their ears the groans of the wounded, and they immediately proposed to become nurses with the army. For some reason, however, they chose work among the freedmen instead. Perhaps they were deterred by the cautious and eloquently expressed reluctance of their father; perhaps their brothers objected to their becoming nurses. In December 1862 they received from LeBaron Russell, Secretary of the Boston Educational Commission, their appointments as teachers. They were instructed to report to Brigadier General Ludovickus Viele, Military Governor of Norfolk, for work on Craney Island. Each received $20 with which to purchase an "outfit"; their salary was to be $25 per month.[8]

The two sisters began work at Craney in January 1863. There they found about 2,000 Negroes, homeless, hungry, and

7. Charles Nutt, *History of Worcester and Its People*, III, 339; *Dictionary of American Biography*, IV, 27.

8. L. B. Russell, Letter of Appointment, December 22, 1862, Chase MSS; Egbert L. Viele, December 6, 1862, Chase MSS. Governor John A. Andrew of Massachusetts sent Russell, a veteran abolitionist, to Port Royal to examine conditions among the Negroes there. See Henry G. Pearson, *The Life of John Andrew*, II, 67 and 82. Egbert Ludovickus Viele of New York was a graduate of the United States Military Academy. He was commissioned brigadier general of volunteers in 1861. When Union forces occupied Norfolk in May 1862, Major General John E. Wool appointed Viele military governor of Norfolk. He was relieved from duty in Virginia in March 1863 and was ordered to Cleveland, Ohio, in August. See U. S. War Department, *The War of the Rebellion: A Compilation of the Official Records of the Union and Confederate Armies*, ser. I, vol. 11, part 1, pp. 634–635; ser. I, vol. 18, p. 567; ser. I, vol. 29, part 2, p. 91. See also Francis Heitman, *Historical Register and Dictionary of the United States Army*, I, 987; and Thomas J. Wertenbaker, *Norfolk: Historic Southern Port*, p. 239 *et seq.* Craney Island lies at the mouth of the Elizabeth River in Norfolk harbor across Hampton Roads from Newport News.

cold, presenting to the staid and somewhat sheltered Quaker spinsters a condition of shocking crudity and depravity. With feverish intensity they worked from dawn to dark—handing out clothing and shoes, patching and sewing, visiting the aged and the ill. They encouraged the industrious, scolded the improvident and the lazy, heard complaints, wrote tender letters for lonely maidens, and at every opportunity (even while teaching sewing) taught the three R's. Through it all, too, they marveled at the strangeness of life in Virginia and at the characteristics of their dusky charges. Lucy, keenly observant and highly articulate, sent lengthy letters to the "Dear Ones at Home" relating the strange experiences which Sarah and she were sharing. Their letters apparently are one of the few sources of information on life among the freedmen in what the twentieth century would call "displaced persons" camps.

Nominally the sisters were under military jurisdiction but their letters show quite clearly that Sarah and Lucy were independent of any rigid control. They worked as labor superintendents as well as teachers, for they hoped to train the Negroes in skills which might be put to use in the coming industrialization of the South. Although the battlefront often was only a few miles away, they continued their work of relief and education. In May 1863 the Negroes were moved to the mainland. The sisters accompanied them, opened schools, and were invaluable aids to the military officers in their efforts to get the freedmen to work on the "government farms."

The summer of 1864, which the Chase sisters spent at home, was a period of cool relief from the heat of Virginia, but the call of conscience was too strong and in the fall they returned to Norfolk. In January 1865 Lucy went to Roanoke Island, where a large number of contrabands presented a great opportunity. In March 1865 they went to Washington, where they visited friends and attended the inaugural ball—"the most magnificent by far ever seen in the U.S.," according to Lucy. A few days after the fall of Richmond, both sisters were members of a party which almost deliriously surveyed the capital of the fallen Confederacy. They then spent five weeks inspecting the schools of the District of Columbia.

The heat of summer drove them to the pleasantly cool, tree-lined streets of Worcester, but again in the fall they volunteered for active duty. Not content to work in quieter areas where schools already had been established and the edge of desire dulled, they asked for commissions to work in Georgia. They returned to Norfolk in November and, with several colleagues, arrived in Savannah in December 1865. A long journey into the hinterland followed, and five difficult months at Columbus, Georgia, apparently convinced the sisters that they conscientiously could serve in less difficult areas. During the summer they sought positions in Washington, Charleston, or Florida, but Sarah, in poor health and with failing eyesight, evidently decided not to risk the dangers of service in the field again. Lucy, the stronger of the two, was then forty-four years old (fourteen years older than Sarah), but she continued to teach until 1869, working in Richmond, Virginia, and Lake City, Florida.

The sisters spent the years between 1870 and 1875 in travel in Europe. Apparently their interest in the Negro, in reform, and in intellectual activity continued to absorb their time and energy after their return to Worcester. Lucy spent much time painting and sculpturing, wrote an occasional article, and encouraged the Negroes of the area in their economic and cultural activities. Sarah, despite her failing sight, planned to translate literary masterpieces, requesting the advice of the learned Elihu Burritt in her search for suitable selections.

In 1902, no doubt impelled by her unquenchable curiosity and an undimmed desire to help suffering mankind, Lucy visited Cuba. But her activity was nearing its end; she died in Worcester in 1909. Sarah died a few years later.

The intelligence, education, and devotion to high ideals of these two Quaker sisters shine through their letters. Lucy's keen eye and facile pen have preserved a unique picture of life in the contraband camps. Her ready wit and bluntness add to the charm of her letters.

The letters are strikingly modern. Sincere and determined teachers and missionaries patiently endure hardship; some are threatened, some are killed. Some Negroes eagerly grasp the key to the door of opportunity—the schoolbook; others appear to be unreliable and shiftless. Teachers, schools, and Negroes are involved in politics, both local and national. Racial prejudice is strong. Negroes are maltreated by Northerners and Southerners. The Misses Chase, the sentimental friend of the freedman and the prejudiced white, both Northern and Southern, the politician pandering to prejudice, and the multi-faceted Negro—all are familiar figures in mid-twentieth-century America. Even the phrases used in the 1860s appear in television, radio, and newspapers a century later.

In editing the letters I have attempted to preserve the original spelling, although the calligraphy has made the task almost impossible at times and errors undoubtedly have been made. A few changes in punctuation have been made in the interest of clarity. Some repetitious and wholly irrelevant material has been omitted. Several individuals have not been identified and some obscure geographical points have not been precisely fixed. In some cases the identification of a person mentioned in the letters probably is impossible now; in others, the principle of diminishing returns seems to be applicable—the grain of fact often may not be worth the labor involved in winnowing the large mass of material in which it lies hidden. This, obviously, is a matter of personal opinion. To those who disagree with me and who disapprove of the process which I have followed, I can only say that I hope that the pleasure which they may derive from reading the letters may be adequate recompense.

The collection is in the library of the American Antiquarian Society, Worcester, Massachusetts. I wish to thank the members of the staff of that institution for their courteous helpfulness. I am especially indebted to the late Dr. Clarence S. Brigham, who made the manuscripts available to me under the most convenient and satisfactory arrangement. I am also indebted to various members of the staffs of the Harvard University Library and of the National Archives. Miss Clara Brown, formerly Reference Librarian of the Joint University Libraries, Nashville, Tennessee, cheerfully responded to my numerous requests for assistance. I am grateful to the Institute for Research in the Social Sciences, Vanderbilt University, for generous financial assistance in the preparation of the manuscript.

I wish also to thank the staff of Vanderbilt University Press, especially Miss Elizabeth Chase. Conventional expressions of gratitude for the assistance of Mrs. Seymour Samuels, Jr., would be quite inadequate. My wife and daughters not only have assisted me in the preparation of the manuscript but have patiently endured the inevitable accompaniments of such an endeavor.

CRANEY ISLAND

Philadelphia, 4th mo. 20th '61

*M*y dear good Father,

I write in some haste to make a request of thee. Will thee please send me by return of mail, thy consent to my going South with the nurses?

I feel fully prepared in every way: Thy consent only is wanted, and I *depend* upon it.

Do not be anxious—if I go—for I shall be no more away from thee than I am here: and Death may be as near when I sit quietly at home, as any where else.

I have enjoyed this life and have no fears for the next. Danger is always near though we may not always see it.

All last night I dreamed most pleasantly of Home.

No one out of the family need know of my going. I shall write again when I receive an answer. I *must* go—and I trust the [sic] will give the desired reply.

Farewell dear Father
Farewell!

My love to all.

[unsigned—SARAH]

13

Salem. Wednesday evening.
[April, 1861]

My very dear Sarah

Thy welcome letter was received this morning, but house cleaning prevented my answering it for the noon mail. Since then its contents have been thought of most seriously and earnestly. If we could only talk. But that being impossible, written words must answer. George and I have talked it all over. Loving thee so dearly as we do and knowing how conscientious thee is and how beautifully thee takes up any cross that duty places in thy path, we give thee our heartiest sympathy. We have no objection to make, *provided* thee has thought of these things: First, with whom thee is to go; under whose leadership, as to their standing character, etc. Secondly, The contingency of what may happen to thyself, and Thirdly, whether, all thy family consenting, thee is *sure* it is best to go. We say this, not to prevent thee from going, but, if thee is strong in thy decision, to add to thy strength by our loving interest All our fears, as well as all our hopes. What do Pliny,[1] Lucy, and Lizzie say? Our Heavenly Father's blessing shall be thine dear Sarah, and Mother is perhaps now repeating that Bible verse of thine, "Many daughters have done virtuously, but *thou excellest them all.*" "Yea, though I walk through the shadow of death, I will fear no evil, for Thou art with me; Thy rod and Thy staff, they comfort me."

Why did I make the remark about thy having a friend of thy own age? Because, from thy letters, I found thee visited and associated with the choicest spirits, but with so much more mature minds, that, although knowing how advantageous it was in most respects, still there was another side. It seems to me, that each year of our lives, should be spent by itself,

1. Pliny Earle Chase, oldest child of Anthony and Lydia Earle Chase. Born at Worcester in 1820, he was graduated from Harvard in 1839, after which he taught in Leicester, Worcester, and Philadelphia. In 1871 he became Professor of Natural Science at Haverford College. He published texts in arithmetic, articles in many scientific journals, and more than 100 papers in the *Proceedings* of the American Philosophical Society. His work in mathematics and science brought him recognition as one of America's prominent scientists. He died at Haverford in 1886. *D.A.B.*, IV, 27; *National Cyclopedia of American Biography*, VI, 53-54.

gaining gradually, but surely. If our companions are much more experienced, it is good, but unless we have our own age for intimate friends also, we lose a great deal. That may not be clear to thee, but it is to me in theory and I could explain it better if we met.

It is most ten o'clock and I must write a line to Charles.[2] This more serious matter has driven news telling from my mind, and as there are no questions to be answered, I must say a good night, with love to Lucy and to thyself, in Which George unites.

We shall want to hear again from thee. Wherever thee goes my own, darling, precious sister "His hand shall lead thee and His right hand uphold thee."

Write soon to thy affectionate sister ELIZA.[3]

It was too bad for me not to receive your fall letters. I think so much of them that it is a great loss for me to miss.

Worcester 4-28. 1861

My very dear Sarah

Thy letter of the 20th inst came to hand last night. What can I say in answer to it? The responsibility is a fearful one —I wish it was not laid upon me. I feel, sometimes, in reference to the present unnatural war, almost willing to step forth in defence of the stars and stripes of our, hitherto, happy and blessed country—the most favored land the sun ever shone upon; but then I consider the present crisis has come upon us without my agency——If true quakerism had prevailed, slavery would have been abolished long ago, and now, instead of brother raising the hand against brother, we should be realizing the fruition of perfect love and har-

2. Charles Augustus Chase, a brother. After graduation from Harvard he worked with the Boston *Daily Advertiser* until early in the Civil War period when he returned to Worcester and succeeded his father as treasurer of Worcester County. He was active in business in his native city, holding office in several financial and commercial firms. He, like his father, was active in civic affairs, serving as an officer of the local art society, the public library, and the Antiquarian Society. He wrote several articles on local history. Nutt, *History of Worcester*, III, 339-340.

3. Eliza Earle Chase was the fourth child and second daughter of Anthony Chase. *Ibid.*, 339.

mony. But let that pass, and to the subject of thy letter. The idea is creditable to thy humanity——It is an impulse of our holiest nature to feel for others woe, and aleviate [*sic*] the suffering fellow creatures when it is in our power. I know there is a panacea in woman's soft and delicate hand, in her look of compassion and soothing words unknown to the science of surgery and medicine. We are all here for a purpose—we have missions, and if we are true to ourselves we shall seek to know what that mission is, and knowing, endeavour to fulfill it. Whatever our suffering, whatever our privation may be, if we come out of it with the consciousness of having been instrumental in saving a brother, a husband, a father, or soothing their pain in the last struggle of human existence, we feel abundantly compensated. We feel that in as much as we have done something, as it were, for the least of Gods creatures, we have done it to Christ. Thus, probably, thou hast reasoned. Hast thou looked on the other picture? Art thou equal to the incidents of the camp—to witnessing mangled bodies and scenes of agony and suffering which no tongue or pen can describe? Is thy experience, thy constitution and health equal to all this? If not, why dost thou go? I disapprove of all wars and fightings, but not of the office of good samaratan [*sic*]. When I meet with suffering humanity I never stop to inquire the cause until I have relieved it, if it is in my power. In the army, in addition to the wounded, there is the sickness incident to man in other employments, requiring careful nursing, hence the necessity of experienced nurses. Is there not an abundant supply of women old in experience ready and willing to do this, without pressing into the service a young, dutiful and beautiful daughter, as dear to her father as his own life, and very precious to numerous brothers and sisters?

I am ignorant of the situation of nurses in the army. Are they cared for and not exposed to danger and insults? This being certain, and thy brothers and sisters approving of thy plans, leave thy father out of the question, why should he interfere with a daughters wishes, "who is of age and can answer for herself" and is responsible for neglect of duty? Ponder the whole matter well, and before deciding, enter into the closet of thy soul and having shut the door, pray to our Father in Heaven to be guided and influenced by the Holy spirit, and thy prayers will be answered.

I shall write to Pliny tomorrow——we are all well——If duty separates us, the prayers of a father who has suffered, mentally, in his pilgrimage thro life, thus far, more than is known or can be, will accompany thee.

Farewell

FATHER

Boston 9 Pinckney St

Nov. 9. [1862]

Your letter of the 1st should, my dear Miss Chase, have received an earlier answer; but I had left Georgetown before it was written, & it only reached me here at home last week. I wish I could give you as definite information as you need; but you shall have my best. Caroline Andrews of Newburyport was driven off the ground in Washington by the Tract Assoc.[1] which regarded the Educational Commission of Boston as poaching on their preserves when that Comm sent her, brave & lovely, to bless with her presence, counsel, & help the dusky fugitives who were sheltered by Government in Washington. I believe you could have no better success there.

My time since June has been so entirely engrossed in the care of the sick & wounded that I have known but little of the condition of the Contrabands at Alex. but I must think that the care which could be given them by two energetic, intelligent & refined women would be a great blessing to them. If Mr Wyman would cordially co-operate & our Educ. Comm would authorize your action, the undertaking seems to me feasible. Could you not come to Boston to say & hear more than letters will carry? On one side squalid wretchedness and ignorance—on the other the high civilization of heart & intellect reaching out a willing hand to comfort & to elevate! No exertion that I can make shall be wanting to forward your

1. Probably the American Tract Society, organized in 1825, which was very active in publishing and distributing religious and reform literature. *Dictionary of American History.*

plan; I will wait to hear from you before introducing it to the Committee on Teachers (of which I am one) of the Educ. Comm. Perhaps we shall send more ladies as teachers to Port Royal—how does that attract you? The success there has been beyond all calculation, even beyond what seemed possible.[2]

Then as to helping the soldiers, there is nothing so much wanted in the hospitals as the service of *ladies,* using that noun in its broadest sense; intelligent refined, judicous, [*sic*] whole-hearted women are needed as the soldiers' protectors & friends in the Hospitals against the avarice & heartlessness & injustice to which the sick & the wounded are often exposed. This, their *incidental* work, is of a most valuable service. I speak from 16 months' knowledge of Surgeons General, Inspectors, Surgeons in Charge, Stewards, &c.

Do come to 9 Pinckney St., & I will be at home when you call, if you will name some hour (*not next Thursday aft.*) I should be sorry that ability as you offer should fail to find the right field of action. My grief at finding myself obliged, by weakness, to leave my gracious work of nursing induces me to encourage you to enter upon one, or the other.

Yrs

HANNAH E STEVENSON [3]

2. In March 1862 a number of teachers and labor superintendents went from New England to Port Royal to teach the freedmen and to supervise the cultivation of long-staple cotton. The teachers were selected and supported by the Boston Educational Commission, apparently the first of the many aid societies, unions, and commissions organized to work among the freedmen. Because of the prominence of many of the sponsors and the great publicity which the work received, the "Port Royal Experiment" became widely known. See Swint, *The Northern Teacher in the South,* pp. 15–16, 44–45; Rose, *Rehearsal for Reconstruction,* Chapter II; Johnson, *Social History of the Sea Islands;* Port Royal Correspondence, The National Archives; and J. H. Chapin, Brief History of the New England Branch of the American Freedmen's Union Commission, in the records of the Bureau of Refugees, Freedmen, and Abandoned Lands, The National Archives.

3. Secretary of the Teachers Committee of the Boston Educational Commission and the same committee under its successor, the New England Freedmen's Aid Society.

Dear Miss Chase,

．．．．．

There are [in Alexandria] now some 700 or 800, receiving govt aid, in the way of shelter, rations, clothing &c; and the field of usefulness is large among the women & children. Capt Wyman has applied for leave to build a large barrack, like the one we saw in Washington, & I trust it may soon be done. That is the only way of securing health, order, decency & improvement. Miss Wilbur received from Capt W. authority to act as visitor & superintendent and she will this week begin her ministry. She would be very glad to have your assistance & sympathy—if you see your way clear to maintenance here. But the Government, for various reasons, will give no other aid than a daily ration,—as they are anxious to report to Congress & the country that the Freedmen *are self-supporting* & cost the Nation nothing. And I regret that our Society has no means to do more, than they are already doing. It seems right & fair to you & to all, that you should know exactly the present state of affairs. You must make a bold venture, independently, if you come. But Miss Wilbur will heartily welcome your cooperation.

Yrs truly—w. h. channing.[1]

Craney Island—Jan 15 '63

To our folks at home

Sarah and I are comfortably established at Dr. Brown's,[1] in a house somewhat lately occupied as head-quarters by Union officers; but built, and occupied by rebels, while Norfolk was in the hands of the Enemy. Like other head-quarters of the

---

1. William H. Channing, Unitarian clergyman and active reformer. He was a nephew of William Ellery Channing. He was a Fourierist, an abolitionist, and an agent on the Underground Railroad. During the war he worked with the Sanitary Commission. *D.A.B.*, IV, 9–10.

---

1. Orlando Brown, Surgeon, 18th Massachusetts Infantry and 29th Massachusetts Infantry; Colonel, 24th U. S. Colored Infantry, and Brevet Brigadier General, Volunteers. He was Superintendent of Negro Affairs under Benjamin Butler, Edward O. C. Ord, and Henry W. Halleck, and was Assistant Commissioner of the Freedmen's Bureau for Virginia in 1866, and from March 1867 to January

Enemy, the house puts to shame our Army Architecture. It is made really picturesque by wooden awnings over the doors and windows. (The awnings and overhanging roofs are designed as protections against the heat.) There are six rooms upon the ground floor and three in the attic. Floors, walls, and ceilings are of Southern pine, giving an air of substantial comfort to the house, which plaster and paper cannot impart. I am writing by the light of a candle held in a candle-stick from Genl Harrison's estate.[2] From the window near me can be seen the estate of one of the Wise family;[3] and a few moments ago I sat writing in the room with (Colored) members of the Washington and Custis families; pretty, and neat girls, and good sewers. I asked them if they could read, they all answered, "No" and very eagerly took their first lesson from me. Waifs of rebel furniture from the region roundabout, beautify the parlor, which wears a carpet with becoming pride. A large room and two or three bureau-drawers, have been placed at our disposal, and we have the promise of a stove.

We see, as yet, no prospect of starving. Chickens, wild-duck, oysters, and Baltimore mutton have already found their way to our table. Relishes, and other light luxuries, do not abound here.

1, 1869. Sympathetic toward the Negroes, he attempted to understand them and to assist them in making the transition from slavery to freedom. Apparently able and conscientious, he was free from the emotional extremes which characterized some of his colleagues. He strongly believed the education of the Negro to be of vital importance but he also emphasized the necessity of cleanliness, industry, and frugality. *Official Records of the Union and Confederate Armies*, ser. III, vol. 3, pp. 1139–1144; Heitman, *Register*, I, 253; Paul S. Peirce, *The Freedmen's Bureau: a Chapter in the History of Reconstruction*, p. 174; Oliver Otis Howard, *Autobiography*, II, 283–284; John A. Carpenter, *Sword and Olive Branch: Oliver Otis Howard*, passim, and William T. Alderson, Jr., "The Influence of Military Rule and the Freedmen's Bureau on Reconstruction in Virginia, 1865–1870" (Unpublished Ph.D. Dissertation, Vanderbilt University, 1952). See also Brown's many letters and reports in the manuscripts of the Bureau of Refugees, Freedmen, and Abandoned Lands, in The National Archives.

2. Probably Berkeley, or Harrison's Landing, built by Benjamin Harrison, the father of the "signer." General George B. McClellan had his headquarters here during July and August, 1862. Writer's Program, *Virginia: A Guide to the Old Dominion*, p. 631. See also Clifford Dowdey, *The Great Plantation*.

3. Probably that of W. F. Wise, which lay between Craney and Cornick Creeks, which flow into the West Branch of the Elizabeth River. *Official Records of the Union and Confederate Armies*, Atlas, plate XXVI.

. . . . .

Craney island is six miles from Norfolk, with which it twice holds daily communication, at government expense. At one point, the river is fordable to the near shore, which is sparsely peopled. There the Dr finds his milk, and there but five miles distant he found rebel roofs for his negro barracks. Government aids him very grudingly [*sic*]. He says he has to fight for every stick of wood which he obtains for the poor creatures. He says Genl Dix[4] lends a ready ear to his every request, and aids him in every way within his power; but his ability is restrained. The island comprises 12 acres. No opportunity is offered for extended agricultural labors, but the Dr designs planting to the very water's edge. He hopes, when we have made the women good sewers, to get an army contract for their needles, and, then, with the mines of wealth in his oyster beds he hopes his community will be self-supporting. He says the N.Y. friends have promised to build him a school-house, and a meeting house. He was delighted with the representatives of that body, with Wm Cranwell particularly. He thought him particularly agreeable, and very handsome. The negroes at Newport News, and other districts in this neighborhood, were recently gathered here, by government order, and, many of them coming as they did from their Master's plantations, feel their deprivations, and look upon Craney Island as a slave-pen. The grumblers see no reason why they could not have been left as they were; ask passes to Norfolk, and elsewhere, that they may find work and wages; but the masses see the promise of the dawn. Dr. B. says it is nonsense to talk of the negroes as being (now) a superior race, and already fitted for freedom. He says they cannot, as yet, compete, by any means, with white laborers; and to talk of them after the manner of ignorant, enthusiastic philanthropists, is giving undue praise to the barbarous teachings of slavery. We are to give them a *chance!* which they have never had.

At one of their prayer-meetings, which we attended, last night, we saw a painful exhibition of their barbarism. Their

4. Major General John Adams Dix, a veteran of the War of 1812, who reentered service in 1861 as a major general, volunteers. He resigned in 1865. Heitman, *Register*, I, 375.

religious feeling is purely emotional; void of principle, and of no practical utility. The Dr says they will rise from prayer and lie or steal, if the way opens therefor. The brother who knelt in prayer had the friendly sing-song. His sentences were incoherent, and aimless—"ohuh Lorder! this afternoonugh, hear our prayerer! this afternoonugh! And dontuh let usuh take helluh by stormuh! this afternoonuh! in heavenuh! Save usuh our father in thisuh trying worlduh, and let usuh go upuh to theeuh for Jesus Christ's sakuh amen!"

They must know what is *right!* in order to worship aright the God of right. Robbed of their all, in slavery, they felt, instinctively, a right to what their masters said they had no claim; and, checked in all directions, they let their passions loose in all directions. The Dr. has a guard of ten soldiers to restrain the negroes from trespassing upon the neighboring shores. He says one of the negroes swore, for a quarter of an hour, that he had not stolen a hog while all the time the hog was in a bag upon his back.

A boy named Friday gave him his name. "Friday is it," said the Dr. "Yaas, Sir, Friday," was the reply. "You said your name was Saturday, did you?" said the Dr. "Yaas Sir." "You are sure its Saturday, are you?" "Yaas, Sir." He says the habit of the Negro is to say whatever he thinks his interrogator wishes him to say. Dr. Brown has already won my respect and faith; he seems to me to be in every way fitted for the difficult task he has undertaken; and I am sure he will inspire as well as direct whatever efforts Sarah and I shall make.

He sees the negro as he is, and knowing his wants can administer to them. I fully believe he possesses the power to touch the secret springs of their consciousness with such skill that success will follow his efforts to direct, control, and educate them. He is intelligent, honest, and kind; and he truly loves his work. His wife also is intelligent and pleasant and heartily sympathizes with her husband in his work—though she is unable to cooperate with him as three young children claim her care. Dr Brown served in the army for a year or more as a surgeon, but he has no time for practice on the island. A kind-hearted Army surgeon, with an assistant, is established here, and one or two other white men are employed as heads of different departments of labor. At twilight, the heads of families flock to the wharf to obtain their daily allowance of wood, which they carry, either balanced on their heads, or swinging under their arms. In squads of ten, led by a colored man, they go for their wood, and for their rations (of meal, bread, bacon, and coffee.) Each hundred reports through a colored leader to the white head of the body, who, in his turn, reports to Dr Brown.

Two women died this morning. Dr B. says the old rate of mortality amongst the negroes was ¼ of 1 pr cent, but it is reduced here to 1/14th. In the lying-in hospital is an old woman who has a certificate from her master testifying to her superior qualities as a mid-wife. She says she only lacks five of making seven hundred children she has helped into the world. Slaves from Hampton are expected daily. (Government negroes) Genl Viele unfortunately told the Negroes, before the issuing of the President's Proclamation, that they were free; and he was obliged to take back his gift. Many negroes, in this neighborhood, came to the Dr to ask him if there was no hope for them. He replied, "What should you do if you knew that you could become free by going to yonder point?" They took the hint, and three hundred went to Fortress Monroe.

Tonight a negro man lifted his hat to Sarah and said "Missuh, please Missuh, may I ask a favor of you, Miss-uh?" Sarah expected to be begged for clothing, but when she said, "Yes," the man said, "Will you be so kind, Miss, as to make me a copy of a b c?" I just heard one of the women in the kitchen, say "You can make a hundred out of any number under the sun, over and over again. Two and two and two, ever so many twos, or any number you have a mind." Her listeners seemed incredulous, and inquired, "Fives? Sixes?" The women are mostly field-hands, and are entirely ignorant of domestic duties. Mrs Brown took one into her kitchen, as a cook, at Newport News (by the way, the woman came in through the window) and found, after having ordered her to make a fire, that she had made it in the oven. Dr Brown designs serving uncooked rations in the future. Skill, neatness, economy and self-independence will be developed thereby. Sarah and I shall rule the roost, for awhile. The Dr expects great moral results from the inevitable calling into exercise of dormant in-born faculties, which must result from any, the smallest degree of independence.

There are now eighteen hundred negroes here; and they continue to arrive. They come almost wholly destitute of clothing, covered with vermin, and extremely ignorant, and incompetent for noble, self-originating action of mind or body, uneducated in principle too as they are they ought to enter freedom through the path of moral restraint. The Dr gives them short practical lessons whenever he drops into one of their prayer meetings. The stir and bustle of a village is about us on this little island. It is but a few weeks since the Dr came here from Newport News, and he has already given giant energies to a giant work. He is now building stables for his mules, adding a wing to his hospital, building more barracks, and looking into the future for his people. Many of the negroes are in tents left here by the soldiers. One brick chimney serves for two tents; the fire-place is in the center of the tent, a mere earth-trench, with an underground flue. We made entrance-calls at several tents, last night. No candles are furnished the negroes, but their soft pine fires give a cheerful light; and, when any woman wishes to sew, she lights a pitch-pine knot, or burns cloth in heated fat. In some of the barracks we found the men and women playing games; in others singing and dancing; and in the meeting we attended, we heard really good music. "I belong to the band, Hallelujah!" is very musical. When singing that exultant, joyful air, the women swayed back and forth, and their dusky faces, and uncouth figures seemed born of the flaming fire-light. Cloudy, Shorty, and Volunteer are already acquaintances of ours; but we are not as yet like *skilled in negro-talk. Mrs. B's little girl said last night, "They have dun called Father to supper."*

Private. I must tell you a word about our journey here. The Superintendent of the Contrabands at Alexandria, a hard-faced man whom Sarah fancies to be earning his way to heaven by *sufferance*—both on his own part, and on the part of all who come in contact with him—found us out, and entertained? us all the way to Baltimore. He was a whirlwind of complaints. He complained of the drunken idle rascals who live on the public treasury; complained of Miss Wilbur, who pays six dollars a week for her board, and does nothing because she's afraid of the smallpox, complained of Friends, saying [that] when the N.Y. Committee visited Alexria [*sic*] he was sick and they could not see things in a favorable light. He said, "You know that Quakers always think if anything's the matter of any-body they are certainly going to die." He pumped us very hard, but found our wells dry. Finally, he found that we were friends. "Oh! that's very nice, You are just the ones to go out." But, we remembered the tone in which he had spoken of friends just before. Narrow and sectarian the man seemed to be.

At Baltimore we were obliged to get passes of the Provost Marshal——"Guards" were (in them) requested to let us pass "without interruption or molestation." We visited a well-ordered hospital in Baltimore. The soldier who conducted us about it said Union feeling is as strong in Baltimore as abolition feeling is at the North. The two I suppose he thought could not be united. On a dirty boat we went to Fortress Monroe, were snubbed by the black, haughty chambermaid; and were told in the morning by a very polite mailagent that "He was very sorry we retired so early, as he had some very nice whiskey-punch prepared for us." But two or three other ladies were on board. There were many military and naval officers on board. Fortress Monroe with Bank's [5] outlying fleet, the Rip-raps,[6] the water alive with wild ducks; the air made white as by falling snow flakes. With an English

5. Nathaniel P. Banks, Massachusetts politician, became major general, volunteers, in 1861. He served on the Virginia front in 1861–62 and in 1863 went to New Orleans to relieve Benjamin Butler. See Fred H. Harrington, *Fighting Politician: Major General N. P. Banks.*

6. A small island between Old Point Comfort and Willoughby's Point; the Federal forces fortified the island. *Official Records of the Union and Confederate Armies,* Atlas, plate XVIII, no. 1; U. S. Navy Department, *Official Records of the Union and Confederate Navies in the War of the Rebellion,* ser. I, vol. 8, map.

l entering the port as a prize all speaking of war
seat of war impressed me as I was never impressed

. . . . .

(LUCY)

Thos will forward to Eliza, Eliza to Charles, Charles will lend
to our contraband society, and then keep.

[January 20, 1863]

Dear home-folks:

Everything about us indicates that we are in the Army!
We realize, too, that we are somewhat exposed to the dangers
incident to "the state of war." A few days ago, Norfolk was
excited by the rumor that Corcoran's legion [1] was cut up,
and that the rebels were marching upon Suffolk. Dr Brown
said if the report was true nothing could save us and we
must be prepared to leave for the Fortress at a moments
notice. The rebels are now within fifteen miles of us in one
direction, within twenty in another, and within thirty in
another. We are under the protection of Heaven alone; neither
Fortress Monroe nor Norfolk avail us, except as places of
refuge; and if the rebels once reach Suffolk, they can easily
march across the country, ford the river, and regain possession of their much coveted fugitives. The Dr doubled the guard
the night of the alarm, stationed them on the ramparts that
they might keep peace without, instead of within—according
to wont,—and gave us a *long candle!* in place of our short
one! to take to our room!

From the roof of our one-storied house we can see Norfolk,
Portsmouth, Newport News, Hampton, and Sewall's Point.
Indeed, we can see them all from the ground. The Merrimac

1. A unit organized and commanded by Michael Corcoran. It also was known
as "The Irish Legion." Corcoran, a native of Ireland, was a hot-tempered and
impetuous officer. He began his career in the New York militia and rose to the
rank of brigadier general, volunteers. The Legion was active in the battles
around Suffolk and Norfolk. Corcoran was accidentally killed in December 1863.
National Cyclopedia of American Biography. IV, 54; Heitman, *Register*, I, 327;
Appleton's Cyclopaedia of American Biography, I, 737; Frederick H. Dyer, compiler, *A Compendium of the War of the Rebellion*, p. 332.

went down near the island, and the Dr kept his large family warm for some days with its *iron-clad*-beams. He has promised Sarah and me some work-boxes from its wood. Bits of the Congress and the Cumberland [2] stand in the room-corners in the shape of canes. "The blockade" reaches within three miles of the island, and we hear it spoken of almost hourly as a line of demarkation [sic]. Craney Island is the only contraband depot in this military department now recognized by government; and it is under absolute military discipline. The clothing-depot is a room adjoining the Dr's office; and, as it cannot be warmed, it is sometimes necessary for us to arrange sewing for our women within his walls. An hour or two with him sets us whirling with the multifarious machinery of the various departments. His factotum comes bustling in, with his census list of numbers, ages, occupations, and former owners. The sergeant of the guard comes in to report his men, and to receive his orders. The Captains of the two island-steam-boats come and go; and mail comes in; and then, as a natural consequence, white-faced-males flock after, each with the same inquiry. Men detailed for carpentry-service on the island come to ask for passes to Norfolk, or the Fortress; or come in to report their return therefrom. The hospital doctor's kind-hearted-assistant, a mere-boy—hurries in with a "requisition" upon his tongue's end from the Lying-in-hospital [sic], stating, to Sarah and me, that one woman is just confined, and that another is about to be; and asking, with unblushing directness for the various articles needed by mother and child.

A wagon passes the window, the guard gather about, lift the cover of a box which it contains—and a stranger passes with the wagon to the wharf. The box contains the body of a soldier who was buried upon the island, and it is now reclaimed by a friend. One of the guard comes in with two colored men (still slaves), saying, "Dr here are two men who crossed the river without passes." "What do you want," asks the Dr. "Massa told me to come over and ask the Dr (Dr Huckins,

2. Federal vessels sunk by the CSS *Merrimac*, March 8, 1862. See David D. Porter, *The Naval History of the Civil War*, pp. 122–133, and Harrison A. Trexler, *The Confederate Ironclad "Virginia" ("Merrimac")*.

the Surgeon) how much he asked for his visits." "And what do *you* want?" "I want to know if the Dr. can come over and see my wife, She's afflicted—She's got something the matter of her leg." Then comes another slave with a written request —from his master to borrow the Dr's horse and carriage. "So you have not left yet?" says the Dr. "No Massa." "Is not your master afraid you will?" say I. "Reckon Massa is," says the slave. Refugees find no immediate asylum here, as the island is under Genl Dix's sole jurisdiction. Then comes a slave-holder for asking sugar, molasses, and vinegar, in exchange for which he gives farm produce. The somewhat intelligent, well-to-do-farmer thinks that "Between the North and the South he and his neighbors are badly off."

Confederate money circulates here, of course, and the neighbors consider themselves specially lucky when they can get hold of U.S. currency. Now, and again, and almost perpetually, comes a black-face to the Dr's wooden window-pane "Massa Dr, I—" "Not massa, I'm not your master, you're not a slave now." "No, massa, but I'm so used to it——"

. . . . .

A son of the Herald was at Newport News at the time of the negroes leaving there, for Craney Island, and was the authority for the statement wh appeared in the Herald that "The negroes have been removed to *Craney Island.* They were accompanied by a quantity of white trash, in the guise of Missionaries."

. . . . .

First-Day evening. An order has just come to the house from the office forbidding us to undress tonight. Our gunboats have been seen pointing towards Norfolk, which has been in a state of more or less excitement for the past week. A steam-boat, which Dr Brown sent to Norfolk to look into the state of things, has returned, with the information that all the steam-boats about Norfolk keep on full head of steam; and that the Galena [3] has opened her batteries towards Portsmouth,—with orders to destroy it if the rebels succeed in tak-

3. A Union ironclad on duty in Hampton Roads. *Official Records of the Union and Confederate Navies,* ser. II, vol. 1, p. 90, and Richard S. West, Jr., *Mr. Lincoln's Navy,* p. 102.

ing it. It is rumored that they have destroyed the telegraph-wires and rail-road this side of Suffolk, thus cutting off our communication with Corcoran. Our Volunteer is ordered to keep up its steam, through the night, and our pickets are to be sent a mile or two out on the main-land. This is war! A few nights ago we saw a large fire in Portsmouth, and from its size and long continuance we fancied that the rebels were destroying the town. The next day brought the news that the secessionists burned seven houses there. Today we saw distinctly from the house top the (permanent) blockading squadron at the mouth of the James River.

Second day, morning. The Dr has gone to Norfolk to accompany Seventy-five able-bodied negroes ordered by the Quartermaster. The Dr thinks they may be wanted to remove the stores; and he says if that is the case, we must move ourselves. Our kind-hearted young Drake, from the hospital, was in the office just now, saying "I shant stir an inch, and leave these poor creatures." "Neither will," the Dr said "I." In case of attack he intends to defend the island, so long as he can, and, when resistance is useless he will surrender. "But," he says, "if we are forewarned of the approach of an overwhelming force, it will be folly to remain, unable, as we shall be, either to defend ourselves, or the negroes."

Drake brings the usual morning report of two or three deaths in the hospital, and one in the barracks. Consumption is sadly prevalent here. The African constitution is certainly very delicate; and the necessary exposure to which our half-clad people are subjected, when going for rations of wood and food, brings coughs and colds into every barrack. I want our good sewing societies to know that we have still nine-hundred unclothed fugitives, and are daily expecting two hundred more. We have great need of broad, coarse, shoes, of stockings, Dresses, coarse and stout, petticoats, and blankets. Our women are ready with their needles. Sarah and I have already employed eighty or ninety of them in the manufacture of beds, and today we shall give dress materials to some of the needy. We consider it feasible to unite study and sewing, so we hang our A.B.C. card upon the walls, and keep heads and fingers busy. For a few days, it has been very cold, and Sarah and

I have shivered in the barracks, which have unglazed windows and wide-open doors. We stand, all day long, having the choice between stretching in a bunk and standing on our feet. The N.Y. friends will soon build a mtg and school-house (in one) and then we shall be able to make ourselves and our women comfortable. *The Dr has just returned* and says his men were wanted to unload stores, not to remove them. He says there is to be, today, a general movement along our whole coast. That we shall be safe unless our army should meet with reverses. Mrs Brown has taken out her travelling-dress, and says she shall put it in repair, in order to be ready for journeying.

We are *subject!* to a very curious cook. It is evident that she has always been used to ruling the roost. She orders her fellow-servants, the children and ourselves. She ordered Sally about last night. "Come, I ant used to so much noise. Ise used to drawin a rockin-chair up to the fire, uh evenins, an bein waited on by my chillun."

There is a great deal of aristocratic feeling amongst the negroes. Criticism upon manners is their acme of disparagement. "I dont know where Sally could uh bin raised. She hant got manners," said our cook. The secessionists left their sentiments behind them on our walls. Yesterday we found these words! "To the infernal Yankees." "We will never be conquered, as long as there is one man left in the sunny South: the only land of the free, and home of the brave." Men and women here are greedy for tobacco. "I'd rather see some tobacco tonight than see my Savior," said one woman the other day. The Negroes have yet to learn to guard in seemly silence sacred things. One of our house-servants, struck with the beauty of a gay dress of Mrs Browns, said to her, "I should be ready to die, if I could get that dress!"

Second-day evening. News has come from various sources tonight that the Merrimac[4] with five other small ironclads

4. A reference to the Confederate ironclad *Merrimac No. 2* or *Virginia No. 2*, launched in May 1862. The possibility that this vessel might appear in Hampton Roads caused consternation among Federal naval officers. In September 1862 Captain John Rodgers of the *USS Galena* warned his superior, Admiral S. P. Lee, that the *Virginia* was a formidable vessel. If she should succeed in running the James, he somewhat hysterically wrote, "Washington, Baltimore, and Norfolk

is again in the neighborhood of Newport News; that the rebels are this side of Blackwater, and that the "incompetent" Galena alone must meet the foe. All reporters say the excitement at Norfolk is intense. I have been listening for a half-hour to a conversation between the Captain of the Volunteer, and various persons from Norfolk. They all think there is cause for alarm. "A *new* kind of parole they'd give us," said one. "We, the last of all people." The Dr says he shall take us to Baltimore, tomorrow; if things still look dark— and if no opening lies that way he will take us to our opposite shore. The Dr thinks there is a feeling of humanity on shore, though there may be no Union feeling. By the way, he is very much respected in the neighborhood on account of the good discipline he maintains here. The steamer from Norfolk has arrived. There are two or three Monitors [5] there ready for the Merrimac! ! !

Ever affcy LUCY 1st month 20th

Craney Island Jany 29th [1863]

Dear home folks;

Having given my word, that our Contraband Society should hear from me, and having very little time at my command, I must ask Charles to lend the Society my last letter, and this also.

---

would reward her success," and he had only the *Monitor* and the *Galena* to oppose her. Lee, in turn, warned Secretary Gideon Welles that the *Galena* was "very vulnerable," and sent the *New Ironsides* (Captain Thomas Turner) to support Rodgers since the " 'Merrimac No. 2' was expected hourly." In January 1863 Lee was still expecting the Confederate ironclad to attack at any moment. He must have been relieved when he learned that she had anchored off Drewry's Bluff. John Rodgers to Admiral S. P. Lee, September 9, 1862; S. P. Lee to Gideon Welles, September 12, 1862; Gideon Welles to Thomas Turner, September 15, 1862; Lee to Rodgers, January 25, 1863; Lee to Welles, February 4, 1863, *Official Records of the Union and Confederate Navies*, ser. I, vol. 8, pp. 14–17, 70, 371, 503.

5. A reference to the armored or ironclad vessels which joined the Federal fleet in Hampton Roads after the battle between the *Monitor* and the *Merrimac*. The *Monitor* foundered off Cape Hatteras in December 1862. Twenty-eight ironclads were in the Federal fleet on the Atlantic coast by December 1862. *Battles and Leaders of the Civil War*, I, 745–758; Porter, *Naval History*, pp. 266, 412–414. The *CSS Merrimac* was sunk off Craney Island, May 11, 1862. *Official Records of the Union and Confederate Navies*, ser. I, vol. 7, pp. 335–336.

. . . . .

I must tell you at the outset, on the authority of Dr Brown, what Sarah and I are *not* doing. In reply to Mrs Viele's inquiry if we were sensible, the Dr said, "Oh, yes, I have not caught either of them trying to give a lesson in Music or Drawing yet." A fine commentary that on adorning the mind while the body is yet unclothed.

. . . . .

You, of course, feel assured of our safety, we also feel assured that we dwell in the midst of alarms while we reign [reside?] in this horrible place. Again, in the Dr's office, I heard two sea-captains and one pilot report a renewed excitement and anxiety in Norfolk, on account of the Monitor having been tugged into port, and that, too, soon after a supposed conflict reported by the sound of guns.[1] We heard the guns here, and one of the Captains declared he saw the flashes of the guns. But no harm came to us and I believe to no one from that direction. Sarah and I still find work for our hands to do in the clothing room. We feel irrestibly [*sic*] impelled to work early, and late, until every refugee upon the Island has tasted one day of comfort, at least, in the shape of clothes. Hundreds are yet to make their first visit to the clothing-room. We have already distributed the large quantity of valuable material which came from Philia, and it is, even now, warming those it was sent to bless. We have not yet found one woman who cannot sew but fearing ingenuity might not be universal, we have cut the cloth before distributing it. I gave a long strip of gingham to one of Col Lee's slaves (from the whitehouse) [2] the other day, supposing she would make from it an apron with a waist; but when

1. Apparently many of Miss Chase's letters were written in the form of a daily record or diary. This seems to be the only plausible explanation for this reference to the *Monitor*, which foundered at sea on December 31, 1862.

2. Probably a slave from the White House plantation of William H. F. (Rooney) Lee, son of Robert E. Lee. The White House plantation was in New Kent County near Richmond. Lee was Colonel of the 9th Virginia Cavalry at this time. White House plantation was the home of Martha Custis when she married George Washington. *D.A.B.*, XI, 134; Douglas Southall Freeman, *Robert E. Lee: A Biography*, IV, *passim;* Writer's Program, *Virginia, A Guide to the Old Dominion,* p. 466.

she appeared with a short, fancy apron and I asked her what it meant, she replied, "Oh, aprons with waists are out of fashion now." One of Col Lee's slaves, bemoaning her isolation here, said, "If I stay on Craney Island all my days, I shan't have a chance to wear out my clothes, and I know I shall keep coming back after I die to see after em! ! I cant help being so fond of my clothes, twas born in me." Dresses made from bed-ticking are favorite week-day garments with the women. The Dr says, "Poor things, we can't blame them for cutting up their bed ticks, they are so comfortless." Mrs Brown says, when the negro-women come here they almost universally wear upon their heads either Tubs or Boilers, whether their bodies are clothed or unclothed.

. . . . .

A perfect mania for thread rages among our Islanders. "Please Maam give me some strands of thread," said woman after woman when she handed us her finished bed-tick. A man, too, who went as a messenger to our sewing-women, begged us for thread; saying, "I live all alone, and I have no one to take a stich [sic] for me." He pronounced himself a good sewer. Some-day I hope we can have a woman-overseer of the wardrobes of the solitary.

2 day Morning. We are, today, practicing homoeopathically in the distribution of needles pins and thread. A quarter of a spool of cotton, one needle; and two pins! to a full grown woman! rolling no one in riches, but enabling the community to be shareholders in our limited stock of necessaries for neatness. Such work may seem to you more insignificant than measuring long lines of tape behind a counter, but based on such a course of action the closest calculation how to best meet the needs of the many, vital needs, too, it is surely, in my eyes, a noble work.

. . . . .

The negro marriage-question [3] puzzles the Dr. A negro man

3. The lack of any legal institution of marriage under slavery and the instability of family life were two points on which the abolitionists had most bitterly attacked slavery. After emancipation the friends of the Negro were often perplexed by the "marriage-question." Mass marriages often were performed—in some instances as many as seventy-five couples took the vows in a single ceremony. See *American Missionary*, VII (April 1, 1863), 88; VII (May 1863), 115; VII (October 1863), 235.

here wishes to retain, for his wife, a woman with whom he has lived happily for a year or more; but another woman upon the Island claims him for her husband, and does not give her consent to a separation; while he declares that his first wife is very ill-tempered and that it is impossible to live with her. The Dr. intends to invite some clergyman to visit the Island to marry all who wish to be married, and to make legal the relation between those who have already married themselves. He wishes to impress the Negroes with the sacredness of the relation. A few nights ago, we had a wedding in our dining-room; perhaps not a "sure enough" wedding. Indeed, the Dr doubting its legality, pronounced them man and wife "By virtue of the authority *assumed* by me." And, also, sent with them to Norfolk, from whence the groom came, a note suggesting the propriety of retying the knot. The bride was a very handsome mulatto, elegant and stately in her bearing. She is a great loss to the Island, having been its most ornamental animated feature. Her dress was always neat and brilliant, and she was always accompanied by a beautiful child in beautiful colors.

A few nights ago, a negro man and two women stole the grave-diggers boat from the hospital, and then stole themselves away; and a few days ago five or six women stole some sheets from a box in a hall; and I was forced to aid in the examination of the culprits. Upon one I found a very suspicious looking petticoat but I could not identify the sheet. Two witnesses testified to the guilt of the accused, but neither the guard-house nor hunger brought the sheets to light. The women protested their innocence in the strongest terms. "If I was as innocent of my sins, as I am of those sheets, I should be sure I should go right home when I die," said one. The guard with their guns brought the women into the office, where the Court-Martial was held. One of the guards said, "The poor women have been knocked about so long with the army, their honesty is frequently challenged. Many will steal, but there are others who would die from want rather than steal."

We were door-way visitors, not long ago, at a dress-ball, where bare necks, and arms shone resplendent with their drapery of jewels and ribbons. There we saw a real Virginia Break-down, on Virginia soil. It made us breathless, to watch the flying movements of the unwearied feet of man and maid. A song, like the sound of buzzing wings, accompanied their feet. "I wish I was a little fly, uh sitting by my sweet-hearts eye. I wish I was uh little bee, uh sittin on my sweethearts knee. I wish I was uh little mouse uh sippin kisses from her mouse" (mouth) [*sic*]. As mouse and mouse do not rhyme, I suggested to Sarah the peculiar fitness of the sub- stitution of Louse for Mouse. From the party, we went to a meeting, where we again saw dancing, after the Shaker fashion. At Dr Brown's suggestion Sarah sang "Joyfully, joyfully." She sang the sweetly, exultant air admirably; the negroes caught the air very quickly, and joined in the chorus. The negro who fell in prayer was very fluent and earnest. He prayed for black and white, for rich and poor, for bond and free. He also prayed that his brethren might not "pull down vengeance upon their naked souls."

First day Sarah and I took two oarsmen and a boat and crossed the river to go to church. After landing, we inquired the way at a house near the shore. We were obliged to knock a great many times, before any-one would wait upon us. And then, when a poor unfortunate, for whom Nature had done Oh! so little! came to the door, and with vinegar pouts and vinegar glances, waited our will. I said to myself Lo! a poor white! We were so sweetly oblivious of her evident ill-will that she finally thawed enough to ask us to walk in.

. . . . .

We had a good deal of talk with three colored men, who told us that a good many slaves still remained with their masters in the neighborhood. Drake, (the hospital steward,) who was with us, Said, "You tell them they are fools to stay." The men seemed satisfied with their own freedom, and in- different to the condition of their fellows; but, as to seem and to be are not necessarily one and the same in *this* latitude it was not safe to judge by appearances. We found one very social and interesting free-negro, living on a small farm, for which he pays $100 a year rent. As figs grow round about us, I have a desire to get some, and so I asked the man if he could tell me whether any of his neighbors had put them up in sugar. "There you're too hard fer me," he replied.

. . . . .

The roseiest [*sic*] of summer sunsets reflected in the many lakelets left by the tide, with the wooded shores at hand, the James River fleet (The Minnesota, Galena, and two or three other gun-boats) within very near view, and our own beloved little village at our feet, made a picture of surpassing beauty. The shaded trees on shore, with the burning lakes on the flats, and the burning-sky above made me dream of the tropics. The Dr & Mrs Brown went to Norfolk when we were over the river, in the morning, and saw a "butternut" prisoner freshly brought in. The Dr was quite excited when we returned, saying it would have been very unsafe for us to have attempted to enter the church. He said where there was an army hospital upon the Island the wife of the Surgeon had the door of the church locked in her face, and missiles thrown at her. "That, too, when we were much less hated than we are now." The Dr said if he had not found us here on his return from Norfolk, he should have hurried after us. He is willing we should go, after he has opened a safe way for us, by letting some of his well-wishers across the river know that we are going.

Jumping rope and swinging were the favorite amusements last first day, but when we were going the rounds in the evening, the Dr stopped all games, and told the sergeant of the guard to allow no playing on Sunday. All play or no play, even on week days, seems to be the theory African. Our handsome and lady-like Custis house-servants said to me, "We never went to a party in our lives. Mother would not let any of her children go to parties. We were as genteelly brought up as white people. Our mother would not let us go with bad company." And one of our sewing-assistants said the other day, "What a very good man Dr Huckins must be, he almost never says anything; I think he must be praying all the time." The contrabands are very mindful of the courtesies due each other. Good day and good health are their daily wishes; given to those they meet; and they are singularly respectful to white-people. Too respectful to fawn and cringe, but ready and expectant to save the whites from all manual labor. A broom in my hand brings them to their feet, they are amazed if I pick up a spool, and most of them show sadly wills unused to will. Yet, with all their willingness, they *are* slow *indeed!* Southern women have often begged Northern abolitionists to sympathize with them, instead of with the slaves and (while the oppressed are still nearer my heart than ever.) I am fast learning to sympathize with the depressed.

To wait and wait, and still to wait, is our lesson of every day. A man has come to the office window for a pass to Norfolk. The Dr is particular in his inquiries when a pass is wanted, fearing a runaway may help himself off with a pass. "What is your name?" "Has that always been your name?" "No, my name used to be ———, but I married my mistress, and now it is (so & so)." All the officials use many precautions before registering names, as the negroes often give false names. Perhaps, after all, no false motive influences them, as they may bear many names in a life-time. They usually need to be asked, repeatedly, for their surnames. They are Judith or John, and nothing more. North Carolina has been sewing lately for Mrs Brown. A woman has this moment gone from me, who wished me write to her sister that another sister died in her tent yesterday "half an hour of the sun." A letter from the one to whom I wrote addressed to the dead has just arrived. The author offered to furnish her sister with money if she needed it, and also begged her to go to Fort Hamilton to visit her. A letter from a woman to her "Dear husband" (who is not here) has been opened, and the woman is discovered to have told her husband that if he does not come to join her, she shall be obliged to get another "Bough"—Boy, I supposed she meant, but the Dr says "No, Beau."

. . . . .

An old-man and a young maiden, whose marriage we shall witness this evening, have just visited our clothing-rooms, and been clad in bridal array. The maiden alone won our sympathy at the outset, but when we had freshened her, her companion said, "I don't want to be a laughing stock, and I don't look fit to stand up along uh her." We agreed with him in opinion, and made his *outside* worthy of his *brides*. Among the slave-holders who, impelled by their needs, often come to the Island is one who says he has not sold one dollars worth of produce since the war began, and that all his negroes have left him. Another has the pleasure of seeing one of his runaways here. The whites rival the negroes in talking of what happens "Heeugh." One of the neighbors told the Dr that since the state of war women-field-hands can be hired for 20, 25, or 30 dollars a year, and men for 40 or 50. A negro who made a nice basket for the Dr, came with it to the office, and told the Dr there was a very disagreeable woman going about the camp who called herself by his name! "Now Dr," the man said, "I don't want her tangled onto me. But I have a daughter at Newport News, and if you'll give me a pass to go fer her, I shall be so glad for she's very anxious to get learning." Every day's tidal ebb, and flow sends solemnly into our presence now the negro stranded on our shores by the war, who forces our sympathies to meet his wants; then the slave-owner either in person or estate, now begging at our hands, now uttering a complaint; and now, Wo's him! houseless and homeless with our faces reflected in his mirrors, our tables heavy with his books, and our wearied heads resting in his easy-chair.

A fine horse and a rockaway just came into our stable from a large farm taken possession of by the Dr a day or two ago. Negroes from here, are already at work preparing *our* estate! for planting. "It is quite time to put in some seeds," say the farmers about here. As none of the farmers in Vir can send "Truck" to N.Y. except by government aid, Dr Brown hopes to have control of the boats, that the expenses of forwarding his "truck" may be covered by his receipts from the farmers he will accommodate. We expect to be flooded, in a few days, with the furniture from our new house. And, tomorrow, another large farm, will fall into our hands. This too, is war! Savage, and cruel! The Dr acts of course under orders. He would consent to the inmates of the houses remaining in their homes; but he says it would be impossible for them to do so. They would provoke the negroes, and the negroes would provoke them. Room in their houses must be found for our overseers, and their furniture would be unsafe. So it seems best to remove them from their estates, if we take possession of their soil.

Dr Brown received a letter a few days ago, from a noisy secessionist from whose estate our negroes had taken wood. "Having frequently heard of your gentlemanly deportment —Mr Marcus did not know how to treat a lady—he would not have allowed the negroes to laugh in derision as I walked off. It is indeed hard having no one to cut my wood (Her slaves have all left her.) The driftwood on the shore, I can get my-self more conveniently than from the woods, besides, I could have sold it several times, but preferred to keep it for my own use, believing that you will see the injustice of it, I leave it with you to do what is right. Very respectfully J. M. Wise."

After taking possession of the farm I spoke of the Dr called a few men and women into his office to test their readiness to work in the field. He told them that what they raise shall be sold, and, after their expenses are met the surplus shall be their own. They were all eager to enter the field. One man went out to bring in a woman he said was an excellent field-hand but he returned with the report that "Ever since her husband went to Washington, she has been living with Com-modore Perry! and she does not want to leave him." One man who was anxious to go said, "Dr, there's no probability of bein (interested interrupted) by them (rebels) Sah is there?" A very bright woman came to Sarah yesterday, and asked her if she would "Expound the Bible to her" saying, "I can read myself, but I am mighty desirous to have you read it to me. I am learning in a broken manner, now." She has, for some-time, been teaching a large class to read. She told us "The white folks didn't think nothin of her after she left off dancing." Mrs Brown said to a very dark girl a few days ago, "Is that very light girl your sister? Why she can't be!" "Yes, she is," replied the girl, "Mother played naughty then." A girl who has been a very useful assistant to us, asked me to write a letter to a friend. She was very well, and hoped her friend was also, wanted her to come to see her, had "nothing more to say at this time present," but, "I have just heard that Henrietta is sold!" ! !

It is very difficult to understand the negroes. South Carolina dialect is unlike that of South [sic] Carolina and Virginia claims little acquaintance with either. Our women tell us which "Bakk" they live in. Oh! how the women besiege us with entreaties! I don't know but I shall fall into Mr. Coleman's habit and pass about the Island with both hands extended and fluttering while I scream, "Shaw! Shaw! Get away from here." I whispered to the Dr at the dance, "I cant afford to give out shoes to be kicked out in this way." Sarah says she expects, the moment, she goes into the yard, tomorrow, to hear our Rockaway exclaim, "I have not had a single thing given me since I came on this Island!" "Move away, white folks are coming." "Let the white folks in," is the cry, when we put our faces within the negroes-doors. "Oh, you'r Secesh," is a favorite insult with them. "Do you think I'll marry any-body as black as you are?" is a very decided cut.

I was very much interested in hearing the Dr commission the "squad-men" to tell their people of his agricultural plans. He has been lecturing them seriously, lately; insisting upon their compelling their charges to keep their quarters clean, to chop their wood in their back-yards! ! to hand their clothes there, and to do other seemly things. One old man, alluding to the life before his men, said, "It makes me feel proud. I think we can talk to them stronger now." The Dr said to them all, "You'r improving, but there's a great deal that ant [?] as I want it, yet." "Yaas, suh," was murmured by many. "But we cant do it all at once," said one man. One of the women ordered to the field said, "I'm so tired doin nothin, makes me no account. I had worked since I came here." We have several dogs at our heels who barked through the perils of the seven days fights. And both our steam-boats served in those battles. One was shelled twice. Our German druggist Sarah found kindling his fire with Hawthorne's "Mosses from an Old Manse." He says he always kindles his fire with books he brought from Newport News. I have been enlarging our stock of threads by making three skeins from one spool of colored cotton, and four skeins from white cotton. Pliny will send to Thos,[4] Pliny to Charles. Charles will keep.

Ever effectionately LUCY. Craney Island, Jan 29 '63

Feb 7 1863

Dear home folks

I am rejoicing with the happy negro in his greed for letters. One word of instruction from a teacher brightens the face of the learner with shining content. Frock coat or shoes, he takes as his due; but every step of his creeping progress into the mysteries of letters elevates his spirit like faith in a brilliant promise. Scattered about the houses of the whites are pleasing, intelligent women, who serve as cooks. One of them told me that she was very willing to take her share of suffering and all who were in the room with us, said they would suffer still more, rather than again become slaves. The woman said she should die very happy, feeling that her children can spend "The balance of their days in freedom, though she had been in bonds." Want of house-room makes it impracticable to form classes at present, but we can assist those we employ directly about us, and may be able in that way, to form a corps of A.B.C. teachers. Five thousand or more bags are to be sent here from the Quarter-Master's Dept for repairs. The carpenters are now preparing a work-room for the needle-women, and, when they gather there I propose reading the Bible to them, and if, practicable, teaching them their letters. "When our ship comes in"! ! it will come in the form of a meeting-and-school-house in one, and, until that auspicious day, we can be helpful to but few.

I laid aside my pen a moment ago to write the following, in the form of a letter. *"My dear Dick:* I hope you will not forget me, and I will not forget you. I am a lady of my word, and I hope you will prove to me that you are a gentleman

4. Thomas Chase, a brother, was Professor of Philology at Haverford College and from 1875 to 1886 was president of that institution. He was editor of a series of Latin textbooks and in 1871 was a member of the American Committee for the Revision of the Bible. Worcester Society of Antiquity, *Collections*, XII (1894), *Worcester Births, Marriages, and Deaths*, Franklin P. Rice, compiler, p. 50; *D.A.B.*, IV, 37.

of yours. I am doing very well on Craney Island. Don think that I dont think as well of you as you do of me. So I write to you, hoping that you will keep the same word you told me in Hampton, that you would not forget me, and that you would come and see me wherever I might be. I shall be a lady of my word, if you are not a gentleman of yours." "Is it to your husband," I said? before commencing. "No," she replied, "To my beau."

. . . . .

The maiden was pretty, coy, and loving. I was really fascinated by her charming bashfulness. We have, in daily attendance upon us, three girls; young to all appearance but one of them has been the mother of one or more children, and another has lost *six* "since she entered the Army."

. . . . .

Mrs Brown's most reliable servant left all her children behind her, with her master, when she ran away. She said one morning her master ordered all the house-servants to the field, a not uncommon custom in busy times, but, when he ordered them into a wagon, she hid away, and saw all the others driven Southward. She said she was perfectly contented with her mistress, was satisfied with her lot, and had, formerly, been willing to live with her mistress all her days; "But, when the Union came along, then, peared-like they would like to kill us. They told us the Yankees was going to send us to Cuba, and goin to eat us up." She said her mistress never sent her to the whipping post because she had such a very bad temper. "But, when she was angry herself and I had not dun nothin she'd lash me and then she'd read the Bible to me till I got qualified [*sic*]." This same woman told Sarah one night that she wanted very much to go to church. Sarah said, "Well, ask Mrs Brown She'll let you." "Ask Mrs. Brown!" said Nancy, "No, indeed I wont ask Mrs Brown. What do you think God would think if I should ask Mrs Brown if I might go to meeting! What ud he think to see me go and ask any man if I might go to church!" I told her today, to get an early supper and hurry off to church. But she went only to return. "What's the matter Nancy?" "Oh, they don't sing to suit me. They didn't rise and fall alike, and they did not put in such words as become the music. Taint Scripture. Then I could not stand outside long and I want going to crowd in. I wont breathe such air. I want to be outside where it can blow all round me. I should go frantic to get squeezed into their dirty rags, and the very sight of them would get something into my hair.''

Lizzie asks if Dr Brown is a New Englander. He is from Connecticut. He is acquainted with Dr Sargent,[1] and he speaks highly of Dr S's professional skill. Of course you all want to know all I can tell you about him. We supposed he was a D.D. having been told before coming here that he was a minister; and so, at our first dinner, we waited for "grace." We told him that we expected to see him with a white choker on, he replied, "You may yet see me with a choker on, if the rebels get me." The Dr is over six feet; large, and handsome, not elegant in manner, but truly graceful in his awkwardness. Very warmhearted and affectionate, though showing in all his relations that he was born to rule. He sways most becomingly the arbitrary law of military discipline. He has a John Donnes-like love for nature, throws himself on the sofa and talks finished pictures of country sights and sounds. We seem to feel the breezes, to hear the leaves rustle overhead, to listen to the babbling brook, and to see the kine come home. I should like to send you a sheet of his country talk. You would have laughed with us to hear him one-day "Tell us our history." "Oh, you've attended two or three courses of Dr Cutler's[2] lectures, you sleep with your windows open, you take the water cure journal, you've had Fowler [3] examine your heads, you've got hair-mittens, and hair-towels, any no of flesh-brushes in your room at home." The Dr shows great capacity for organization. His community was planted here but yesterday; but, directed by his brain, it has already made

1. Possibly Dudley A. Sargent, M.D., a graduate of Yale, who was a member of the faculty of Harvard. Thomas W. Herringshaw (ed.), *Herringshaw's Encyclopedia of American Biography of the Nineteenth Century*, p. 817.

2. Probably Hannah M. Tracey Cutler, a teacher and homeopathic physician. *Appleton's*, II, 46.

3. Orson S. Fowler, phrenologist. He published many books and articles on phrenology and on marriage. See John D. Davies, *Phrenology: Fad and Science: a 19th-Century American Crusade*.

for itself a picturesque village. It meets daily many of its daily wants and hopes to meet *your* want, for early spring vegetables. Fifty or sixty white people, are, at present, subject to the Dr's oversight; and what they have done today, and what they shall do tomorrow are studies for the Dr's brain. Twenty of the whites constitute the guard. One is head-oyster-man (He superintends the planting of oysters) another is a blacksmith, and several form a squad of carpenters (soldiers detailed for work on the Island.) All the whites are connected with the army. Even our house-walls tell us that we are in the army. Black target-circles adorn our bed-room walls, and parlor and dining-room vie with the homes of the dead—great in wall names. Everybody is glaringly invited not to spit upon my chamber-floor. And there is no lack of written indications that the 10th N.Y. Regt was determined to "furnish ample information" to all who came after that it was "The first Regiment that landed on this island." "Whence shall our wood come," is the Dr's cry just now.

· · · · ·

We went to Pigs-point,[4] memorable in the early days of the present war, passed rebel rifle-pits and abatti, and drove over a large camping-ground of a Georgia Regiment. The large, substantial barracks, still standing, are of mud-cemented logs; and, if their excellent roofs had not found their way to our "Quarters," the village would seem to invite emigrants. The barracks enclose a square; they are near each-other; and it is supposed they were designed to serve as barricades against infantry. The universal custom in this country of building outside chimneys was not lost sight of by the builders of those barracks. Of mud and sticks the chimneys were built, and they still stand, pointing a moral and telling a tale. Opposite Pigs-point is Newport News, near whose shore we saw the Minnesota and Galena at anchor. We saw the yucca not in pots and housed, but thriving on the sandy wayside banks.

4. Pigs Point at the mouth of the Nansemond River, approximately five miles west of Craney Island. A Confederate battery was stationed there during the Suffolk-Norfolk campaign. *Official Records of the Union and Confederate Armies,* Atlas, plate XXVI, no. 4.

. . . . .

At low tide women and boys wade into the water to dig for
clams. They reap a very scanty harvest, and they are forced to
reap it with sticks. A *spade!* is a sure *clam-send!* and lucky is
the chap who can hold one for an hour. I am afraid a little
boy we caught in the act, a few days ago, hardly counted
sixty minutes for his hour. "Hullo, my lad," said the Dr,
"what's your name?" "America, Sir." "Well, take that spade
right back to Mr Miller" (Chief of Police, who superintends
the daily sweeping of the Island, and who, for some special
purpose, had put the spade in the boys hand). "Take it right
back, America, or I'll give you United States," said the Dr
playfully. "Pocahontas" came to me yesterday for shoes;
but poor "Queen Victoria" is yet unclothed. Hannibal had
a new coat this morning, and Abe Lincoln *cried,* in honor of
his new birth, and, if not, because "He had not had a rag
of clothing since he came into the army." Certainly before he
had a rag of clothing after he came into the army. A tatter
demallion modestly asked the Dr today for a pair of pantaloons. "Why, Uncle, have not you a better pair?" "Yaas suh,
Ise got one better pair." "Well, Uncle, what do you want
another pair for?" "Well suh they've got a hole in each of
the knees, and some holes behind." Appearances seemed to
indicate that those he had on had holes behind, though I could
not so affirm, as he spread his hands upon the affected part
when he turned his face from us to pass through the door.
Two very old men bent with age, were made both comfortable
and grateful this morning. Freedom came too late to them to
teach them their right to gratify their wants; and every look
and movement was servile. But, as happy as children with new
toys, they smiled and bowed, and declared to the four walls,
"These are gentlemen and ladies waiting on us."

. . . . .

The frowning Providence sent a frowning multitude to our
doors all day yesterday, and we were forced to break our good
rule of distributing clothing by districts. All through the morning our entry was filled with the shivering, driven early from
their wet beds, and coming from their empty fire-places to
seek cold comfort in our cheerless hall. The most destitute

could not, of course, come out, and, most unwillingly, we gave shoes to those who manifested their *toes* to us, feeling that there were, shivering by empty fire-places *feet* manifested in their entirety. The stock of women's shoes was soon exhausted, and we were forced to distribute to the women men's shoes. It seemed as cruel to rob the men, but it was cruel to deny the women; and from one dose of cruelty my conscience sought refuge in performing another, and I was forced to send sick and shivering women home with their worthless shoes. Many are entirely destitute of bed-clothing, and we were unable to meet half the need by sending out our entire stock of clean, white, hospital-blankets. Even today we learn of many new cases of extreme need. One young, motherless girl, who has been here several weeks, has been without sufficient clothing to keep her warm by day, and has had neither bed nor coverlet by nights and has set up through the long watches of every night! Cases of long continued suffering which has escaped observation are not rare here. Women are taken sick and die without entering the hospital or letting their wants be known. It is the duty of the Squad-Master to report the sick, but many lie in silent suffering cared for by their companions and shrinking from calling on the Dr.

. . . . .

It may interest you to know that we occupy a decidedly "airy situation." Tell Arthur that "the wind whistles after us." I am afraid it would be necessary for Dr Collins, if he should visit us here, to "Hold his hat on" even when our windows are closed. The winds, when they are abroad, have free sweep across our island, and they howled like ravenous wolves, all day yesterday. It is only necessary, at all times, to draw a chair near the wall, if we wish to gauge the amount of air stirring abroad. When the balmy South is true to her traditions, gentle breezes fan our brows, but, when Northern fury sickens [?] her, the sharp teeth of fiery dragons pierce us, and threaten to carry us off. Last night, cross-winds swept over our bed, and wove a network of frost about us, and I know of two more than Tom who were cold. I have not told you of half the expedients to which the Dr resorted to defy the storm. When we were coming from the office to our dinners men were hacking the cannon-carriages in pieces. "That looks like the coming of peace," I said, "as well as like coming to pieces." An armed guard was stationed all day at the redout [*sic*], to guard the wood as it was brought in across the ford. The Dr was filled with anxiety, all day, lest the ford should become impassable.

. . . . .

If we live through the fiery ordeal of this winter we may be able to travel about the country to test the heat of brick-ovens by crawling into them after the coals have been removed. The Dr catechised Nancy last evening, and found she needed no religious teacher. "Nancy do you believe in so much excitement as your people work themselves into when in meetings?" "No, sir, I dont." "What do you think of, Nancy?" "Oh its self, they can deceive man, but they can't deceive God. They sees each other doing so; and so they does it." "Where is heaven, Nancy." "Heaven can be here below sir, as well as above." "What sort of a place is it, Nancy?" "I cant tell temporarily, that is discerned spiritually." "Do you think hair will be straight there, Nancy?" "Oh, yes sir, hair will be straight there." "Do you think the slave-holders will go to heaven?" "If Massa's good he'll go to heaven with all the rest of the just." "What is your idea of God, Nancy?" "He's all in a smile," said Nancy, adding, after a pause, "he smiles on the just, and he frowns on the unjust." "What is your idea of the Devil?" "He's *meesable*, he's *meesable*." "Well, what does he look like?" "Well, the Devil has got such a disagreeable look that it's out of my power to tell how he do look. He drags his tail, too, oh, its so disagreeable. He looks naturally; sometimes like a man, sometimes like a beast." "Well Nancy what do you think about baptism?" "Its one of Gods commandments. He say if we neglect one commandment, we neglect all." "Do you think no one will be saved who is not baptized?" "It is the pure in heart what see God," said Nancy. Oh how charming Nancy is! I really love to be ruled by her. She is motherly, kind, fond as one's aunt, and indulgent as a grandma.

Sarah and I are very happy here, happy enough to say many times that we are very happy.

Sarah wrote a little letter full of enthusiasm two weeks or more ago but it did not get into an envelope. To be in at the birth! is it not something to rejoice in? Great plans that are not yet afoot but are creeping into strength and promise spring daily, from the Dr's brain, shining with the prestige of success of their antecedents. It is certainly very good for us to be here. Men selected for farming came into the office today, all eager to work, and all expressing strongly their desire to have their families accompany them. "Well, Squire Nixon (the name the man gave as his own) do you wish to go upon a farm, to have for yourself half that you raise, and perhaps more?" said the Dr. "Yes suh, no more required suh than that suh." "Well Champion what do you say?" "I suppose when we get there, you'll let us have our families, like you said suh?" "Well Knowledge are you going?" "Yes, suh, that's my intention, exactly what I cum fir."

Some of the men, having recently arrived here from Norfolk, the Dr took their names; their condition, before entering the army, occupation since, and amount of wages they have received from government. Two or three said they were free. "Well," said the Dr to one self-styled free-man "Why did you leave?" "Oh, I cum to look fer you all suh, when the others did suh." Cross-questioning showed that all were slaves. "I dont care about the work," said one man, "but I'm might afraid when you aint round they'll interfere with us and kill us." One or two of the carpenter's squad were sent for, but "I'd rather use tools, suh, if its left for me to decide, suh," promptly said the foreman, when the Dr put the chance in his way, at which all the others leaped. I have not told you that Uncle Sam slipped Craney Island into his pocket when he ran away from his mother, so you see we are really in the *Old Dominion* and not on rebel soil, after all. We are obliged, on Craney, to take a public journey every time we visit our *private house*—to put fairly out to sea. But, at such times, and at all times, I find myself ignoring the crowd. I am too busy, and every-body I pass is too busy to heed the concerns of others. We are as independent of our fellow-islanders as Broadway denizens are of each-other. But, when I go into the village! I am abashed like a country-girl who thinks all Broadway staring at her. Dont think the village outlies our twelve acres. It lies in the rear of the house and the office. "Sounds from home" come to us at night in the tattoo at our gate (the head-quarters) and, in the morning, the reveille is sweeter than the storied lark when it bids us to rise. The oratorio of the creation cannot vie with the sunsets here! Night after night, they glow like our warmest and most golden summer skies! and a step gives us the whole horizon-circle! Water too, all about us, and always about us! Water and sky —and around us work, work too which we love to do.

You all seem anxious about our health. I think we shall be well and strong here. Sarah, is, just now suffering somewhat from a cold, and I was hardly my best self for a few days, but we both believe that the climate will agree with us. Lo, on my first page rain-drops, from the roof when I sat writing at the parlor-table!

Ever lovingly, LUCY.

Craney Is.
forwarded 3d mo. 4th [1863]

Dear folks at home.

You are doubtless aware that the whole Army of the Potomac is ordered into our near-neighborhood. If a moment of leisure comes, we talk of making it a visit. Last seventh and first days we were in a state of some anxiety, arising from a report brought here by a trembling negro from the mainland—that five butternuts had been seen across the river. Five too many of the seen; and who can number the unseen! thought the Dr. who grasped his pistol, summoned the Sergeant of the guard and sent off an armed force, hoping to make captive the intruders, but though many confirmed the negroes story, the guard returned without even the shell of a cracked butternut. On First-day, Dr Brown sent Dr Huckins and his assistant to gather information about the mysterious five. They learned that the intruders came down the Nansemund river passing our picket-boat in a fog—and were seen by two of our pickets on the land, but as they were five against two our pickets did not molest them!! They visited the old Georgia Camp, where we mine chimneys and *pluck* roofs; and, as they were dressed in Georgia uniform they may have come to look after roof-trees. But our prize escaped us, no doubt prizing its escape.

Dr Huckins came home with a wheel from the Pig-point battery, so he considered his journey far from fruitless. Dr Brown is now the proprietor of five or six confiscated farms so the local prejudice against him is of a decided butternut hue, and we think there is some danger of his being attacked when taking his lonely rides from farm to farm.

2d mo 27th. I wrote the above, after two or three days illness. I thought myself well, wrote seven or eight letters (many of them on business) went into my work, was torn into shreds by an army of colored besiegers, and sent to bed with a fever; and now, on the ninth day am calling my feebleness strength and trying to write to you. Sarah is in the field again. Her three drops of verat verat[1] [?] three times a day, and my calomel-pill, (the first that ever dared intrude within the prejudiced precincts of my mouth) did not kill us, and may have cured us. At any rate, we believe fully in Dr Brown's medical skill——I left Dr Brown the proprietor of five or six farms, behold him now the proprietor of twelve or fourteen! Of the fourteen, or to be added to it, is Gov Wise's[2] farm, seven miles from Norfolk. We shall probably hail from Nor-

1. Probably veratrum viride, a drug obtained from the rhizome and roots of the American hellibore, sometimes called Indian poke or tickleweed. It was first used by ''eclectic'' physicians. It is a heart depressant and may be used in the treatment of high blood pressure, but it must be used with caution, since there may be severe side-effects. See Arthur Osol, *et al.*, *Dispensatory of the United States*, pp. 1267–1270.

2. Henry A. Wise, Governor of Virginia, 1856–1860. He was a member of Congress and Minister to Brazil. As governor at the time of the John Brown affair, Wise was excoriated by the abolitionist press. He was commissioned brigadier general in the Confederate Army in May 1861 and was promoted to major general in April 1865. His plantation, Rolleston, was on the East Branch of the Elizabeth River. The Chase sisters began a school on Wise's farm, and the Governor's former slaves, learning to read on the estate of their former master, aroused widespread comment among friends of the freedmen. Apparently the school originally was in the carriage-house, for this building was enlarged by the American Missionary Association in 1864 so that Professor A. W. Eastman could care for 300 pupils there. Barton H. Wise, *The Life of Henry A. Wise of Virginia: 1806–1876*, pp. 371, 373–375; *D.A.B.*, XX, 423–425; *American Missionary*, VIII (November, 1864), 260.

folk, when you hear from us again. Dr Brown has been ordered to make the city his headquarters. His doing so, will save the Gov an annual expense of seventeen thousand dollars in the daily sending of two Steam-boats to and fro in the Dr's business. Norfolk becoming his head-quarters the commissary stores will be removed there, and boats will be sent here two or three times a week. Although Norfolk will be our special field of labor, we shall come here semi-weekly and continue our interest in our first charge. I cannot tell you what a trial it is to us to leave this Isd this Gaza—this wilderness— has become very dear to us. This sandy bleak Isd cut off from the world is the whole world, and enough of the world for us ——Dirty, dilapidated, south-side *City* of Norfolk intruding its white faces and civilized habits upon us! ! Out upon it! Dr Brown has been privately informed that govt may ere long, take possession of the Isd for a hospital station. If it should, the women and children would join us in Norfolk.

All our squad-men except the wood-choppers, (even the grave-diggers) have gone upon *our* farms. Their good, as well as the relief of government, being considered in the arrangement. The Dr gave them their choice between working jointly, or on separate patches. Each man his own row—was the invariably, promptly expressed choice.

. . . . .

In order to test Gov. Andrew's chance of success in his rumored soldier-hunting tour[3] to the Isd the Dr said, "Well,

3. John A. Andrew, Governor of Massachusetts, an active abolitionist and strong supporter of Lincoln's war policies, was active in recruiting Negro troops for service in the Union forces. He organized the 54th and 55th Regiments, United States Colored Troops, pioneer units of their type. In March 1863 he sent an agent to Fortress Monroe to investigate the possibility of recruiting Negroes for service in Massachusetts regiments. The state bounty of $50 was to be paid to each recruit and each man was to be credited to the Massachusetts quota; thus the state would be relieved of a heavy financial burden. Andrew with the consent of Secretary Stanton sent LeBaron Russell to Ft. Monroe to examine the condition of the contrabands there. Russell reported that the Negroes had been defrauded and abused. His scheme was not approved by the War Department. General John A. Dix, then in command of the Norfolk area, wanted to send several thousand Negroes to the north but opposed the arming of escaped or captured slaves. Andrew objected to Dix's plan and Secretary Stanton agreed with Andrew. Pearson, *Life of John A. Andrew*, II, Chapter II; William Schouler, *A History of Massachusetts in the Civil War*, I, 376–378, 416.

my men how would you like to be soldiers?'' "To go into the Army?'' A low murmuring grunt of distaste accompanied by a slight restless shuffle was the response. "I think I'm making the best soldier now, sir or shall be when I get my axe,'' said one man, his heading rising with every word, and his face kindling with pride in manly labor which not only earnes [sic] its reward but hopes to get it too. Each man takes his family, and, in so doing, assumes the responsibility of its support.

. . . . .

Think of the seven league boots in which Dr Brown compasses his acres! To Fortress Monroe, Norfolk, Suffolk, Portsmouth, and the round of his farms he sometimes goes in one day. Every-day adds to his care. Lighters are to [be] bought, manure is to be found, tools must be at hand, and men with hands to use them. Quarters for the men and their families must be provided, the one amount of rations sent to every house and carts must be found to operate with the men, the machinery of the Isd must also have its daily share of oil, and Dr Brown must count the drops for every hub. From the stables of Norfolk, and the Army stables of Suffolk, the Dr gets his manure. One day a lighter of manure sinks at Norfolk, sinking with it eight hundred dollars in value.

. . . . .

Genl Viele beaf [sic] (would there more beaf about the man) tries him beyond endurance with his caution and vascillation.

. . . . .

A good Sunday-School teacher he would have made! The officers in Norfolk are generally disaffected toward Viele. Gen V. tells the Dr that he does not dare to open schools for the contrabands in Norfolk! So we shall remain here, and keep house by ourselves.

Think of Butlers schools in New Orleans![4] I am as near boiling with indignation, as it is possible for a cool-blooded member of the Society of friends to be. Beyond the luke-warm

4. Soon after assuming command at New Orleans, General Benjamin F. Butler expressed great concern over the prevalence of treasonable ideas in the schools of the city. All teachers of ''secesh'' sympathies were replaced by ''loyal'' teachers and new schools were opened for the Negroes. Willie M. Caskey, *Secession and Restoration of Louisiana*, pp. 51–52.

point I surely am. Because the refugees in Norfolk are arbitrarily kept unlettered, I agonize to give them what they so much crave. Craney Islanders may and will hold books in their hands (all thanks where thanks are due!) It is those who cannot, who cry loudest to us.

Major Beauvais,[5] Provost-Marshal of Norfolk, aids the Dr to the extent of his power. He seems to be an honest man of the right stamp. "That is what you black Republicans have done," said Gen V. to the Dr one day. "I am a black Repub." said Beauvais, "and I am proud to own it."

Our impetuous Dr stirs the blood in everybodys veins. "I never saw any-body like you," said Beauvais to him, yesterday. "You come in coolly, and say, 'I want a ware-house,' and you must have it before the shower is over. I expect you'll ask for a city next." "Well, the city is yours, with one scratch of your pen," said the Dr. "I know it," said Beauvais, "and I could take every house to the ground if I chose, but I should expect my own to come tumbling about my ears."

A lady Secessionist went into Beauvais office yesterday, while Mr. Young,[6] of the Boston Herald (who has been a guest here for the last week) was there, and handed the major playfully what she called a Southern badge. That badge is now on our parlor-table. It is a cluster of hyacinth and arborvitae, tied with red white and red. Major Beauvais refused to accept it and Mr Young asked for it. The lady forged a pass, got one of the clerks to sign it, was hunted for three days, found & brought back to the city. She is a Dr's wife.

A woman was brought in yesterday who attempted to smuggle millinery-goods. "Genl Viele gave me leave to take necessaries," she urged. "Millinery goods are not necessaries," said Major Beauvais. The office is daily thronged with secessionists: seeking papers, and exemptions from confiscation, making complaints, and begging for indulgences. One of Mrs. Brown's girls thinks, "Perhaps if I go to Norfolk I can get

5. Alvin E. Bovay, Major, 19th Wisconsin Infantry, Provost Marshal at Norfolk. Heitman, *Register*, II, 82; Dyer, *Compendium*, p. 239; *Official Records of the Union and Confederate Armies*, ser. II, vol. 6, p. 106.

6. Probably William Young of the Boston *Herald* and the New York *Herald*. J. Cutler Andrews, *The North Reports the Civil War*, pp. 503, 508–509, 759; Bernard A. Weisberger, *Reporters for the Union*.

a husband." "But you have one," says Mrs. B. "Oh, yes, but I have not seen him since last August, and I have not got any-one to take care of me. How'd you like that?" The cook lays down her fork, and says, "I think if I fall in love, I must marry again. I dont know whether my husband is living or not, he left me in Hampton." Nancy, My Nancy, poor Nancy, says, "Ive only got *one* man, and he's away; left me here like a rotton [*sic*] stick to drop down and die, and my children, I al-ways look out when the boat comes, thinking its my children. I could rule my grown-up children better than I see other people rule little children." "Why dont you get Miss Lucy well?" says the Dr. "I'd uh got her well in one day, if 't had been left to me," said Nancy, "but she's in the Lord's hands. Its as He says He'll do it at his leisure, He's slow and sure."

. . . . .

Now comes Nancy's turn to be sick—Sarah was taken sick —I kept her company. Sally took to her bed, then Milly was sick, and, one day, while we were all sick, Nancy came stum-bling into our room, saying, "Oh, how tired I am." "Why, whats the matter Nancy, what have you been doing?" "Its what I haven't done, that tires me." "You see nothin goes on, nowhere, without me overseein it. You see Mrs Brown, she can study whats right before her; but she cant sit down in one spot, and study all round." As Nancy would be helpful, I asked her to hand me my watch. "Ise used to hangin up watches, and takin on em down. Missis, she used to have me sleep on the floor by her bed, and hand her watch every hour of the night." Each day Nancy grew weaker, and we tried to keep her in bed; but she would steal into our room. Sarah said to her, one day "Why, Nancy, you ought to be in bed. What are you here for?" "I cant lie in bed, fer I think every-thing goes wrong, if Nancy an't about. I laid there, and I thought, now there ant any-body doing any-thing fer Muss Lucy. Im sure she's sufferin fer attention. So I looked in a few minutes ago, and she did not say any-thing, but she looked distressed, and I knew she was sufferin fer all sorts of things, and wouldn't say a word, because Nancy want round, and there want nobody to do any-thing." Nancy told us she laid awake one night, adding, "I heern my teeth knock together, plain as I dunno how, and the chills searchin me. I aint got strength enough to draw up my entrails." On the very rare mornings when the Dr is not out of bed at four o'clock Nancy is apt to rouse him with "Dr Brown get up. Its high time you were up."

Our young Ary, one of our clothing-room assistants, pines for a young child she was forced to leave behind her when she ran away and which died, soon after she left it. She looked long, and fondly, one day, at a child's skirt, saying, "Once that belonged to some dear little baby." She told us her story, one day. "Young Master was the father of my baby, and he was very fond of it. He made me dress it clean, three times a day, and he was never tired of playing with it and calling it pet names. One day the nurse put it in a tub of water and got a grit in its eye, and I thought he'd go mad about it. We always played together from the time we were little children. Old Master was the richest man in Virginia. He's all out doors secesh. His sons were Union and Anti-Slavery. Oh, how he would quarrel with them, and swear to them! He'd make his daughters kiss the bible, every morning, and say they would not give anyone a rasher of meat. Ive seen ten cargoes of negroes sold on his plantation, at once. They came and tied young Masters hands and feet together, and took him off to the war. He used to write to me, and a young lady who was in love with his brother used to read me his letters." "Did your Master's sisters know how intimate you were with him?" I aked. "Oh, yes, indeed," she said, "and they were all as fond of me as he was, and of the baby too. The baby was very white, and looked just like him. When the cavalry came and took off young Master's brother, I had gone to the point, four miles, and got a woman to mind my baby while I was gone. Master's brother rode up to me and said, 'Don't go back Ary——I'll take charge of the child. It shall go to my house, hurry to the Union Army.' And the next thing I knew, in four weeks, the babys father wrote me that baby had died. He said I must not grieve, that it was a great deal better off now than it would be with me. That he should try very hard to get to the Union, but he was afraid he could not. That if I found any-body I loved, I must marry him, and try to be happy. He used to say he should go mad if I left him. He always stood up for the North, and found fault with the South. His mother came from the North. O, baby could walk, and could say almost any-thing. He would not let me have any-thing to do with colored men; he said they weren't good enough for me. He was my cousin, and he named the baby for his uncle.''

"How old are you," said Mrs Brown to a woman one day. "Oh, I ant but thirty-five. I ant done breedin yet. I reckon breedin ages a woman." "I ant done breedin yet" is a frequent statement here. We are in Virginia. Anne Devor, another of our clothing-women, says she was always hired out to her husband, at first for ten dollars a month, then for five, and then for nothing, because she was breeding. (She has lost her six children.) Both Ary and Anne are now sitting with my writing-class, both greedy learners. Ary says her young Master constantly begged her to learn to read and write, but she says she was so happy with him she did not care about his teaching her, and now she wishes she had not lost her opportunity. "I can stumble along right smart," said an old man, when asked by Miss Smith if he could read. . . .

My temporary school-room was in a barrack whose space was monopolized by bunks, and as no admittance was not on our sign-board, the eager children crowded pestilentially around us. Until our schools can be organized, we are forced to give divided attention to good readers, indifferent readers, and A. B. C. Darians; but we find no difficulty in keeping the fixed attention of all, and in making the lessons equally profitable to all. By enlivening easy-reading with oral instruction each mind is kept interested, the beginner dwelling on the little word and the little thought, and the more mature grasping what we put within his reach. . . .

Sandy and his wife have just been called behind my chair by the Dr. "Well Sandy, will your wife be comfortable at Fort Norfolk if I let her join you there?" "Well, Lucy, where's your other husband?" "They sent him off Christmas before last sir." "I don't know about these things. In the North we should not allow such things. You don't love this husband, so well as you did your other, do you Lucy?" "Yes, sir, better." "Well, if he should go off, and some fine-looking man should come along, what should you do?" "I'll never have another husband sir, if I ever get destituted of this one." "But, supposing your other husband should come and claim you?" "Well, where's your other wife Sandy?" "She's the only one I ever contained Sir." "Well, supposing you take a notion to take some other wife, some day?" "The way I've felt Dr, ever since I was a boy, was if ever I saw a woman I loved well enough to marry, to stick to her as long as I could." "Then you think you'll never leave her Sandy?" "I put myself with her suh to do as well with her, Suh, as long as I can stay with her, suh." "Did you ever want to go into the army Sandy?" "Yes, Sir, I did, indeed, sir. That Seven days battle at Gaines' Hill [sic], I wanted to go into, dreadful bad, but they would not let me, Suh." "Do you think many of your people would be willing to fight?" "Oh yes suh from now to Saturday night you'd have all you wanted Suh!" "Would you be willing to fight, rather than go back into slavery?" "Yes, Suh. I wouldn't ha come away Suh, if I hadn't felt willin to fight suh. I have been in some scrimmages. I drove an army-wagon in Hooker's division three months and two days." "Well, Sandy you've got a nice wife and Lucy you've got a nice husband. When you get to Fort Norfolk have the chaplain of some regiment marry you." Sandy literally pulled his wool when he bade us goodnight. I note all conversations on the spot so the language is sure. One man, who stood before me a few nights ago, wore in his fore-lock a wooden comb, of the fashion of those Thomas distributed largely among the lousy beggars of Italy.

Have I told you the favorite gracious courtesy mutually exchanged by fond lovers? A real dolce-far-niente, sunny Sunday luxury? Hunting for hair-walkers. No mothers caress is fonder, no lovers embrace more welcome—if appearances are not deceitful—a smile of satisfaction and sweet peace lights the face that nestles in a lap—and the joy of well-doing kindles the face of the seeker. Nought abashed, the work goes on, pass by who may.

Did I tell you of the Dr's checking our inward progress on our first-attempt to enter an evening meeting? "Be careful."

"Keep back." "Dont get too near." Charmingly respectful and considerate of the solemnity of the occasion thought I, is the Dr. But poor Sarah, blushing at her hoops, felt mortified by the Dr's seeming allusion to her intrusive fence, whose bars poked impudent infringement into the very faces of the worshipping crowd. We no sooner entered our house, than Sarah discussed with Mrs B. the feasibility of laying aside her hoops permanently. Mrs B. wondering at the strange suggestion, said 'twould never do to deprive our colored sisters of the delight they find in our expanded borders. It was only after another, and clearer warning that we found the Dr's consideration was for us, alone. He did not want us to take more life away from the meeting than we carried into it! At the last m'tg we attended, the Dr preached a sermon on practical religion. He loses no opportunity to impress upon the noisy worshippers that boisterous Amens, wild, dancing-dervish flourishes—, "Oh thats the Devil," exclamations—Yu-ooo's, raw-aw-aw's, Ru-u-u-uh's and pandemoniamics generally, do not constitute religion.

If the Dr had studied to be simple and direct in his thought and language, he could not have been happier than he was when he tried to tell them how to live and how to worship. His talking always tends to cultivate intelligent thought, and every listener kindles with appreciation; while "That's so, Dr." "Thank you, suh." "Thats the way." "We know it." is heard on all sides. . . . I can truly say, white-man though I am, that I have, with the Negro, "a feeling sense" of this state of transition. Lo! an episode! Every hour of my life here is strange: it is not the past; it is not the future, and, with all the chances and changes of war it does not seem to be the present either. Carlyle is right. Quashee[7] *does* love to lie in the sun.

. . . . .

There are no out-at-sea accomodations on the front of the Isd and though tubs, daily emptied at low-tide, serve as substitutes, "the flag of truce," as the Dr calls it, "is always hung out." He thinks the flag would serve to deter any designing rebels from invading the Isd.

7. Thomas Carlyle uses the term "Quashee" in "Occasional Discourse on the Nigger Question." *The Works of Thomas Carlyle*, XXIX, 348–383.

. . . . .

I have never told you of my ridiculous fondness for Army-bread. Potomac-river bread, I call it since the Dr tried to sweeten it for my palate by telling me that it was made with the dirty water about Norfolk. Not losing my relish for it, he threatened to tell me something worse about it, but it is still sweet and good. The Quartermaster in Norfolk deserves great praise. More delicious beek [*sic*] and mutton that [*sic*] we have had here uniformly I never ate. Today we are house-keepers, living alone. Come and see us, one and all, sure of a welcome.

. . . . .

The N.Y. 99th Regt,[8] has pocketed thousands from the sale of colored men. Mr. Young saw slave money and watch at the Provost Marshal's in Norfolk.

Ever lovingly LUCY

[April 1, 1863
6th letter]

Dear Ones at home:

"*I* doe want to go on a ery farm." "*I* doe want to leave Crane Island" is now the cry of the women unused to field-labor, and of some of the timid men, who, made aware by painful experience, that, in these war-times, one knows not what a day will bring forth, prefer the comparative security of the Island, to the uncertainties of the distant main-land. Heart-broken too, some of them are! Husbands are with the army, they know not where. They are alone, with no one to comfort them. "All my children have died, since I came into the army," I hear lonely mothers say, every day. A good old, mother-soul came out into the darkness last evening, (while I stood waiting for Mr King to open the school-room for me) and said "Is that Miss Lucy? Wont you come in, and sit by the fire?" And she ushered me in right sweetly. Gave me a warm seat, stooped to the stature of her broom, fresh from

8. The 99th New York, originally the "Union Coast Guard," was sent to Fortress Monroe in 1861. In 1863 it became a part of Viele's Seventh Army Corps. It served in the operations in coastal Virginia and North Carolina. Dyer, *Compendium*, p. 1444.

the green-pine tree, made her hearth clean and attractive, lighted a new pine-knot, and held it, more gracefully than hand of stone can do. And told me of her husband with the rebels—her only remaining child of nine sold, she feared, "down South. My last child died two weeks ago. She was so high and she was amazing helpful. She could sew and knit. She could spin and weave, and mind the chickens, and tend the children. Oh I should go wild, if I had not any children to look upon." A feeble cry from the bunk and she rose, and took in her arms a young infant, a motherless child, her charge. "My desire is mighty to hear from my husband," she said. Sad faces were around her, and each had her sad story to tell. They seemed willing to go upon farms. One of them said, "I think all of us have a good deal to be thankful for, just think, we haven't been sick since we've been *travelling*." "Travellers" indeed they are, poor creatures. Coming from nowhere, and going nowhere. "We went to Yorktown first, then to Hampton, then to Craney Island, then to Newport News, then here again, and now we must go again; but I am willing, for I like the Union folks better than our folks," said one woman last night. Our home-girls and many others, have pitched their tents on many fields since they "entered the army." I told Mary-Jane last night that her aunt was going to a farm today, and gave her leave to go with her, but she begged me to let her stay with us, and live with us when we go to Norfolk. "I shant leave Miss Lucy and Miss Sarah as long as they stay here," said our Ary, fond and true. "And I'll stay with them wherever they go, if they'll let me." Ary came to us when the Browns left, said not a word about staying, and heard not a word, but *claims* us, and keeps with us; and means, evidently to leave the running away for us to do. The dear child was in tears, all last evening. "We must leave the Island," grieved her.

Old Sukey, our house-cleaner, asked Ary one day, where she got her straight black hair. "My father gave it to me," she said. She told us that her father "Left word, on a piece of paper, that he loved her as well as he did his other children, and that he wished her, as his youngest, to have the largest share, requesting his oldest child to take charge of it, until she came of age, but before that day, the war broke out." She often speaks of her fathers affection for her, and says; "If my father had lived I should have been free. . . ."

They warm my heart, these warm-hearted people. One almost worships the wealth of love with which God has blessed them, and willingly forgives the barbarous assaults they make on ones patience and forbearance, remembering that slavery alone is responsible for the scars which so disfigure them. The aristocratic pride of the F.F.Vs, is here to trouble us. "I an't going with those North Carolina niggers," say the F.F.Vs, when they are called to go to the farms. "I'm willing to go any-where, where the Union folks put me," some say. "I think we ought to be thankful that they think so much of us." "I'm willing to do any-thing but be put outside the lines." "I wouldn't uh come away, if I hadn't uh been." They chuckle with satisfaction, and a feeling of reverence [?] when they say, "The Union-folks own all the States now." Proud as they are of speaking of the wealth of their old masters—("Oh, Master was very rich, he owned five farms, and five hundred negroes!") their pride and importance is greatly increased, now they are in the hands of the "Union," who owns all the estates of all their masters! We asked a colored woman we met in Norfolk, to whom she belonged. She said, "I don't know, I reckon I'm Massa Lincoln's slave now. . . ."

I wrote this letter, for Fanny, Mrs. Brown's cook. "Your mother is ceasted (deceased) [sic], and your sister Sally. I am right well, I thank you. All your inquiring friends and sisters is all well." Nancy said, after I closed her letter, "I hope I shall hear from it very soon. It will consolate me great satisfaction." When North Carolina came to bid Mrs Brown good-bye, she told us that her daughter was recently confined, and was "as well as could be respected, maam." She said she herself had had a great many children. "I used to have one, every Christmas, but when I had six, I put a stop to it, and only had one every other year. I think they have too many children here. I think the business better kind uh dry up till things is more settled." Nancy, mourning over her absent children, said, "They did every-thing for me except eat. . . ."

Our school children delight us. Their bright faces, bright

heads, and bright little ways would win us easily to make pets of them, if we had time to think of them except as parts of one great whole. I wonder if white children pore over books as my colored little ones do! And I wonder, also, if any white child ever leaped into the mastery of the penmanship of his own name with the agility which characterizes my little children. I told Dr. Russell that I let pot-hook's go hang, and rushed my scholars in one day, from little A to their full names. All do not learn so rapidly, and I do not approve of writing-made-easy plans. But five slates is all I possess, and, as each scholar is ambitious to write, I feel obliged to hurry their little fingers. I let them pass from letter to letter, only when they form them well; and, knowing that a tomorrow may take them from me, I strive to stimulate and fix their ambition to write by letting them see that they really can write their own names. Even Nancy, old as she is, wrote her letters, at once, as well as if she had been a month at the writing-desk. Perhaps if I was more used to "beginners" my amazement and delight would not be so acute. In answer to a letter I recd from New York, a few days ago, I asked from the Friends a thousand slates, which I look for very impatiently.

Eliza Dodge led me to expect to be obliged to make the negro dialect a study, but I have found no difficulty in understanding it. I do not aspire to graduate elegant talkers from my school, but I try to teach the children that *a c t* does not spell "at," *m u s t* does not spell "mus," *n o r* is not "nur," and *a r e* is not "ur." Sarah and I take our kerosene-lamp, occasionally, to the school-room, and call in the sweepers, and squad-men, who are busy during the day. There is something truly solemn in the earnestness shown by the men-students. They are so warm, and emphatic, too, in their expressions of thankfulness that I feel crushed by *my own sense of obligation.* Perhaps my little nephews would like to hear my scholars spell? What does D i n n e r spell? "Dinner." What does s-u-p-p-e-r spell? "Supper." What does H o o d spell? "Breffust," screams a little boy who has kept his mouth open and his eyes fixed on me during the whole lesson. I hang a card on the wall, and point to Be set. "B-e (be) s-e-t (set)." "Beginning to set." I point to sleep—s-l-e-e-p. "Sheep."

"No, sheep is s-h-e-e-p." "Oh, yes, that's lamb," screams a little voice, for all my children scream, and I am forced, as Sarah says, "to outscream the screamiest."

We have found a number who learned to read in slavery. Before our school was opened, we asked Jane Washington, a good reader, if she would not teach the children in her neighborhood. She said, "Fur as I am able I do teach people in this camp. Fur as I know the A.B.C. book I teach my children. I had all the chance when I was young, to learn with my owners." Men come home tired with their labors, sit in their door-ways, with their *open books,* till dusk drives them to the fire-light and are joined at their fire-sides by their little ones, with whom they "Stumble along right smart."

. . . . .

Harrison's Landing is the name of our spirited boy; our wood-chopper and errand-boy. I want to see you all here, and I wish every-body I love would cross my threshold; but I am not at all eager to make a display of my housekeeping. If you want any-thing done just do it yourself, seems to be the maxim of the Islanders. "Mary Jane, put some warm water in this jug, and clean it for molasses," I say before tea. After tea, I say again, "Mary Jane, put some warm water in this jug, and clean it for molasses." I go to bed. In the morning, I say, "Mary Jane, put some warm water in this jug, and clean it for molasses." Two days afterwards I clean it myself. "Oh, your fire is going out, Mary Jane, put in some wood." In ten minutes the fire goes out, and put in the wood myself. "You may boil some eggs, Mary Jane, put the tea-kettle on, and let the water fairly boil." "It has boiled, some time ago, Maam."

Before Dr Brown left us the reins were in our hands one day, while Mrs Brown was in Norfolk. At dinner-time the mutton came on cold, and we sent it to the cook, to be warmed in the oven. Not coming in, in due season, we went out to look after it, and found it in the center of the kitchen-floor; while cook, waiter, and other attendants were eating their dinners puss-in-the-corner fashion. To gather about the table is not the negro fashion. Facing the corner wall, like a naughty child in durance, is their habit. White people are looked upon as intruders in their kitchens. We put broom and brush at work, vigorously, the moment the kitchen was ours; and fondly trusted our garnished closets would remain clean, but a day had not worn away before everything had slipped from the bag, (which had lost its string) and was most emphatically "lying round loose." Ground-coffee, hard-tack, pork, ham, tin, earthen, and glass-ware, with my cherished Potomac-bread jumbled into hodge-podge, strewed the shelves. . . .

Milk is a fluid that does not circulate here. Meat we are sometimes without, and all the oysters we get we send as a gift to Dr. Brown. Potatoes too, are wanting, both because they cannot be had at the Commissarys, and because those left us by Dr. Brown, left themselves with fifty children Sarah called into the attic, when she was unable to go to the school-room. "What shall we have, rice and homminy [sic], or mush and rice?" I ask Sarah in the morning. "Shall we have rice and boiled eggs?" says Sarah at noon. "Lets have mush" we both say at tea-time. I am really learning to like Southern corn, and I am convinced that it maintains a more amicable agreement with the stomach than yellow-meal does. If you could eat the negroes corn-cake, you would no longer ask for scalding water, milk, eggs, soda, or yeast for your "Indian-cake."

Comes one day, in a pitcher, some milk, a present from Mr. Moss, a half pint it is, but we prepare for a pudding for dinner, promise ourselves chocolate for supper; design to reserve a cup-full to make cake to serve as a treat to Dr and Mrs Brown, when they call on us, and show great want of calculation in our great calculations. Chocolate we *will* have. I measure the chocolate, hold the pot while Mary Jane pours water into it, say "Enough" when there is enough, and am satisfied, since I feel sure that we shall have chocolate as thick as cream, if we don't have cream for our chocolate. Comes to the table a pot filled to the brim, and every pitcher in the house vacantly declares it "Hasn't had a drop of milk in it since it came into the army!" Oh! I never loved a dear Gazelle[1] &c !! Morning comes. We are hungry, but cool. Yes,

1. From Thomas Moore, "Lalla Rookh," *The Poetical Works of Thomas Moore,* p. 419:
> I never nursed a dear gazelle,
> To glad me with its soft black eye,
> But when it came to know me well,
> And love me, it was sure to die!

quite cool and collected. "Harrisons Landing, did you say there was no bread at the commissary?" What shall I do. We have no yeast.——I highly approve of soda, when tisn't to be had; and it was never so high in my estimation as now. "No meat, you say, Harrison?" "Beans and pork we'll have for dinner, Mary Jane." Home from school and into the kitchen, to find Mary Jane mashing the beans into pulp. "Because they an't done enough Maam." Sarah said she was tired of mush, and had hoped to find variety in beans, but there was mush again.

Sunday comes, and we go to Norfolk, and in Commodore Pegrims[2] house (where Dr Brown makes himself very comfortable). We find "The Virginia Housewife, or Methodical Cook." [3] We pocket it (with leave) fancying we are carrying a larder to the Island, but when every receipt calls its roll of ingredients, we are obliged to answer, "Absent without leave."

Order refusing to reign in the kitchen, we are determined to attune the parlor. Desiring to know we were clean, that we might have a reason for feeling clean, we set Sukey to washing the chairs. After she had washed rebels, unionists, and contrabands from their backs, she, resting from her labors in each one, wiped out her work by wiping herself into them. When I asked Mary-Jane, this evening, to hand me a glass of water, I called her attention to the unclean tumbler, which she speedily made clean with the towel to which I was indebted for clean feet.

. . . . .

All seem to prefer *wearing the tare* to taking the stich [stitch]. Dresses given out one day for wear look the day next as if they should be called in for repair. I have clothed two women, today, who have been through the winter without petticoats, their dresses and chemises alone covering them. I have no doubt there are still many equally destitute. "Clothe

2. Robert B. Pegram, C.S.N. After his resignation from the service of the United States he became a captain in the naval forces of Virginia. He was in command of the Norfolk Navy Yard after its evacuation by Union forces. *Appleton's*, IV, 700.

3. Washington, D. C.: Davis and Force, 1824. The fourth edition was published in 1839.

them in squads, Clothe them in squads, Miss Chase" has been Mr Coleman's command, from the first. "I'll send them to you. You wont know who were clothed before you came." "Pray don't give out irregularly." "They lie so, you'll be constantly deceived." I saw, at the outset, the absolute necessity of meeting the greatest want, let it be in "Granville's squad," or in "Uncle Billy's" in the tents or in "No 5 Barrack"; but my judgment was set aside. Next winter, even, will find some unclothed from *our* stores, and if we keep up our system of *order,* many of the most needy must suffer. We strive to guard against deception, by keeping a list of articles and recipients. But that is not all the safe-guard we need. Sarah and I, finding six or eight rolls of Georgia gray upon the storeroom shelves, set ourselves at work, almost immediately after we came, in cutting them into dresses; cutting waists and sleeves, and preparing linings. Feeling that not a moment should be lost, while there was nakedness in the camp, and creeping ourselves with sympathetic chills, we worked upon them until we were exhausted. But our forty-five or fifty dresses never came to light. They were Georgia-grays! and, falling not into field-hands, were made into under-skirts! Shoes here are an anxiety to us. They stand in such need of insurance against fire. Whether cold, or warm, a blaze attracts the negro, and into the hottest fire he plants his shoes.

We were at home, last Sunday and made the circuit of the ramparts, for the second time only, since I came upon the Island. Within one or two minutes walk from the house and the office, is a view of great beauty, and surpassing interest. Norfolk and Portsmouth can be seen from our parlor windows, Sewall's Point [4] from our bed-room. But the view of which I speak, adds to the picture, Fortress Monroe, Hampton, Newport-News, and Pigs Point, and the waters are ever alive with sail-boats and steam-boats. A week ago, the Army of the Potomac moved from Newport News to Suffolk, and for several days gun-boats and transports passed the Island in rapid succession. . . .

My steps were constantly dogged by whining and complain-

4. South of Fortress Monroe about five miles northeast of Craney Island. *Official Records of the Union and Confederate Armies,* Atlas, plate XXVI, no. 4.

ing beggars. "Oh, cant you let me enjoy myself! I've been here three months, and have had no time, till now, to look about the Island. Why you'll make me afraid of you all, and I shan't dare to look about me again." "I never tease white folks, I don't go near you. I have not had a thing given me since I came here. If I only had some shoes, I could get along, I didn't bring nothing with me. This here top-frock is all I've got," with similar original, novel, and interesting statements. If we wish to see a little home-life, and enter a tent or barrack, after the fathers have come in from their work to sit at their own fire-sides, we raise discord, and mar our picture, before we have fairly looked upon it. "Oh what a bad cough you have!" I say. "She wouldn't have a cough, if she had some shoes," says a surly matron, who pokes the fire, and proffers us no hospitality. When waylaid in a city, from morn till night, the most benevolent can conscientiously say to the beggar, "I haven't the wherewithal." Doubting somewhat, to be sure, but silenced, the beggar turns away, with a "God bless you," with no curse following after you and blessed yourself by your will to do, you pass on, with your moral courage unabated. But woe rests on her who holds the key to the store-house on Craney Island! She knows the gift and the power to give are hers, and the Islanders know it also. She knows the needy are many and the greedy and lying are more, that she may withhold where she should give; and that error in judgment may work mischief. When one pair of shoes is in the store-room, and one hundred feet go bare, she wonders which of the fifty will, next week, walk into her grave, because her feet are unshod:—wishes she knew today, as well as she will know then. When Philia sends a dozen shawls, and every woman who comes to the clothing-room declares she has nothing for her shoulders, she wonders if she does right, when she sends the strong and healthy from the door, and piles again her dozen shawls, reserving them for the old and sickly. "Please Maam, give me a comforter, I've only one thin blanket," says every-body. One thin-blanket is not enough in the airy-barracks on windy Craney Island, but there are some without the thin-blanket, and a double gift to any-one enrages a whole barrack. We must not only guard against robbing the needy, by giving to the comfortable, but we must strive so to regulate our charities as not to educate paupers, and to *demoralize ourselves;* and the task is no small one.

Norfolk March 30th. No one is allowed in the streets here, after 9 P M without the pass-word, and every citizen has been forced to give up his fire-arms. A few nights ago, the pickets at Fort Norfolk were fired upon and an attempt was made to rescue the prisoners. The same night an attempt was made to burn the Customs House here. Randall, a boy the Dr brought from the Isd, was mobbed a few weeks ago, because he was a "Union-man's nigger." Secession-feeling is rampant here; and the women are often noisy and disagreeable. When Sarah was crossing the ferry, she was entertained by two of the F.F's, who talked loudly against Massachusetts. Dr Brown commanded some ladies, one day, on the ferry-boat, to hold their tongues. He said their impudence was intolerable. Upon Henry A. Wise's farm, the Dr found a poor man, whom he allowed to stay, until repeated fits of intoxication compelled him to remove him. After which step, the Gov's brother sent to the Dr's overseer a violent letter of remonstrance. "Please inform the Dr. that while I do not wish to threaten, I will be heard by a candid world, even if my appeal must be made through her Britannic Majesty herself." A notoriously eloquent family is the Wise family. This letter was made doubly ludicrous by a rich expenditure of rhetoric. The Dr offers us the care of the negroes on the Wise farm, Gov Wise's house for our own, and his beautiful estate for our enjoyment. But we think, when it becomes necessary to leave the Island, we shall take charge of the negroes on two adjoining farms. One hundred and fifty negroes will be under our care near Portsmouth. I suppose we shall also have some supervision of most of the scattered Islanders. When schools were opened in Portsmouth, a slave-holder there said, "The schools will destroy fifty-thousand dollars worth of my property." One of our main-land neighbors, at the Island, is disgusted at the very thought that any-body could be found so silly as to come out here to teach the negroes! "I'd poison a Yankee, in a moment, if I could get a chance," she says. Another neighbor, who has lost all his negroes, says, piteously, "I should not have cared, if they'd only given me notice that they were going!" Poor man, they went and left no sign! no farewell fitly spoken!

I am beginning to take quite a fancy to Norfolk, dull and dead though it is. It is beautifully situated; many of its houses are fine, and most of them are home-like, and pleasant; and its streets are (now, certainly) kept very clean. Business is dull here. No jeweller has taken the oath, and the jewellers are not allowed to sell, though they can make repairs. "Sunday morning used to be the great market-day. There is so little business done here now, no store-keeper cares whether he opens or not."

Sarah and I heard a sermon in the Episcopal Church[5] which I suppose was designed to be discerned by spiritual ears; the ears of Southern spirits but whose literal interpretation was unmistakably Let my people go out of darkness into light, out of slavery into freedom. State St and Wall St would have cried, "A rabid anti slavery discourse!" if their ears had heard it. "The chains of slavery are galling, though they be wreathed with roses." "The house of bondage is a prison-house, however ornamented its architecture." "Your deliverer has come, the boon of freedom is offered you." "Who would choose slavery, when freedom might be his?" "The children of the bond-woman shall not be heirs with the children of the freed-woman." "The Romans held slaves, but the slaves might become free." And so talked the man, on and on, for a hour. The slaves in the gallery stooping over the balustrade, and giving keen attention to every word and the people, motionless, keeping their eyes fixed on the preacher, and putting on airs of patience, and acquiescence. The minister was from Portsmouth. I presume his hearers did not question his soundness, but, knowing not what ears were there to hear, they might have doubted the propriety of the man's mode of treatment of the subject. The church is the oldest in the town, having been built in 16—. It is very light and pleasant. The singing was excellent. The congregation had the air of decayed gentility. Well-kept men in well-kept

5. Probably St. Paul's. The building used in 1863 was erected in 1739. Wertenbaker, *Norfolk*, p. 25.

Spanish Cloaks, and women making the most of well-kept finery of past days . . . .

The Dr. no longer thinks Genl Viele will supersede Genl King[6] tho' he said to him, the other day—"When shall we have you for our King? You are, you know our heir-apparent." Military discipline seems to be very lax here. I wonder the guard are not required to report treason on the ferry-boats. Miss Smith heard a noisy lady say, on the boat, "I wish all the Unionists had one neck, that one blow might sever the head from the body." Travelling secessia is obliged to go under the Stars and Stripes in crossing the ferry; and I suppose the forced recognition of protection adds gall to the already envenomed tongue. The ferry-flag once waved before the Provost Marshal's office, in the Custom-house; but, as Norfolk would walk around it, and not under it, it was hung where Norfolk must, would and should, go *under it*. Dr. Hand passed a night with the Brown's, last week and told them of the bitterness of Southern feeling at Suffolk. He said an Adjutant called recently at a house which the officers frequent, as guests, and was there introduced to a young-lady caller, who immediately raised herself, and said, "I wish I had a pistol, and I would shoot you." The Adjutant replied, "You must excuse me, if I do not know exactly how to respond to such a salutation. It is a style unknown among the ladies at the North, and I have never been educated how fitly to meet such advances." The next day, the Adj. asked Dr Hand if he would like an excellent house for hospital-purposes, adding, "I know of one where a rabid secessionist lives." The Dr took steps toward taking the house, but when the old father humbly begged pardon for his rash daughter, he desisted. He said to Mrs Brown, "It is as hard for me, as it [is] for Genl Viele, to turn women and children out of house and home."

I rode, today with the Dr, upon one of his twenty-odd farms, the only one I have visited. It is charmingly situated upon Tanners creek.[7] The water sweeps in a curve before the door-

6. Rufus King of New York. A graduate of West Point, he became a brigadier general of volunteers in 1861. Heitman, *Register*, I, 600; *D.A.B.*, X, 400.

7. An estuary of the Elizabeth River, north of Norfolk and about two miles northeast of Craney Island and three miles south of Sewall's Point. *Official Records of the Union and Confederate Armies*, Atlas, plate XXVI, no. 4.

way; narrows the strip of land about the house, and flows on either side of it. We took turnips from the ground, saw cabbages of large dimensions, peas promising plenty, and that speedily, and talked of the tobacco and cotton to be.

Monday morning. While we were waiting in the Dr's office, this morning, for our boat, Mrs. Gayl [?] and her daughter— from our first confiscated farm—came in to beg a bed-stead and a chair from the Dr. The daughter was young, and very pretty, but fire was in her eye and fury on her lips. While they were in waiting the Dr received an order from Genl Dix put in his hand (designed to overrule Genl Viele's conciliatory courtesies,) to retain, in safe-keeping, all property found upon the confiscated estates, except such articles as he (the Dr) might permit the occupants to carry away with them. "Well, you promised me the chair before you received this." The daughter encouraged her mother in making appeals, and the Dr said, "When your daughter comes here with the stars in her hair and the red, white and blue in her bonnet, I'll see what I can do." "You'll never see that," said the daughter. "I'll starve, first." "Oh, you'll be a good Union woman, some day," said the Dr. "Never." "Do you know what the ladies did Fast-day?" "Fast-day, what Fast-day," said the Dr. "Why, last Friday, the President's Fast." "Oh, did Prest Lincoln proclaim a fast, for last Friday?" "No, Prest Davis, our Prest." "Oh, I've heard of the man," said the Dr. "Yes, I reckon you have," said the miss, "and reckon your army has too, and will hear of him again, very soon." "You would not let us go to Church Fast-day, and I'll tell you what we did. The ladies fasted and prayed at home." "Did you fast?" asked the Dr. "Yes, indeed I did, I took a cup of coffee in the morning, and I did not take anything else all day." "Well," said the Dr "I never saw you half so pleasant, as you are this morning, if you would fast very often, you'd soon fast all the Secesh out of you." "Hmmm I dont wish to do that. I'll never do that."

A very little girl said to Ary, in Portsmouth, "I don't like

8. Possibly Mrs. I. Cale, whose home was on the west branch of the Elizabeth River, opposite Cornick Creek. *Official Records of the Union and Confederate Armies*, Atlas, plate XXVI.

you, I'm secesh, I don't like any-body who came from the North. I don't like my mother because she came from the North." On our way from Norfolk we stopped at Fort Norfolk, to see the wife of the surgeon, who has repeatedly called on us.

. . . . .

Secession-ladies have been in the habit of flocking to the Fort, and talking treason noisily. Mrs. Ensign heard some ladies threatening to "make the Yankees leap," the day of the attack. A lady from Richmond arrived in Norfolk within a few days.—In rebel-correspondence, recently received, it is stated that boats from Norfolk run the blockade three times a week. The lady of the badge (who forged a pass in the office of the Pvt Marshal,) has finally succeeded in running the blockade.—Between here and Norfolk, we see [a] little white flag floating over the wreck of the Merrimac.

At low-tide the boiler of the Merrimac can be seen. From an old boiler at Fort Norfolk,[9] and from the doors of the barracks the soldiers have made ornaments, and have made fortunes by selling "Bits of the Merrimac." Our copper bolt and our wood were taken by Mr Kings own hands. With my own hands, I bore away from Pigs Point, shrapnel, and made my horse bear away a lignum vitae cannon-wheel. Mrs Brown found, in her house, a letter from—Pegrim [sic] who commanded the battery at Pig Point. He said all the harm he could do the enemy was to grin and make faces at them. Newport News lies opposite the Point. The James River, and the Nansemund were protected by it (supposed to be). We found cannon in the fort, one still mounted. Seven of the cannon were casemated. The land-sides were protected by breast-works, and the quicksands outside the casemates were forced to inertia by elaborate wickerwork. The chimneys are standing of a well to-do-house, which stood within the fortifications. Flowers were blossoming in the garden, and I brought away roots from the soil. Our ride took us through the Louisiana and Georgia Camps. The Louisiana Camp, which in an early

9. A Union fort at the entrance of the eastern branch of the Elizabeth River about one-half mile northwest of the city of Norfolk. The fort was directly across the Elizabeth River from Pinner's Point. It now is on Front Street, Norfolk. *Official Records of the Union and Confederate Armies*, Atlas, plate XXVI, no. 4; *Virginia Guide*, p. 250.

letter I called the Georgia Camp, has given its last log to our fires. The Dr was very much distressed, early in the work of destruction, by finding the houses deserted in which two or three colored families had been sheltered, and he called his workmen to account, thinking they might have molested the people. But he learned that they fled from fear of their former master, who since they set up for themselves, and refused to come and go at his bidding threatened to burn them out if they did not speedily leave his soil. The Georgia Camp was built upon twelve broad streets. The rebels burned the barracks— cold comfort for us Islanders.

Peach-orchards abound in these regions. We passed several in our ride. Three weeks ago the peach-trees were in blossom in Dr Brown's yard. It has always been supposed that peace alone enables a man to sit under his own vine and fig tree, but to war, alone Dr Brown is indebted for the beautiful fig-trees which now promise him fruit. A large evergreen mulberry stands before Dr Browns door. The live-oak, branching like an apple-tree with leaves like a berry is one of the glories of this region. The magnolia is common here, and other beautiful ornamental evergreens, whose names I could learn if I could succeed in finding a native who knows them.

"Have you ever been married, Miss Lucy?" asked one of our very few kind-tempered and sympathetic women (whose goodness is patent.) "Nor Miss Sarah either?" "Well, a good husband is very comfortable, but its mighty bad to have a bad one." My kitchen "people" quarreled today about the question of honor due each other. One of the boys was an overseer, and he demanded of the others to call him overseer. Mary Jane said, "My master would kill any-body who called *any-body* but a white person Missis." Ary boasted of her white blood and all the others became at once enraged. "Well, how near do you think my child was to being white? My father was white, and his father was white." "Well," said one "Just tell me how many folks it takes to make a white person?" Ary was obliged to answer, "One white man and one white woman."

Ever very affectionately

LUCY

Craney Isd. April 1st '63

THE MAINLAND, VIRGINIA

[Sarah and Lucy to Father, no date, 1863?]

*M*y dear Papa,

How will it please thee to look on thy daughters faces on paper? In anticipation of seeing them soon. Sarah is nearly well. I suppose the conflict will open again speedily, and we may be unable to find a transport; if we are, we shall leave by the last of the month the regular way. We have green corn and tomatoes in our market, and figs, and the most delicious of berries and apples in great abundance.

. . . . .

Love to all from thy aff daughter

LUCY

My dear father,

If this climate was not dangerous for Northerners I should spend all the ink and paper it would take to get thee out here to see the wondrous vegetation of this most beautiful country. Every day I wish father could see this tree or that view——In the Fall I trust thee will come——The second Summer is telling on my constitution. I feel that if I ever wish to be good for anything again I should go North immediately but the feeling that I may never see Norfolk again if once I turn away makes it almost impossible to go——Such rich mines of purest love as are here I never dreamt of——"Bless de Lord da goes Miss Sarah, de good Lord foller her every step" and "dah's my lady. I prays for her every day and de children will as long as dey live"—how many times a day I hear expressions of this kind which make me happy and stimulate me to higher endeavor——The over estimation in which I am held humbles me with the knowledge of my shortcomings but makes me constantly endeavor to do my best in all things.

Farewell with love to all—thy ever affct daughter

SARAH

Whitehead Farm No. 1
5th mo. 1863
[June 13, 1863]

Dear Ones at home:

Sarah and I are domiciled with the man who wrote the following, to Dr Brown; "Dr Brown, Sir I wish you would be kind enough to let me know if those ladys that were at my house to day are coming up here to teach school if they are I shall be obliged to move my family for we have never been used to Negro equality nor to White Ladys going in the kitchens and kissing the Negroes. Sir, I am a union man and ever shall be but I am not an abolitionist nor never can be as fer you I believe you are a perfect Gentleman you have always treated me as such and I am willing to do all I can for you and the Government but if you allow those Ladys to live on the farm you will get very little work done by the Negroes and it will end my peace fer this year as fer Mr. Giny [?] he need not give himself any trouble about their teaching my children I am able to school my children as yet without sending them to a Negro school.

Yours Respectfully,
Wm Wakefield, Overseer"

. . . . .

Sarah glories in being nomenclator of the first babe among the new-born freemen upon Gov. Wise's estate. "John Brown Wise" he is hight, and Sarah highted him, and she stood on Gov Wise's threshold, when she said "This be thy name!" I had the pleasure of taking the inventory of Gov Wise's household goods.[1] I handled every dish of his superb dining-sets (said) [sic] I wondered if his blood-stained fingers gave the rosy hue to his finger-bowls; counted his very neat and pretty carpets; sat on the sofa where he has found rest, and which, he, perhaps, is now longing for. Saw his books, papers, and pictures, and thought How long it would be before he would see any of them again. I could not help mourning with the Wise-mourners, when I saw the carefully saved noses, handles, and covers, of very old and probably sacred pieces of china; and I really wanted to put them again into the hands that once itched to cement them. Gov Wise's farm is upon the East branch of the Elizth river, which makes a sharp turn around his estate, and heightens its picturesque beauty. Noble ash-trees stand on his lawn and the house, though old, is large, and wears a certain air of country stateliness. Six or eight negroes were left by his family in their old quarters. They told me they had no wish to see him back again; and they spoke of him with little affection. One woman told me she often heard the Gov talk with his family and friends about John Brown. The Govs elegant family-carriage stopped the way at my

1. When the area was occupied by Union forces, Wise's property was confiscated. Barton H. Wise asserts that before "the protegees of the Freedmen's Bureau" took over the farm, its "furniture, bric-a-brac, pictures, and household articles" had been carried to Fortress Monroe by military forces. Apparently Miss Chase made an inventory of the Governor's effects when they were seized. In the summer of 1866 General John M. Schofield ordered Wise's property returned, and numerous articles were located at the fortress, in the officer's quarters, and elsewhere. Others were later returned from Washington at Schofield's insistence. Rolleston was returned to Wise in 1868 on orders of General E. R. S. Canby. Wise, *Life of Wise*, pp. 372-375.

front-door, this very morning, and I was honored with an invitation to ride upon its cushioned-seat. To the Gov. we are indebted for our milk and butter——Sarah and I, for the time being, are sole proprietors of one of his cows. . . .

As little milk as she can give gives the cow, and as poor (perhaps, also, as much and as rich) and her butter is not golden. Then to the tender mercies of Gov Wise's carriage I trusted myself, and, on the comfortless seat I sacrificed the vigor of my back-bone. The roads are hard to travel, and we expect in vain when we fancy the Virginians will mend any of their ways. Level as New Jersey is the country, round about, but over hill, then into hollow rolls the carriage, tumblety-bump; and, after rain has fallen, horse and wheel plough through mire (when the mire does not hold them fast.) A drive in any direction takes one through the woodlands, which are novel, and of surpassing beauty. The Southern pine, of delicate foliage, shoots its straight shaft far up into the blue; the hanging moss festoons the branches, and brambly vines luxuriant and various, bind all the motley trees in close fellowship. The foliage of the trees is more delicate than that of our forest-trees, the leaves sport in the breeze [?] more freely, and more grace and beauty crown the Southern trees. The farm-houses, (Every-body out of town lived! on a farm) are invariably distant from the street, to which a gate by the roadside gives them communication. The houses are generally small, and unpretending; but those that have fallen into our hands are mostly very handsomely furnished, and, as good luck did have it whether it would or no, are charmingly planted on the river-banks. On the Bradford-farm we pant for breath; there, the woods fell for one-man's comfort, and the encircling woods of the hollow-square where his house is planted say "There is no beyond." And you believe them and you hope for nothing, and care for nothing, but keep on sighing because there is nothing. Martha Chase is shut in by woods on the Baker farm; but her horizon politely retires a quarter of a mile from her presence, and a road that starts from the plain and hides in the woodland premises something with its perpetual, "Come and see."

But no house with its outside kitchen and negro-quarters

can look lonely. Outside kitchen!! Sarah's and my horror by day and our servant's chamber by night! We run to it, scream to it, send to it, try hard to get something done in it, and try still harder to get something brought out of it. It is our hay-stack, and every-thing that belongs in the house is the pin we must hunt for there. We have four regular servants; and volunteer-aids, unnumbered; but, if we call on Polly, she summons Betty; and "Mary Jane do this," is sure to wake the echo, "Oh, Albert, whar's Albert!" Our kitchen is a heart-wearying treadmill. We can't get ahead of our smutty servants and their smutty kettles. A kettle clean, and in waiting for its stated work is a kettle that can not, could not and will not be seen! Our china is washed in our parlor, that porcelain and delf need not mar each other; but when the stores go from parlor to kitchen the china goes also; the silver seeks society, and goes with the saucer, the pitchers go to the pump; because we have four pails, and because they are very small and be-cause the cistern is a great way off, and when they come back they stop in the kitchen because they don't belong there, and because that is going visiting. All the "people" stop "in the kitchen" also, because they don't belong there and because we tell them so. And our some-time smoking food stops in the kitchen, because its long past meal-time, and it did not happen to find its way into the parlor half an hour too early. From our large, four-sided, Craney Island house we came to our present crowded quarters, and when we put our stores into our parlor-closet, the uninvited, a host that no man could number, came in to partake of them. While I write, I listen to the music of falling grains of rice which the flies work from a dish to the floor. If the sugar bowl is uncovered for a moment, the black-ness of blackness enshrouds it, and, like lumps of (negro) sugar the flies lie piled to its mouth. How hard it rains! thought Mr Lovell and we, as we woke in the mornings. The flies make their mark, emphatically, upon current literature. They work faster than I do, and fill all my sheets in advance of my pen.

Our other dark little friends, who swarm about us do their best to relieve us of the pests. They fan us while we eat, and while we sleep. Oh! give me a slave to fan me while I sleep! (as the poet did not say) They would fain worship us, the little things. I suspect my head will fall a victim—not to the fever and ague, but to the fevre de negre, which is to scratch the head of himself or any other. I, one day, foolishly gave up my head to four little beseigers who robbed my head to enrich their own. They drew my torn hair over their wool, appealing to each other for compliments on their good looks. They like to handle us, to pull at our hoops, and hang about us. We find we can't keep them at a distance, so we let them creep, kitten-like into our parlor, remembering we are in Virginia, and doing as the Virginians do. But we are obliged to deny them the coveted comfort of a seat in our rocking chair, since my fine-toothed comb has detected in my head what was once seen on a church-going lady's bonnet. . . .

Soldiers and their horses are constantly in our door-yard. Suffolk is pouring its hordes upon us. Genl Getty[2] has taken one of our farms for his head-quarters, and is running a line of intrenchments through two or three others; and we expect the labor upon five or six must be sacrificed to the invading friend (?) Two or three fortifications are building very near us, and we confidently look for the war to come into Africa.

Four days ago, an order came from head quarters to send out pickets to seize all negroes and their teams on the highway without passes. And I, with my permanent pass, was startled by being stopped just beyond a picket-station near home, by some dusty soldiers, who demanded my pass. I asked for an explanation, and was allowed to pass on with Shorty whom the soldiers coveted. Very few people have passes for an in-definite period; and one soldier said to the other, "She's got the very best kind of a pass." On our return from the farm, three other wandering soldiers screamed out to Shorty, "You'd better look out, or you'll be confiscated." Whenever our servants have wished to go to near farms I have written passes for them; and yesterday, knowing that all men who cannot give a good account of themselves are to be put at work

2. Brigadier General George Washington Getty was placed in command of a division in the area in March and in September was given command of the area between the James and Albemarle Sound, exclusive of Norfolk and Portsmouth. *Official Records of the Union and Confederate Armies,* ser. I, vol. 29, part 2, pp. 226–227; *D.A.B.,* VII, 230–231.

upon the fortifications, I wrote "My servants," on the boys passes. Thanks to the accident of my living on a Government Farm, and holding a pass which takes me to all the Farms in this Department, my passes *pass;* and I saw my boys again.

On the Farm where Genl Getty and his staff are quartered is a flaxen haired blonde, the fairest of the fair; who sits alone and sings and paints. Four or five months ago, when the Dr took the farm, he found her living upon it, with a slave woman belonging to Mr Wilson, who was in the rebel-army. He cross-questioned her with little satisfaction, and was convinced she was a spy. He tried to convince her that it was unwise for her to remain; and he urged her to join her friends. Finding, two months ago, that she was frequently visited by officers, he begged her to come and live under our protection, but she refused. Determined to do all in his power to protect her, he obtained from Genl Viele an order forbidding soldiers to trespass upon Government farms and caused the order to be posted upon that farm, and upon neighboring farms. Pretty and accomplished though she is, the colored woman cannot be made to acknowledge herself to be her mother but the neighbors know that the black and white are mother and child. . . .

When I made my first visit to the nearest farm the overseer's wife tracked into the kitchen after me, and said, "I should like to know why folks don't go round giving white children books and slates!" My time was too precious to heed the intruder, and so I went on with my talk to the negroes. Mrs Armstrong, standing six feet high, was determined to show me the extreme *lowness* of her stature as a Virginia white! and, while I offered a book to a woman near me, said, "Jane, what's the use of your learning to read, I'd like to know. You're a great deal too old, you cant learn." So Jane refused my book and slate, and "Did not wish to learn!" A few days ago, I visited the farm again, with clothing; and Mrs Armstrong (having, I suppose learned that I represented power it was wise in her to respect) was extremely gracious with her, "Miss Chase, would you like this?" "Oh yes, Polly, study all you can and learn, you ant a bit too old to learn." "Have you got a book, Jane?" "Oh Moses, you've got one, that's right."

Upon one of the farms this letter was handed me for Dr Brown.

"Mr Willis Criss has been hear and wanted me to have him, and I dont want to have aneything to do with him and I dont him [sic] to come here whare I am. Mr Jerimiah Standing has been hear and has ben hear ever since last Cristmust on the place and I want to take him as my Husband and he has ben my husband ever since he has ben hear. I want to keep him as my husband. Mr Criss has ben hear and has threatened to kill my husband. I want you to keep him a way from hear and he does not belong to the farm at tall. Hannah Standing."

Coming from the Wise farm a few days ago, we picked, up five miles from Norfolk an old negro man with a runaway's pack on his back. He misunderstood our driver's inquiry and said, "No, I shant go back tonight, I reckon I'll stop awhile." We told him to jump into our clothing-tumbler and we found he was taking his first free walk. Refugees crowd into Norfolk and Portsmouth. The colored residents hold weekly charity meetings to aid them and government strives to feed them, and give them work, but hundreds are overlooked. While we were at the Wise farm a woman and two children found an asylum there—an asylum in the human stable, now washed and made clean by the blood of John Brown!

"What do you need?" We say as clothing-women. Not being understood, we say, "What do you want?" To which in the language, that is plainer than words, there is one invariable reply, "Whatever I can get!" With no means of knowing what is greed and is need our anxiety and responsibility is unceasing and wearsome. We dined at a distant farm, the other day, and the colored cook, who had taken great pains to make the table attractive, to us, said, after dinner "I should have been very much interested if you had not eaten dinner here." Sarah handed an old man, (a good reader,) a testament, and he inquired eagerly, if he should find "Revolutions in it." Our servants ask if they shall "Pull any rubugs for us." If they shall pick "snaps" (string-beans) for dinner. If they shall "Cup the cow." Laugh, convulsively, whenever we say, "Hark!" to each other. Saying they never heard anything but

"Stop!" The mail! the mail! and the mail carrier. Excuse my short letter.

Ever lovingly LUCY,
Portsmouth Va—June 13 1863

Boston, Sept. 14th, 1863.

My dear Miss Chase,

I have your letter of the 8th inst. I take special note of the contents. I wish I could do something towards a remedy for the abuses you speak of, & I have no doubt I could accomplish some good by continuing to act under the commission which I received from Secy Stanton last fall under which I did some service to the blacks at Fort Monroe & vicinity. The Secy would I think be glad to have me examine & report again, but I should hardly do so without another conference with him.

Meantime I am at present very much occupied in selecting a new company of teachers for Newbern & of teachers & superintendents of plantations at Port Royal, & I think also of going to Port Royal by Genl. Saxton's[1] repeated invitations as soon as I can get away. I do not see therefore that I can go to Norfolk just now, although I see the importance of it & would like to do it. I will endeavor through Dr Howe to have some changes made, & may also see Mr Sumner on the subject in a day or two. I think Mr Stanton would at once take notice of any well authenticated facts of the kind you name, & issue such orders as would correct the evil to a great extent. . . .

The suggestions on the other pages of your letter, in regard

1. Rufus Saxton of Massachusetts, a graduate of the Military Academy, was a captain in the Quartermaster Corps in 1861, became brigadier general, volunteers, in 1862 and major general in 1865. As commanding officer of the Sea Islands area and as assistant commissioner of the Freedmen's Bureau, he strongly supported the plans of Edward L. Pierce, Secretary Chase, and other friends of the Negro to carry out the dramatic "Port Royal experiment." Saxon was dismissed in January 1866 and was replaced by Robert K. Scott. See Johnson, *A Social History of the Sea Islands*, pp. 171–195; Pierce, "The Freedmen at Port Royal," *Atlantic Monthly*, XII (September 1863), 291–315; Mrs. A. M. French, *Slavery in South Carolina and the Ex-Slaves: or, the Port Royal Mission;* Pearson (ed.), *Letters from Port Royal, passim; Journal of Charlotte Forten*, Billington (ed.), pp. 20–29; and Rose, *Rehearsal for Reconstruction, passim.*

to the farms, seem to me very judicious, & I hope they will be carried out. I wish the policy of Govt. were more defined in regard to the districts "excepted" from the Presidents proclamation. They never should have been "excepted."

Hoping soon to hear further from you on these subjects, I am very truly yours.

L B RUSSELL   Miss Lucy Chase   Norfolk Va

Fort. Monroe Sept. 25/63

Miss Chase

Dear Madam

Your very business like letter was thankfully recd. All these things, if they do not afford light, they develop facts, by which I am in hopes of getting evidence by which I can pay all to whom anything is justly due.

Lieut. Sykes made no payrolls but sent me his books & went off. If he had made pay rolls & certified them, I could probably have got the proper officer to vouch for him & draw the money. I shall pursue the matter to the utmost. We have not a yard of shirting, if any comes that can be spared will hold it for your people, but, *your* people are fast becoming *our* people, & if you could see the huge barrells of clothing that they bring you would no longer be in doubt where the immense quantities were swallowed up last season. Dr. Brown represents you have no men left & if so what can you do with shirting? Now if you will follow your people to our new Contraband Home for them, & look after them there, we will supply all good men not only with shirts, but with work & pay. Or they can build themselves little cabins & take their families on to a little farm & take care of themselves, or they can find situations possibly elsewhere. See copy of letter enclosed. I could find a hundred places for them but for their children. What do you say about going to the Home. It is to be not only a Home, but a kind of Hotel for them to tarry at as they come in & go out. As Genl Naglee[1] is left out we expect a large increase of arrivals. Gov.

1. Henry Morris Naglee, graduate of the U. S. Military Academy, Lieutenant Colonel, 16th U. S. Infantry in 1861; became brigadier general, volunteers, in February 1862. He served in the defense of Washington, in the Peninsula cam-

Andrew has broke down all barriers, & we propose to tempt all slaves yet with their masters within 50 or 100 miles to take up their beds &c & walk this way. Is there any harm in that? If your people are in danger or in any way suffering we could now take them in at the Home & here somehow until we can make better accommodations for them. Dr. Brown is off & I know not if they can be got over before he returns. If so who can attend to it and how many are there left, Men, women, and children each. Dr. Brown said that there were several large stoves for warming large rooms, how is that, how many, how large, & is there much pipe with them. If you will trouble yourself to make inquiries & report, I will try to perfect the work

Yrs. truly
C. B. WILDER[2]
CAPT. & A.Q.M.

ENCLOSURE

COPY

Clarkson Hall, No 115 Cherry St
Philadelphia Sept 22 1863.

Mr C B Wilder
    Fort Monroe Va
        Dear Sir
        You will see by this, that I am in charge of an employ-
ment office for Colored persons. The demand is very great at
this time and all the more since the New York riots. I write to
ask if you think the way can be opened to get a number of both
women and girls to this City from Norfolk, and the Fortress.
I can get them good homes, and I cannot think that their suffer-

---

paigns, and in North Carolina and South Carolina. In 1863 he was placed in command of the 7th Army Corps and of the District of Virginia. He was transferred to Vicksburg in September 1863. *Appleton's*, IV, 476; *Official Records of the Union and Confederate Armies*, ser. I, vol. 29, part 2, pp. 226–227.

2. Captain Charles B. Wilder of Massachusetts. He was assistant quartermaster, volunteers, in 1863 and was superintendent of contrabands in Virginia in the area north of the James. Heitman, *Register*, I, 1035; *Official Records of the Union and Confederate Armies*, ser. I, vol. 18, pp. 570–571; ser. III, vol. 3, pp. 1139–1144.

ing will be less this winter than last, at the above places. Please do me the favor, if it will not be too much trouble, to tell me whether or no, you think anything can be accomplished by coming to the Fortress.

I think now I shall have to go to Washington before I can accomplish much from that source, and at the same time I might down [*sic*] to Norfolk. Please let me know if you know anything, [of] Mr Benjamin Bozeman, who was at Newport News while I was there. Yours Respectfully

Signed   JOHN OLIVER

Craney Island, Sepr 30th 1863

Dear ones at home:

This last day of Sepr. 1863 is the last day of the occupation of Craney Island by the Contrabands! Two hundred negroes have just left for Hampton; and Sarah and I are awaiting the arrival of a Norfolk boat, that we may accompany the remaining negroes to Norfolk. Memorable indeed, will be these last days on the Island. Yesterday afternoon, the John Tucker,[1] a huge steamer, "came into port," bringing orders for all destined for Norfolk to be ready for an early boat today, and designing, herself, to hurry away to Hampton with negroes and with bed and board of the contrabands; but though the beds were packed when she came, the boards were still in barracks, and though the eager "Travellers" snatched at their own rooftrees, the tide fell before their work was done; and they stayed to help us remember our last night on Craney Island!

After dark, Sarah and I took a pour prendre conge stroll, when we longed for you all to bear us company. Fires were blazing in the fire-places of the lonely chimneys, and picturesque groups were crooning over the embers. Out on the plain blazed fires, the centre of just such groups as you have

1. A transport frequently used by Federal forces in the area, also called *C. Vanderbilt* or *Charlotte Vanderbilt*, not to be confused with the *U.S.S. Vanderbilt. Official Records of the Union and Confederate Armies*, Index, p. 991; Wheaton J. Lane, *Commodore Vanderbilt, An Epic of the Steam Age*, pp. 175–179.

heard of! "Groups for a painter!" As we drew near one circle, we Oh'd for a Darley, a Walter Brown,[2] or a lead pencil. Facing us, sat an old man, with his withered, whisker-shaded face almost lost under his slouched hat; with his shoulders comfortably and cozily raised, as if to fondle his good-natured cheeks; and with his hands resting on the shoulders of a little child who stood between his knees. Around him stood all ages, sexes, sizes and conditions, but prominent amongst them all was the pomegranite-cheeked young mother, the young wife of the old man upon whose loving and really lovely face all eyes were fixed, because her hand held the skillet, with its promise of supper. That out-stretched hand, grasping the long iron handle, its kindred in color, the golden steaming corn-cake, the fond and hungry children, the crackling fire, doing its best in a picturesque way, outlining each figure til it became a shining mark, the evening darkness, the desert plain, the long rows of house-deserted chimneys, the water all around and very near, and Sarah and I looking upon it all!

· · · · ·

At one of the fire-places, whose sides were as numerous as the points of the compass, our welcome was very hearty. The good-dame said, "When my husband came it was 'God bless Miss Chase, God bless Miss Chase, God bless Miss Chase,' all the time! and I said, 'Who is Miss Chase?' He said, 'Oh, she's a good lady, if hadn't been for her I could never have got to the Island!'" "Yes, yes," said the man, "I shall love you always. I shall love you as long as I live." Sarah told me that when she came to the Isd she found him at the office, eager to get permission to come to Craney Island for his family, for whom he had already built a house. Permission was refused him, but my sister entreated in his behalf, and not in vain, and he was happy and his wife was happy, and they were both thankful. Around one fire the boys had gathered to dance and make merry. The door of a fallen barrack was their springboard, and upon it they performed their jigs and horn-pipes, keeping time to a variety of strange accompaniments the rapid

2. Felix O. C. Darley, American artist and illustrator; Walter F. Brown, a Boston artist. Mantle Fielding, *Dictionary of American Painters, Sculptors, & Engravers*, pp. 44-45, 87.

and regular falling of the hands upon the knees, the beating of feet, or the pleasing accompaniment of a tenor and base voice singing alternate strains of music. Of one of their Union songs I remember a few words "Richmond town is burning down." "High diddle diddle inctum inctum ah." The byplays and interludes were as good as the play. If a well-to-do dancer had his coat-sleeve pulled or was threatened with a tripe [*sic*] he turned from his partner, and almost before he was missed, was rolling and tumbling with his teaser in the sand. Then all were challenged when one boy said, "You can't spell every." "Ev -ev ry ry- evry," said one and another each trying, all interested, and those who could say, with the pride of sure knowledge, "Ev- ev, Er-er- Ever-y," looking, for a moment, every inch the pedagogue. Spelling is with them an exciting pastime. When at work toting the barrack-boards to the wharf, men, women and children spelled aloud for their own private ears, though we heard now and then "B-o-a-r-d, Board," "H-o-u-s-e, House."

Under the fallen roofs some of the evening fires were built. In doors and out many families were preparing for a feast of rats! Under every barrack the dogs have found more rats than they had power to worry. One hundred and sixty huge rats were found under one barrack. Let many or few come to light, when the floors are raised, the negroes eagerly seize them, skin them, cook them and eat them. "Oh, they taste like chickens," you are told. "What are you cooking, Aunty?" "Some calls em squirrels, but they'r altogether too tame for squirrels; I call em pigs. They ran all round my head last night, crying 'Peat weet.' They've lived long enough on my good things to be good eating. One night they ate up the whole of my ration of meal and meat, and now I'm going to take my pay. I reckon they'r as good eatin as possum. They only eat bread, and such like. I don't see any-body around here that won't eat em, any way. They say no, at first, but I have not seen any-one who did not say yes, after the first taste."

Sarah and I walked from barrack to barrack to say Good-bye. Every-body was packed or packing, but every-one had a smile for us. Though most of those we found upon the Island were recent refugees from Suffolk, (and strangers to us) our relation to them is much more intimate and sympathetic than it was with most of our last winter's friends. They are a superior class; have but recently become paupers and are not demoralized by long clinging to the skirts of the army; (from which insecure position the last winter Craney Islanders were so frequently shaken—dropped as they were at Yorktown, to be dropped again at Hampton, then again in Craney Island, then to be removed to Newport News, only for a season, to be turned back again to Craney Island upon the arrival of Corcoran's Legion at Newport News.) Then, too, they do not beg of us (probably because we came empty-handed) and consequently have no refusals from us. And, as we are "White folks" it "seems like home" they say, "to have us about," and they are really glad to see us.

From the barracks, we went, last night, to a religious meeting, where we heard a preacher worthy of a high seat in our Newport synagogue. He is from Gates County, N. Carolina,[3] and I feel very sure that he must have lived very near Friends, for his musical intoning can have been picked up nowhere but in Friends meeting; and his mode of appeal, of argument, and of illustration were decidedly Quaker-like.

. . . . .

Sarah's stay here has been a fortnight; while I have been here a week. We have taught the children, visited the sick, clothed some of the most needy, and done what we could to make the road easy for those who are seeking to join their families. One woman who always came to the school at the first sound of the bell, said to me, one morning, "I feel so anxious to learn! Every once in awhile I come to the name of God,—and the love of it, the name is so sweet, I can't help trying to learn!" We often hear the negroes singing this— "Jesus been here, been here, been here,—Dun bless my soul, and gone." Some of them show, unmistakably, that their souls are blessed.

3. Gates County, North Carolina, lies between Perquimans and Hartford Counties in eastern North Carolina, directly south of Norfolk. This was among the earliest areas of Quaker settlement in North Carolina. The Society in this area was weakened by western migration but was still active at the time of the Civil War. See Stephen B. Weeks, *Southern Quakers and Slavery, passim.*

. . . . .

Sarah's stores for the sick, were, by mischance, left at Norfolk. The well on the Island were suffering for food; and we had nothing with which to tempt the convalescing. The Island has, until recently, been freely supplied with sweet potatoes from one of the Dr's farms, three or four miles from the Island; but a few days ago, Mr Lessing received an order from the Commander of the Pass-boat near Norfolk forbidding the removal of potatoes from the farm. Failing to receive rations from town, it being supposed there that each day would be the peoples last on the Island, none were sent, sweet potatoes were our main dependence. For several days, the people have lived on half rations; and have been obliged to work hard in tearing down and removing barracks. Sarah and I, contrary to good military order, had made, some days before, very satisfactory visits to the farm, and designed going again, on second day last. We were unable to go when the car cried, "I wait" and so lost a chance of being made prisoners. Our sweet potato cart with its potatoes, was seized and taken to the farm, but the horse and driver were allowed to return. Mr Bidgood,[4] the owner of the farm, had come home, and we supposed took advantage of the fact that there was no overseer upon the farm, and that the farm is now outside the lines, and getting the Comr of the gun-boat into his buggy, he won him to his side.

. . . . .

Oct. 1st/ Last night Sarah suggested to Mr Moss that all the beans in the commissary should be cooked at the cook-house, and distributed; so we watched with interest, all news of the progress of the cooking. The beans were few and dried peas and meal were added to the stew, but yet all were not fed. Of meal every-body had enough, so they could hardly be said to be starving, but when good things are lacking, the negroes say "They have nothing to eat.—" They tire of meal, of course; and many of the so lately well-to-do Suffolk people would go hungry before they would make it their staff of life.

4. A reference to Henry or Cornelius Bedgwood, who owned land occupied by the contraband camp on Craney Island. Report of Captain Orlando Brown to General John A. Dix, January 19, 1863, in Chase MSS.

Some grumbled this morning when we went our rounds; and most of the people, tired of looking for the moment of departure, "Should be glad when they saw the last of Craney Island." One jolly soul, who hurried in to a barrack as we were hurrying out of it said to her friends, "Oh I'm sorry she's gone; I love to hear her talk; she talks so pretty." She stepped forward to us, and said, "Oh, it's so funny not to have anything to eat." It was funny to us to see the different faces put by different dispositions upon the same hard fact. A few days ago, Mr Hand forbad vegetable carts from the mainland to vend their wares on the Island; and the loss of garden-"truck" aggravated the mental suffering, and perhaps accounted wholly for the complaints.

It was a very novel sight to look out in the morning upon ten or twelve market carts, the centre of a greedy crowd. A market on Craney Island would seem to be as unprofitable as coals in Newcastle though from a far different reason. . . .

The Island was cold, and bare, and strange to us, when we first made its acquaintance; and it was, in all respects, so savage that it seemed to be the truth I spoke when I said, The tents were left by the Arabs when they silently stole away. The waiting Islanders sit, in these last days, in their doorways, wondering what the future has in store for them. "I want to get a foundation and go to work," said one to me, "I should enjoy my health better, I know; Ise always used to work."

Few of them were aware, until we told them, that each man will have a few acres of land attached to his cabin. "Oh, that's a blessing," said one. One mother rejoiced for her children. "They'r all hemmed in here. They've always run all about the corn-fields, and climbed the apple-trees." "What to be done this winter?" asked a man. "To those whats exposed to take their families empty-handed, that's what I want to know." One asked me how "We hands whom that's worked at Suffolk could get their pay. Capt Sykes is a more punctualar man than to go away and carry the books." One man gave us a reason for many of the slaves near the lines remaining still with their masters. "Because they ant willing to go through no supper-ments."

When Genl Foster[5] visited the Island he ordered large open-
ings to be made in a roofs of the barracks; and they have
served, admirably, to keep sickness out in dry weather, and
to let it in, in wet weather. In every rain-storm floors and
beds were flooded, and colds came after, in due season. When
the Genl ordered the removal of the people Dr Huckins
thought it as well to take the logs from the rebel-built cabins
for fuel, as to send to the woods on the main-land; so one cabin
furnished back-logs for all the cabins. But Dr Clark spared
the remaining houses. One of the negroes said to me "We had
to tear down the houses on account of we colored population
having something to burn."

. . . . .

Octr 2nd. No boat for us yesterday; but today a tug and a
barge came early. Upon the tug stepped Mr King, Sarah and
myself; and into the barge went the colored people, with all
their worldly goods. We left upon the Island, the Commissary
and the Druggist with a few colored men to complete the
destruction of the barracks.

. . . . .

It was a very pretty sight to look upon the confused crowd
of the animate and inanimate floating at our side. Barrel-heads
and human heads, canvas-bags without number, all in-doors
turned out of doors; looking strangely "not at home." All en-
livened by dashes of brilliant color on the head of or shoulders,
and in the faces too, for there is an amazing variety in the
hue African. Give me some vermillion, some blue, and some
white, and you shall see a tint to be proud of. Lo, behold, *this*
is the blood that runs in *my* family. Now give me some
cadmium, golden cadmium, the very "Rays of the Sun"——
Dont be afraid to take too much of it. No matter if 'tis the most
costly of colors shall it not picture the blood of the F.F.V's.

5. Major General John Gray Foster of New Hampshire, a graduate of the
Military Academy and, for a time, a member of the faculty. He rose rapidly in
rank during the Civil War, becoming major general, volunteers, in July 1862.
He was engineer in charge of fortifications at the surrender of Fort Sumter.
He was placed in command of the Department of the South in May 1864.
Heitman, *Register*, I, 431; *D.A.B.*, VI, 549–550; *Official Records of the Union
and Confederate Armies*, ser. I, vol. 27, part 3, p. 723; Butler, *Butler's Book*,
p. 897.

The blood of the F.F.V.'s, enriched and beautified by its admixture with the sang d'Afrique? Give me some Lake too, some Prussian blue and some white. But I wont neglect the darker skins. The warm chesnut [*sic*] nut color, shining as the nut from which it borrows its name; enriched and glowing as no white complexion can be with its rosy blood. Purples that might well be called "Royal!"—and Browns of many shades—I notice as much individuality in the faces of Negroes as I do in those of the whites. Their features are so much lost in the single shadow with which Nature has veiled their faces, that I once fancied that they would be hard to find and recognize. Every shade that light drops upon our faces lifts some feature into greater prominence. But black Sue looks herself as well as white Sue.

. . . . .

We hope to go, in a few days, to the farms where they will be established. No one can grieve over the loss of Craney Island; but we sympathize with the many loyalists cut off from market by the change of "Lines." A loyal German at Pig Point can reach no market with his sweet potatoes, and must go without flour. He showed his loyalty some months ago, by releasing from prison in Richmond a Union officer, whom he kept secreted for a month in his own house. Of course he is only one of many. Farmers break their contracts with Negroes unscrupulously. Some taunt the negro with his loss of protection, and refuse to share the harvest with him. One farmer steadily refuses to share a large crop with his negro workman "Because he does not pay him twenty-five dollars he owes him." Knowing well that without a market the negro cannot get $25. I called the attention of the Adjt Genl to these cases, and he proposes securing the crops, and dividing with the negroes. He says there is no legal way by which to aid the German; but he promises to hire a lighter (of course no govt steamer can be employed) and bring up the potatoes making an exception of the German. We have a very familiar acquaintance with the Adj Genl and his wife. We broke his wife down, you know, in our buggy, one day; and then we all broke down together one day, in one of the Dr's large, three-seated carriages. I had interested them in the flaxen haired, blue-eyed girl, and her negro mother, on the Wilson farm, and we were on our way to see her.

. . . . .

We are frequently charmed with the delicacy and tenderness with which the Negroes express affection for each other. They know how to love, and how to remember. We sometimes witness the unexpected meeting of scattered members of a family. When the John Tucker was at the C. Isd wharf a little girl who had wondered where she should go, as she had no friends to go with, or to go to, strolled upon the deck of the steamer and found in one of the hands her father! After reaching Norfolk there were other surprising meetings and recognitions. Sarah assisted many to find their friends, and she found homes for some, and work for others. For some young boys she found work upon the fort near us, with the promise of ten dollars a month. Sarah teaches at the fort, first days, and she exults over the progress of her pupils. We are near the war-fields, still.

. . . . .

The guard on our bridge are from a regt just come to town; and they seem to be as ignorant of military proprieties as they are of military officers. The evening of the same night the P. Marshal and his wife took tea with us, and as they seemed inclined to hurry away early, I said I would send my guard to the bridge to tell the sargeant that Maj. Beauvais would cross late in the evening. "I dont believe Maj Beauvais sent you, he would have sent a written order. Besides, I don't know him from Jeff Davis," was the tale brought back, so the Maj thought it as well to leave before the bridge was drawn. I looked from my window just now into a cloud of dust, and saw forty horses tied in one knot led by an artilleryman. They were followed by other troops and multitudes of horses which were knotted together.

Just now too, the four little children we have in our family, wild always, and irrepressibly playful, made such a bustle at our elbows that Sarah cried "Hark!" with amazing spirit. All hushed at once but the always unquenchable Albert, who burst out in a muffled growl. Little, few-years-old Bennie, his dignified rebuker, who is as solemn in the parlor as he is play-

ful in the kitchen, and who puts censure in his eye and surprise and sorrow on his young lips whenever the other children fail in showing due respect to "white folks" joined with
Annie, (whose merriment is never below the gushing point,)
in sternly reminding Albert that "Miss Sarah said Hark."
"Oh! I thought she said Bark!" said ingenious Albert. Annie
said, just now, to Sarah, "What do you think I have found?"
"Oh, a louse." "Is it a body-louse," said Sarah. "What do
you call lice found upon the body?" "Jeff Davis's Calvary,"
said Bennie. A gentleman from Yorktown told us a secession
song in honor of Jeff Davis and his steed——

> Jeff Davis rides a fine bay mare,
> While Lincoln rides a mule.
> Jeff Davis is a gentleman,
> But Lincoln is a fool.[6]

The Adj Genl says the rebel mail brings to light many
curious caricatures of Lincoln. His face to perfection, but always set upon foreign shoulders. When the Adj Genl was
speaking the other day, the excellent opportunity offered for
the escape of criminals by the removal of officers, he said
many would slip free, through Naglee's removal. Among them
was the Capt of a boat, then lying at the wharf. The boat
brought into port eighteen hundred gallons of whiskey secreted
beneath her iron-sheathing. In the Genl office is now a loaf
of bread in which a whiskey flask was buried. The loaf was
found in a soldiers mess-box which was undergoing examination at the Custom House and the tin flask was discovered
through a small crack in the loaf. Every body declares the
loaf was baked in the flask; and I suppose the whiskey may

6. See Frank Moore (ed.), *Anecdotes, Poetry, and Incidents of the War: North
and South, 1860–1865*, p. 251, for a somewhat different version: "A Secesh girl
thus wrote to her cousin, who was a prisoner at Camp Morton, Indianapolis:
> 'I will be for Jeffdavise til the tenisee river
> freazes over, and then be for him, and scratch
> on the ice
>> Jeffdavise rides a white horse,
>> Lincoln rides a mule,
>> Jeffdavise is a gentleman,
>> And Lincoln is a fule.' "

have been introduced through a very small tube. Measures are to be taken to discover the firm enriching itself in this strange contraband fashion. We sometimes see officers breaking whiskey casks and pouring their contents into the gutters. We see little boys too, dipping their hands as in to a brook into the filthy, street-running stream.

Ever yr's

LUCY

Oct 5th Va '63

Office Ass't Quartermaster

Norfolk, Va., Sept 30th 1863

Mr Emerson

Will send the tug White with Barge to Crany Island to bring away niggers.

B.C.E. GOODWIN

CAPT & AAQ

Norfolk, Va. Nov. 29th 1863

My dear Miss Lowell:[1]

Let me congratulate you on your new "Organization." You work at home, and my sister and I work here, and we all give thanks for the day that has dawned, and for the work it has brought with it. I will trust myself in your hands, especially since the Moth Socy will keep me tied to its apron strings. I thank you, kindly, for your willingness to call me one of you. And I will gladly write to you occasionally.

Two or three days ago, 4 hundred negroes followed on the

1. Probably Miss Anna Lowell of the New England Freedmen's Aid Society. The Boston, New York, Philadelphia, Cincinnati, and Chicago aid societies combined in 1863, forming the United States Commission for the Relief of National Freedmen. This group, after a series of withdrawals and additions, became the American Freedmen's Aid Commission. After a heated controversy over segregation in relief and education and a hardly less acrimonious discussion of the function of the aid society as an evangelistic organization, the Freedmen's Aid Commission was joined in 1865 by the American Union Commission. In 1866 the new organization assumed the name "American Freedmen's Union Commission." See Parmelee, "Freedmen's Aid Societies," *Negro Education*, pp. 269–271.

heels of a force sent out from Norfolk in search of guerillas, and now we find them at our doors. Two weeks ago, four hundred other negroes, accepting a cordial invitation from colored soldiers, came to town. Not to spend the winter, not to tarry but a night, but with their faces firmly turned forever and a day from their homes? Such floods we look for all through the winter.

The dark flock run out of their clothes, and run away from their beds, [page missing]

... you will "fit" if we will measure, is it not so? I have never found it necessary to send directions for cutting and making. Let all material be stout. Shirts made of bagging, or something of the nature of linen-crash, are very desirable. Colored shirts of stout cloth are useful. Stout pantaloons for men and boys are always wanted. Stout dresses too, for women. Baby-clothes are in great demand. Sewing materials, shoes, and knitting yarn, we look for, (but don't find) in each box we open.

We want everything! At all times! And in all quantities! Is that intelligible? It is so very true, that I feel very much disinclined to tell Societies of any special need. Why should not some societies send shoes only, others shirts, other dresses, and all send what they can most easily secure? "A little of all, if you please"—though, I am willing to say, since I speak not for myself.

I wish you could go with my sister and myself into Hall's Jail Yard, and to the Pest House, just after the arrival of refugees. Tumbling about amongst boxes, beds, tables, and tubs, the little ones with their shining eyes and frolicsome ways, sing "Jubilee" for the whole community. While the more anxious parents sit on table-corners, or lean against the brick walls, too unsettled in the face of an uncertain future to find rest either for body or mind. My sister saw many reunions yesterday. One woman came to her, leading a girl of eighteen, and said, "See my daughter, they sold her away from me when she was just old enough to rock a cradle, and see how they've done her bad, see how they've cut her up. From her head to her feet she is scarred just as you see her face."

A man from one of the farms just came to me for a blanket, saying, "I make out tolerably well myself, but my children, you see it grieves my mind."

I feel obliged to confine my charities to refugees, and to the laborers on Govt farms, though Norfolk and Portsmouth swarm with pauper-stricken negroes. Ten acre lots are offered the refugees, and until their own hands have raised the cabins, Dr. Brown finds homes for them. Genl Butler has made house-taking so easy that the Dr proposes putting them into houses in town. With our new Genls here and at the Fortress,[2] we hope to be recognized as a "Department" worthy of reverential deportment from the powers that be.

Our general care-taking includes, of course, teaching, in

2. Brigadier General Benjamin F. Butler was placed in command of the Virginia-North Carolina area on November 2, 1863, and Brigadier General Isaac J. Wistar replaced H. M. Naglee in command of the Yorktown sub-district. Naglee was transferred to Vicksburg. A strict disciplinarian with a somewhat harsh temper, Wistar found conditions among the contrabands "disgusting." The Army officers on duty were unscrupulous and incompetent drunkards, he asserted, and the Negroes were "lying about without any order under any ragged shelter they could get, in every stage of filth, poverty, disease and death." See Isaac J. Wistar, *Autobiography*, p. 417. Wistar took firm control of the situation and cleared a large area of adjacent land, which was laid out in lots of two to four acres, on which rude huts were constructed. The soldiers (and the Misses Chase) called this settlement "Slabtown." The Negroes were farming, gathering oysters, and working at various tasks, and their prosperity attracted "from the enterprising people of New England," said Wistar, "numerous cranks or self-styled missionaries of both sexes, who infested Slabtown in ever-increasing numbers" and who were "by no means averse to extracting a pecuniary profit from their pious labors" (p. 438). Not all were "scamps," however, for some, according to Wistar, really believed in "the equality or superiority of the negro race, and that all that was necessary for the demonstration of that new-found fact was to teach the darkey to sing hymns and read the newspapers, while supported at public expense. . . ." (p. 439). Wistar says that he received the missionaries and sent them on to their charges at Slabtown until one of them was found guilty of having tied a number of Negroes to trees for having refused to permit him to re-marry them at twenty-five cents "a pair." Though Wistar did not consider the price "unreasonable for a good article of connubial felicity, backed by a solid New England guarantee," he was incensed when he found that the marriage fee originally had been $5.00 and had been reduced only because of the poverty of the Negroes. See also Heitman, *Register*, I, 1052; *Official Records of the Union and Confederate Armies*, ser. I, vol. 29, part 2, pp. 226–227; Benjamin F. Butler, *Correspondence*, IV, 9–11, 31. The village also was known as "Acreville." It is now Lackey, Va. Morton, " 'Contrabands' and Quakers in the Virginia Peninsula," *Virginia Magazine of History and Biography*, LXI (October 1953), pp. 419–429.

which our success has been brilliant (so much I say for the African, alone.) Yesterday, my sister repeated an oft-repeated experiment of ours.

She formed a class of the new-comers at the Jail-Yard, and made of them discipline-drillers and *boys of letters!* in a few moments. Satchels and school-bells make truants and idlers; but, to the dark ones who have broken through the fence of *witholding,* [sic] and have run into golden opportunities, round O and crooked S are a surprise and delight. And the picking-up propensity which slavery engendered in the pinched African, stimulated anew by enlarged opportunity makes thrifty husbandmen of them all. So they shoulder the ax a-x, pick up the b-o-x box, play with c-a-t and d-o-g and fill their baskets with a multitude of words.

Will you be so kind as to tell Miss Stevenson that we think her proposition to send another teacher to Norfolk a wise one. We will promise to find work for her, and will give her a home with us.

Tell her to bring bed-tick and bedding, and, if she fancies good things, preserves.

Yours,
LUCY CHASE

Norfolk, Va. Novr. 29th

[Norfolk, Jan. 25, 1864]

My dear Miss Lowell!

All boxes sent to me will reach me. Col. Kinsman [1] *respects* them. So, if you forward those prepared for me, I shall probably receive them. 231 one of your boxes was marked. I received all. In future, I will try to send Mr Atkinson the numbers.

1. Josiah Burnham Kinsman of Maine was appointed Superintendent of Negro Affairs for Virginia and North Carolina in December 1863. The area south of the James River was to be administered by Orlando Brown (then Captain), that north of the James was under Captain Charles B. Wilder, and Chaplain Horace James was Superintendent for North Carolina. Lieutenant Colonel Kinsman was brevetted colonel for his service in this position, and by March 1865 he had attained the rank of major general, volunteers. Heitman, *Register,* I, 602; Benjamin Butler, "General Orders No. 46," December 5, 1863, *Official Records of the Union and Confederate Armies,* ser. III, vol. 3, pp. 1139–1144.

Norfolk, Jany 25 '64

Upon the government farms the men are ploughing. The blue birds sing, and we, as well as they, fancy the year has leaped into spring. We glory in the moonlight. It stays longer with us than it does at home; and is far brighter.

A week ago, a stranger came to us, recommended by a member of the Freedmen's Aid Ass in Phila and she is so much of an elephant that we are puzzled to know what to do with her. She is an orphan from Western Virginia. Her parents were strong Unionists. Her father freed five-hundred slaves, thereby winning the ill-will of his neighbors; and they only awaited her sick mother's death to set fire to her house, and destroy all her household goods. She found friends in Baltimore and Philadelphia who would willingly pay her board at the North; but, hearing that many persons are aiding the Contrabands, she came to Norfolk zealous to help them. She has evidently been brought up luxuriously; but her natural intelligence is small, and her education imperfect. She is very anxious to teach, and wonders that a school is not given her for the asking. She is a good-hearted girl, very eager to help when she sees any-one busy, but wholly incompetent for house-work, and strangely wandering in all her ways. We allow her to assist us in our school, and she shows a good deal of tact, when she gives her mind to her work. She is wildly and charmingly impassioned, when she talks of her suffering and its cause, and is really heroic and exalted in her happy satisfaction in having done as Peah and Meah would have had her do. She is a representative, no doubt, of a class of Vir wonders, of whom we know nothing. She puzzles and entertains us.

. . . . .

Patience has an ample field to perfect its work here.

The small-pox rages alarmingly. When patients are dismissed from the hospital their clothing is burned, and they draw upon me for raiments. I have urged, in vain the importance of looking into each case, in order to learn if the means of a patient will permit of his drawing upon his own private chest at home; but the Drs and stewards laugh at me; and since I must compromise, I do the best I can, and so send old and patched articles. The chances are not slight that the patient

is well to do, or his friends foolish. In the first case, the clothing would be rejected (after reaching home;) and, in the
second place, it would be burned, by frightened paupers. So
it is wise to send old clothes. It is a sanitary necessity, consequently a necessary charity, that the patients should be
clothed.

. . . . .

Yrs truly

LUCY CHASE

Sunday, Jany 24th 1864

New York Feb. 13/64

My dear Miss Chase,

I have to acknowledge the receipt of three letters from
you, dated Jan. 24th, Feb. 1st and 3d.

I was very glad to hear from our sacks of clothing, and I
read your letter to our ladies. It is a great encouragement to
them to hear that the garments they prepared reached their
destination and were what was needed.

You give a list of articles which are most needed, but you do
not mention *dresses*. I suppose dresses were left out by accident, as they must be among the first wants. We have made
up a great many dresses for women, in the shape of skirts and
sacques.

. . . . .

You and your sister are engaged in a noble work. You are
laying the foundations of many generations. May you be
Divinely guided. There is something grand in this effort of
the North to lift up the freedmen. It seems to me that God
never laid so great a work upon one generation as he has on
this. How often the words of Cope come to me,

> "We are living, we are dwelling
> In a grand and awful time
> In an age on ages telling
> To be living is sublime!"

I mentioned to Mr Beecher[1] what you said about his lec-

1. Henry Ward Beecher, prominent preacher and abolitionist. See Paxten
Hibben, *Henry Ward Beecher: An American Portrait.*

turing in Norfolk. He smiled and said it would be some time before he should get there, but he hoped, before he died, to speak in every one of the slave states.

In your letter of Feb. 1st you present a new field for benevolent action, and one certainly of great importance. These white children should be cared for and instructed, as well as the blacks. Would it be practicable to gather these children into the colored schools, or would the prejudices of the parents make it impossible? I know of no way in which this wicked prejudice could so well [be] overcome as by having the children of blacks and whites go to school together. This is the practice in Boston. Separate schools for the colored children were abolished many years ago, and the plan has worked well. Would it not be well for all our teachers at the South to invite the white children around them to come into their schools? If the parents dislike the idea at first, they may on second thought conclude that they had better submit to it, than to have their children grow up without education.

I talked with Mr Beecher about doing something for the white children, and he said we must take care of the black children first. There is however a large class at the North, who do not feel inclined to do anything for the colored people; they are the right ones to take up the poor whites. I hope they may be moved to do it. Those merchants, who sent such a liberal present, the other day, to the poor whites in Savannah, might easily do this work, if they could be roused up to feel its importance.

With my best wishes and prayers for your health and prosperity in the good work to which you are called, I remain

Yours truly

MRS LEWIS TAPPAN [2]

2. Wife of Lewis Tappan, New York merchant, financier, and reformer. Tappan was one of the founders of the American Anti-Slavery Society, a member of the Amistad Committee, and treasurer of the American Missionary Association. D.A.B., XVIII, 303–304; Annie H. Abel and Frank J. Klingberg (eds.), A Side-light on Anglo-American Relations, 1839–1858.

Dear friend

We forwarded to thee on the 22nd two barrels more clothing which I hope will reach thee in less time the others have
been on the way. I learned from New York that the others were
still there on the eighteenth but that they would go on the
next Government Steamer. It seems there was some misunderstanding about the express. It seems to be the opinion of the
Society that in all cases when the parents of the children are
able to pay something for the clothes they have that they
should do even though it may be only half price or less. They
will value the articles more will learn more self reliance and
feel more self respect than if they depend entirely upon
charity and thou can return the money to us to be expended
again in more material. But we would not have thee fail to
give wherever they are really destitute. I have been very sorry
to hear that Sarah Chase has been so poorly—tell her from me
that she must take better care of herself that it is wrong for
her not to and please give my love to them both.

The articles sent are as follows:

18 flannel skirts	$18.00
22 cotton flannel do	12.00
20 striped shirts	12.00
27 chemises	14.50
26 aprons	2.50
4 spencers	2.50
4 sacks	2.00
7 dresses	26.00
4 prs stockings	2.00
10 handkerchief	1.68
1 sack &c	1.00
2 prs pants	1.00
1 jacket	1.00
1 suit boy clothes	2.00

it is very difficult to get the boys clothes we would like to. I

The Mainland, Virginia 105

have thought that a little boy might do very well with a good flannel petticoat and a good long sleeved apron

15 calico dresses	18.00
10 flannel skirts	8.00
14 chemises	9.00
10 aprons	4.00
1 delaine dress	4.00
2 skirts	1.50
5 prs woolen pants	6.00
5 jackets	9.00

1 cape	1.00
2 overcoats	2.00
1 pr pants	1.00
1 skirt	.50
2 boy's suits	.75
1 spencer	.25
1 sack	.25
5 aprons	.50
1 sack	.10
1 blanket	.15
1 pr stockings	.50
1 shirt	.50
15 prs pants	2.00
1 suit boy's clothes	1.00
13 prs shoes	12.00
12 towels paper & soap	2.00

all in the other barrel are new and all down to the mark in this

Thine very truly

ANN B. EARLE
(MRS. EDWARD EARLE, TREAS)

Norfolk Va 1864

Norfolk is a Dole place three years ago i was Dasant to
say that i was free but thank God i can say so now the man
i lived with is named W W hall he says that Woebelong to
him in hell and he says that he wishes that yankees was at
the Devel when i came a way i Diden no my a b c he had sould
my brothers and sisters and would have sould me and mother
and father if he coud for he had us paced upsen to richmond
to sell he sead that the yankees had horns and thaer eyes was
be hind them and thay had but one and thay us to [illegible]
thay us to beat me this man was a negro byer he says before
meny years he will be Doin the same bisniss he ses that the
rebles will be her in may thank God that yankees come mond
he was goin to send us to richmond the next monday that
yankees come satday night he carad my brother away he sad
that youal black that you all had for legs like a hors and had
one eye before and one behind and a horn on each side

EMMA BOLT [COLT?]

[Yorktown, May 19th, 1864]

Dear Eliza,

We were delighted to receive thy last letter. Delighted to
hear from all of you, and delighted to get general news.

·   ·   ·   ·   ·

Out of the window, at my right, long streets of negro-cabins
stretch over the table-land—a complete city. Fifty cabins—
Low, pigmy door-ways, open into their narrow, dimly-lighted
single halls. Absolute neatness surrounds the cabins, which
are unfortunately crowded, and are in many instances without
garden patches. This neat little log house, with the schoolhouse
on one hand, and the store on the other, stands on a little slope
overlooking the village. Looking itself symbolic of the benefi-
cence which emanates from it. Beyond the village lies the
fort enclosing Genl Cornwallis's head-quarters and a number
of other houses, one of which is the head-quarters of Gen.
Carr,[1] successor to Gen. Wistar. Gen. Washington's head-

1. Joseph Bradford Carr, Brigadier General, Volunteers, was in command of
the Yorktown area in May 1864. *Official Records of the Union and Confederate
Armies*, ser. I, vol. 36, part 3, p. 431.

quarters, are within sight, and Gen McClellan's fortifications
are within a few minutes walk. The soil is sandy, broken, and
billowy, and, as we ride about the district, we think of the
barren moors where dwelt "that Eyre Jane we read about,"
as Sarah said.

. . . . .

First day. Yesterday we went to Williamsburg, a ride
crowded with interest. We drove through wasted plantations,
all of whose fences were sent up in smoke by the soldiers. We
passed Fort Magruder,[2] a formidable fort, with seven large
redoubts, some of which are garrissoned. A large negro village
is near, and many houses have sprung up to meet the various
needs of the large force, until recently quartered there. Williamsburg is now the oldest city in the country. Jamestown
is no longer a city. It is a city in the wilderness. Williamsburg
is a Conn. valley village in feature. The streets are wide, the
houses old, and picturesque, with sharp roofs & dormer windows. Radiant now with rose-draped porches. Thee may remember that the rebels left a multitude of insane in their
Asylum in Williamsburg.[3] Those patients have been, from
that day to this, in the charge of army officers. We entered the
gate-way of the premises, and were fascinated with the boxed-
up treasures of spreading lawns, blooming hedge-rows,
parallel elms, spacious buildings, with columns and corridors.
(Beautiful, because irregular.) Many old men were walking
in the shade, or seated under the elms. One came to us. "This
is the place of principalities and powers Powers I take to
mean power of numbers; strength of will. Here beautiful
woman dies with no one help." [sic] "There" pointing to
the women's quarters, "Cruel negro [sic] lord it over the
white man." "All the patients are noisy secessionists," the

2. Fort Magruder, part of the Confederate defense works in the Williamsburg-
Yorktown area, lay east of Williamsburg at the intersection of the Yorktown road
and the Hampton road about one and one-half miles form Williamsburg. It was
the site of the battle of May 4–5, 1862. Alexander S. Webb, *The Peninsula:
McClellan's Campaign of 1862*, p. 67.

3. In the shift of control from Virginia to the Federal forces under McClellan,
the Lunatic Asylum (later, the Eastern State Hospital) suffered severely. Its
staff scattered and its inmates were inadequately cared for. See Virginia,
Calendar of Virginia State Papers, XI, 471–497.

steward told us. The one with whom we talked told us he was a cruel master.

At the head of Main St. stand the ruins of Wm and Mary's College and we took our basketed lunch within its walls. Madison,[4] Monroe, Genl Scott, Chief Justice Marshall graduated there. Halfway down the pretty street, a desolated church faces the desolated court-house, and govt horses are stabled in the basement of each, while vacancy has taken the place of all the inner architecture. We visited the "oldest church,"[5] under the favor of the half-crazed, black secessionist sexton, who sported a big-headed foil for a cane, and wore a button, a candelabra drop, and a triangle hanging from his buttonhole. We asked him their significance and he said the button means "Be faithful." The triangle means the trinity. The rebels removed the pews, and made of the church a hospital. "We tried to prevent them," the sexton said, "but they excisted." "This house was once a house of grace, now disease and sickness fills the place," said the sexton. "Who was the author of those lines?" I inquired. "I offers em to you now, myself," he replied. A tablet upon the church wall tells of somebody whose "Other felicity ware crowned by his happy marriage with——She died and left behind her a most hopeful progeny." Some of the tombstones mention that the great Panjandrum himself attended the funeral.

On First-day we went with Eunice Congdon to Acre-town, a mile or two distant, and taught the children of the village

4. Miss Chase is in error here. James Madison received the A.B. degree from the College of New Jersey in 1771. *D.A.B.*, XII, 184–193; Irving Brant, *James Madison*, Ch. V.

5. Bruton Parish Church. The building which Miss Chase saw was completed in 1715. The marble tablet referred to is in the choir.

Neare this marble lyes	his happy marridg with Rebbecka
Ye Honble Daniel Parke	the daughter of George Evelyn
of the County of Essex Esq. who	of the County of Surry Esq. She dyed
was one of his Majesties' Counsellors	the 2d of January Anno 1672 at Long
and sometime Secretary of the	Ditton in ye County of Surry and
Collony of Virgia. He dyed the 6th of	left behind her
March anno 1679.	a most hopefull
His other felicites were crowned by	Progeny.

William A. R. Goodwin, *Bruton Parish Church Restored and Its Historic Environment*, p. 111.

in an unfinished school-house which the friends are erecting. Into that school-house they design putting colored teachers. We were very much excited by the spectacle of rebel earth-works in the neighborhood. Long lines of parallels, with zig-zag communications, protected by forts, all so complete as to be intelligible, with Heinzelman's [6] opposing breast-works start-ingly near. Acre-town was built by Gen. Wistar. The cabins are well-built, of uniform size, not crowded, fence-inclosed, with the door-ways within the gates, the acres adjoining, and noth-ing unclean to be seen either in front, or in the rear. The negroes when first driven upon the plains, found homes in the woods, and in the power-magazines under ground. Gen Wistar finding the negroes dying rapidly in the Forts at Yorktown and Gloucester point,[7] sent them out unto the open, and sentimentalists call him unfeeling. All might have died if they had remained in the Forts. I imagine Wistar is what Butler thinks him to be, a man of rare judgment and ability. Impatient, to be sure, and unwilling to tell the curious and imprudent the whys and wherefores of his movements.

Yesterday we drove over McClellans roads upon Wormleys Creek [8] and saw many of its works. Long lines of zig-zag. We visited a masked battery of the rebels upon the rivers-shore. It was planted upon the arc of a natural circle screened by trees. An English officer who visited it said it was the prettiest masked battery he had ever seen. Upon the shore near the battery we picked up rare shells unknown in Northern waters. We passed California Joes tree, and visited the house where Washingtons terms of capitulation were signed by Corn-

6. Samuel P. Heintzelman, a graduate of West Point and a veteran of the Mexican War who was active in the battles in eastern Virginia. Defeated by Thomas J. Jackson in the Valley of Virginia in 1862, he was assigned to duty in the Washington area. *D.A.B.*, VII, 505–506; Heitman, *Register*, I, 521.

7. The Confederate defenses included heavy batteries at Gloucester Point across the York from Yorktown.

8. A small stream which flows into the York River southeast of Yorktown. Its tributary ravines lay quite near the Yorktown fortifications and sharp skirmishes took place along its banks during McClellan's siege of Yorktown, April 4 to May 5. *Official Records of the Union and Confederate Armies*, ser. I, vol. 11, part 1, pp. 316–321.

wallis.[9] It was McClellans head-quarters also. All of these spots are within walking distance of the mission-house. The friends have already done a great work here. They have nearly three hundred pupils in their day school, and they have a large night-school of adults. The Trojans came here with Eunice Congdon; and her predecessors and associates have accomplished wonders in cultivating the morality of the community.

. . . . .

[Unsigned, in Lucy's hand]

June 5 [1864]

Dear Ones at home.

. . . . .

We have decided that it will be best for us to continue housekeeping, but we want you to see our present home. Dr. Brown's secret detective (once Chief of Police in New York) is trying to find for us a furnished house. We shall hunger and thirst for our present view, which, modified by atmospheric changes, is new to us every day.

. . . . .

The mists and fogs and sunshine; soft air, and summer flowers, have brought the South right back again, and we want Lizzie to hurry back again. I meant to have her take to you some of our second crop of apples. The trees continue to blossom; and some of them have a great many young apples upon them. The cherry and peach trees are also in blossom. Roses still abound, rich in variety.

. . . . .

The autumn tints upon the leaves seem like smiles from home, and make me want to shake hands in the woods with

9. The conference in which the articles of capitulation were drawn up took place in the Moore House. It was located ''half-a-mile behind the right of the American first parallel.'' The articles were actually signed in the trenches. Douglas Southall Freeman, *George Washington: A Biography*, V, 382, 385; Charles E. Hatch, Jr., and Thomas M. Pitkin (eds.), *Yorktown: Climax of the Revolution.* Apparently McClellan's headquarters was not in the Moore House, but in a wood nearby. *Official Records of the Union and Confederate Armies,* Atlas, plate XIX, no. 2.

Blake Brown & Co.[1] But we don't have the beautiful Gum-tree with its English-ivy shaped leaves,—green, graceful, and abundant in the summer, and, in the fall, rich bronze in the sunshine, and purple, almost to blackness, in the shade. Neither do we have the beautiful hanging-moss, which festoons the gray oaks. The live oak we dont have, with its willow-shaped leaves. An evergreen too. And the male mulberry is a stranger at home, is it not? Its glossy laurel-shaped leaves are glorious all through the winter. Stately trees, with thorny spikes invading their sides now bear heavy clusters of purple berries, but we dont know what they are. The "What is it" is all around us. The negroes say "Dont know" when we ask the names of things; and as we dont want to trouble the whites to "Don't know," when we know, right well, that they do know, we satisfy ourselves with admiring. We are making last visits for the winter to some of the distant farms.

. . . . .

We frequently think, after leaving home for town only, that we will visit some farm, and we remember our passes only when they are called for. Sometimes our story serves for a pass, and, sometimes we cannot pass. The picket-stations annoy us greatly. In going to some of the farms we pass through a rebel intrenched camp, and through the "Alabama Camp" village of log-huts. A Negro family by putting a fence around some of the houses have made a cozy homestead in the wilderness. Our draw-bridge annoys us, and as it wont stay shut we shall be glad when we are shut of it. We can always arrange to have it closed for us, if we know, before leaving home, that we shall not return until after eight; but, as unforeseen events sometimes detain us, we sometimes are turned off upon the hospitality of our few town friends. The night we took tea with Lizzie at Dr Brown's I sent to the Genl requesting a pass at whatever time we might choose to cross. When we handed the pass, the guard said, "This is very peculiar. When did you get this?" "This evening," I said. Then I added, "What difference does it make?" "A

1. Probably James H. Blake, painter and teacher, of Somerville, Massachusetts. Fielding, *Dictionary of American Painters*, p. 31.

great deal of difference to me," said the guard. I suppose he fancied I should be awed into silence by his oracularly ambiguous speeches, but I startled him by saying, "Is not the pass dated the 27th?" "Yes," he replied. "Is not that to-day?" I said. "Yes." "Well," I said "Why should the Gen choose to change the date?" (He had said, "It makes a great deal of difference to me, whether it was written yesterday.") "I understand," said the man, "they wont even pass bearers of despatches!" "Is not that an order from Gen. Barnes?"[2] I inquired. "Yes, it is." "Well, he is Military Governor, and I should imagine you would reverence his authority." The ignoramus let us pass.

So many streams that we wish to cross here, are left unbridged, that delays, deception, and unsuccess are in accordance with good order. Two or three days ago, having left our pass at home, I obtained one from the Adjt Genl but a stupid picket, not knowing who was Adjt. Genl refused it, and so we took our horse out of the carriage, and trotted Albert to town to the Genl giving him an outdated pass drawn up for me by Genl Barnes. I wrote, in pencil, upon the pass, Genl B. Sir: I find at the picket-station that this pass wont pass. May I ask you to make the pass passable?

Today, the Genl asked me why I did not go to him whenever I wished any favor. ("Come in person," he said, gallantly—) "Because you are a General," I said. "And *you* are a lady," he said—bowing low. "Ladies come constantly to me with much more trifling requests that your's." "That is why I stay away," I said. "Cela ne faut rien," said the Genl. "Do yur work through me," said Dr Brown. "No, do it through me," said Genl. Barnes, and so on we talked for several minutes.

These occasional social chances are very refreshing to us. And now, after months of lonely living, we hope for a semi-civilized season.

．　．　．　．　．

2. James Barnes of Boston graduated from West Point in the class of 1829 with Joseph E. Johnston and Robert E. Lee. He was placed in command of the Norfolk-Portsmouth area in August 1863. *D.A.B.*, I, 630–631.

I spoke of Gen. Barnes, I find, when I laid aside my pen. I told some of you that I took to his door a box of our beautiful November apples and apple blossoms, telling him upon the cover of the box, they were "Contrabands to Nature for Genl Barnes's inspection." His son, a New York horticulturist, saw the blossoms and growing fruit, and said he ne'er saw the like before. Mrs Barnes, and her lovely daughter joined the Gen and staid here until he was removed. Mrs Barnes was a Vir. But she is strongly anti-slavery, and I one day heard her utter her sentiments freely to another Vr lady, the wife of an U.S. officer. Mrs. Barnes is a very elegant woman. She was very kind and sweet to us, and kissed us, with tears in her eyes when she left Norfolk. We called on her the evening before she left and heard a grand serenade from Post band. Her husband left a few days before she did. We felt personally attached to him, and determined to see the military display on the occasion of his leaving. It was really a grand spectacle. The colored brigade formed a hollow square around the green in front of his house. While the white troops, with flashing bayonets and streaming banners, paraded impatiently while biding the General's time. He—tall, handsome, and elegant— stood upon his porch, welcoming the officers who mounted his steps, while his wife and daughter sat near him receiving the compliments of the occasion. Every-body talks of flashing bayonets and streaming banners, even when the provocation is exceeding small but we all realized, for the first time, the exceeding beauty of sun-stricken steel and floating colors glazed by sunbeams. It was so sunny and so Southern we revelled in it. A son of Genl Barnes was Capt. of the Minnesota,[3] and his lovely wife from Philia was in the Generals family. She was an enthusiastic admirer of Philips Brooks,[4] and gave me his famous thanksgiving sermon. From that day

3. John S. Barnes, Lieutenant Commander, USN, was a fleet captain in the North Atlantic Blockading Squadron under Admiral S. P. Lee, Commander of the Squadron. Barnes was on the *Minnesota,* but Lieutenant Commander J. H. Upshur was captain of the ship. *Official Records of the Union and Confederate Navies,* ser. I, vol. 9, p. 592 ff.

4. Phillips Brooks, rector of Holy Trinity, Philadelphia, and Trinity, Boston. *D.A.B.,* III, 83–88.

to this we have had many Generals. Wild,[5] Graham,[6] and Shepley.[7] Mrs Wild we knew. I don't know whether I ever told you much of our beautiful home at Ferry Point,[8] where we were in Norfolk, but outside of it, and looked upon Norfolk and Portsmouth over the water.

· · · · ·

Having around us forty or fifty beautiful and charming lady teachers we have not taken time to visit them, but, we sometimes meet them very pleasantly. I will tell you sometime, at length, about my pleasant interview with Gen Butler. People from far and near look in upon us, very often. Mr Hale (who is now in camp at the front) called on us two or three times while Sarah was in bed with her sore-stricken eye-lid. James Miles now (with Augustus wounded and at Fortress Monroe) has been twice to see us. The Adj Genl took us to Gottschalks [9] concert and to see Laura Keene,[10] a courtesy which we highly appreciated, because they were the first public entertainments which we had enjoyed here.

· · · · ·

5. Edward A. Wild of Massachusetts, who rose from captain in the 1st Massachusetts Infantry in 1861 to brigadier general, volunteers, by 1863. Heitman, *Register*, I, 1034.

6. Charles K. Graham of New York was a colonel of 4th New York Infantry in 1862 and brevet major general, volunteers, by 1865. Heitman, *Register*, I, 467.

7. George Foster Shepley, a Maine politician and a friend of General Benjamin Butler, was military governor of New Orleans in 1862 and in May 1864, was placed in command of the District of Eastern Virginia. *D.A.B.*, XVII, 78–79; *Official Records of the Union and Confederate Armies*, ser. I, vol. 40, part 2, p. 256; Heitman, *Register*, I, 881.

8. Ferry Point or Washington Point at the confluence of the east and west branches of the Elizabeth River.

9. Louis Moreau Gottschalk, "the American pianist of his day." He studied with Berlioz and after a brilliant career in Europe returned to America in 1853. Between 1862 and 1865 he gave over 1,100 concerts. *D.A.B.*, VII, 441–442; Vernon Loggins, *Where the World Ends: The Life of Louis Moreau Gottschalk*. See also Louis M. Gottschalk, *Notes of a Pianist*.

10. Well-known English actress, who came to America in 1852. She was the first woman to be successful as a manager and producer in the United States. In 1863 she resumed her active career on the stage. She was playing in *Our American Cousin* at Ford's Theatre when President Lincoln was assassinated. *D.A.B.*, X, 283–284.

Eliza will thee please to write for me to Fidelia Bridges,[11] asking her if she will be in Salem in Aug. or Sep. and asking her to let me know at once, where I can meet her, in either of these months, to be a pupil for one or two weeks. I *must* refresh myself by painting. I should write but I dont know where she is. I hope I shall hear speedily from her. We may decide to remain with the soldiers through July. If we do, we shall give several hours a day to the contrabands. But we *may* go home the first of July. Our *visit* in Philia will be on our way back. If anything should cause Gen. Butler to leave this department we may, instead of returning here, go to Richmond, or to Washington, where we have been asked to go. I wish you could have seen the woods here in April, alive with a multiplicity of blossoming dogwood (not poisonous like ours,) and fragrant, and wondrously beautiful with the golden Jessamine, whose perfume Fanny Butler calls the richest on earth. The beautiful, drooping bells of the red honey-suckle, wild and luxuriant, here, burning like drops of sunshine on many a leaf and branch. Now the laurel towers into a tree and bears large and rosy blossoms. The magnolias are in bloom and "The rose blossoms like a wilderness!"

. . . . .

I want to fill a whole sheet about the hospitals. As all when able to be moved are hurried North, none but the sore-distressed patients remain in our hospitals. We talked with men gasping with lungs shot away, with men bleeding to death, saying "I'm beginning to grow cold." Saw a poor boy raving with a bullet in his head which could not be found though the wound had been probed four inches deep. Wrote letters for men with amputated limbs, and internal wounds; and spent a great deal of time in a ward devoted to patients with gangrene and erysipelas. Many of the poor fellows are grieving because they have received from home no return for letters they have sent telling of their wounds. The Christian Commission is doing a great and noble work in Hampton. Unlike

11. A Massachusetts painter, born in Salem in 1835. Her work was chiefly landscapes and nature scenes. George C. Groce and David H. Wallace, *The New York Historical Society's Dictionary of Artists in America: 1564–1860*, p. 80.

the Sanitary Commission[12] it is not the agent of the Govt and does not require a surplus demand for its comforts. Fortress Monroe is alive with the Army. On our way to Yorktown we stood on the wharf when more than a hundred wounded men were taken from a transport to the hospitals. We talked with many fresh from the field; and found them hopeful and believing. A hundred prisoners were marched by us while we stood there, and a hundred convalescents were put upon a steamer to be brought to our Portsmouth Hospital. I will write again and send to Newport as you may *all* be there.

Aff.

LUCY

Norfolk Va July 1st 1864

My Dear Friends

... Have I told you that I hope, if I am in the field next winter, to furnish remunerative work to women? I can command as many sewing machines as I may desire, but I think it unwise simply to teach the use of them. To teach it too to women unlikely to go far from Norfolk, where many private machines are now lying idle while their owners beg work from door to door. Now, if the Government will let the machines sew for it, the machine-worker can be furnished with present means of support and those who become experts, may secure here, or elsewhere, permanent situations in manufacturing establishments. That will be one spoke in my grand industrial wheel. I have already put into the hands of a shoemaker five sets of tools, for apprentices, all of whom shall

12. The United States Sanitary Commission, led by Henry W. Bellows and Frederick Law Olmsted, was a powerful adjunct to the Federal medical service. Entirely voluntary in character, it raised supplies, employed agents and inspectors, and cared for the wounded and the sick. The Christian Commission was an agency for religious activity among the Union soldiers. It "represented Protestant ministers, the Y.M.C.A., and the American Tract Society." Its leaders charged that the Sanitary Commission was un-Christian and unworthy. This difference of opinion between those who placed religious activity before relief and education and those who saw need for immediate practical action also appeared in the freedmen's aid and education movement. William Q. Maxwell, *Lincoln's Fifth Wheel; The Political History of the United States Sanitary Commission*, and Ira V. Brown, *Lyman Abbott: Christian Evolutionist*.

be cripples, incapable of active work. But some efforts, even
on a large scale, could not meet my demand for *Ready opportunity for labor with the assurance of a ready reward.* Let
the transmutation of dollars into clothing cease at the North
——Stores for the negroes are now liberally supported, at all
their central camps. Those persons who find employment at
the hands of chance and circumstance can avail themselves
of the opportunity furnished at these stores to buy at less
than market prices, and they may well thank the good fortune
that has made two feet sufficient for each one to stand upon,
and two hands quite enough for his main-stay. To each we
(all of us) furnished opportunity and now we further honor
them by *leaving them alone.* But why should we increase the
misfortune and degradation of those who have drifted away
from all things needful for their physical comfort, and now
find themselves stranded on our fallow shores? They open
their mouths and we feed them, and they stretch out their
arms and we clothe them. "Yes," we say, "heads *were* made
to push with, hands *were* made to work with." "There is
work for you now, at the North, but you mustn't go there.
There'll be work for you here, at the South, when the war is
over! ! Here's a nice broad shelf we of the North have made
for you. Pocket your hands and tuck up your feet, you wont
need them here. Crawl upon it. Leave all to us. We won't let
you fall off." This is what you of the North (or rather we,
your representatives) have done. But there is a highway,
that leads to Independence, which the negro would gladly
travel, if the North would pave it. Every foot-fall therein
should be labor which would bring the sweat to his brow, and
weariness to his frame. But the courage, in his heart, would
be freshened by that sweat and it would be a crown of manli-
ness to his brow. On the stage, at the North, you have "The
Ticket-of-leave-Man." When our *houses* of opportunity are
opened here, the negro shall enter them with his ticket of
leave to be a *man.* Let come that day, O Government! Even in
these burning days, with the thermometer 100° in the shade,
our benighted friends still work vigorously at [one word
illegible] planting. One is sometimes oppressed by the moral
significance of the solemn earnestness they exhibit. We have

100 hard working students in our night school, which is presided over by Miss Smith and Miss Collins, members of our family. Some of our scholars come to us fresh from Richmond and its vicinity.

Far out, on a sandy point, stretching into the ocean, stands Cape Henry lighthouse. Opposite it lies the dark point of Cape Charles, whose lighthouse was destroyed, not long ago, by the rebels. A plan to destroy Cape Henry lighthouse, and to murder its guard, was recently detected, so increased vigilance is maintained there night and day. A colored company is stationed there—isolated, solitary, and inactive. It is officered by noble men who are ambitious for the welfare and reputation of their company. One of them appealed to my sister and myself, some time ago, for books, and we determined to visit them so that we might learn their actual wants. On the very day of our arrival, their captain received some primmers [*sic*], from a tract society, and he declared to us his intention to put one into each man's hands. We gathered the men and found their zeal needed no quickening. They were very apt, and those who knew no *letters,* learned a number of words, in the one lesson we gave them. To one of the men, my sister said, "Are you free now to run and do just as you please?" "Oh no," he said, "I'm free to hold myself, to learne [*sic*], to show my best behavior to everybody, to serve my country, and to be always a gentleman but I'm not free to do anything else. I want to do all I can to show the white people our race is of some account." Books and teachers find the colored man, even if his home is the wilderness, and I know they will brighten the days of the soldiers on Cape Henry, like blooming flowers in its sandy waste.

.   .   .   .   .

Far from town, and near Cape Henry, we saw an *occupied* schoolhouse, the first we had seen in Virginia, and curiosity prompted us to visit it. The teacher, a young Virginian, told us the house was used for a public school before the war, and she had permission to teach a private school there. She had but three scholars, but they were bright and well advanced. Scattered about in the woodlands, in all directions, in this part of Virginia, are tidy school-houses and pretty churches;

but the school-master is far abroad, and the minister is away, and so are the people.

Since I wrote you last, my sister and I have made a delightful visit to Yorktown. It is now very easy for us to leave our own school, and so we readily assented to a very urgent invitation, from the Phila. friends (who are doing a large missionary work there) to aid them in organizing their schools which had for some time been struggling to secure a permanent foothold. Yorktown would be a fine point for a Northern tourist to visit. There one may see what the Negro can do with small opportunities, and may learne [sic] how surely the effort of his white patron meets with a speedy reward. A mile from the fort is Sabletown, a village of 500 negro cabins; while a half mile beyond it, is Acretown, a neat, negro village built by Genl. Wistar. Each cabin is enclosed with its acre, by a curiously interlaced slab-fence (the universal cabin enclosure in these parts). The acre [sic] are contiguous in their rear, so air and space are meted out in double measures. The cabins are built of an uniform patern [sic] and absolute neatness is enforced upon the premises, by military authority. There the friends have built a school-house which, like the one at Sabletown, is occupied as a church on Sundays. A large Sunday-school is also kept, in each place. Uniform neatness, taste, and cleanliness characterize the dress worn on Sundays. The combination of colors, known at the North as "niggerfied," are seldom, if ever, seen here (in the South). Upon a hill, a few rods above Sabletown, the friends have built a mission-house, a school-house, and a store. To the mission-house the people flock for sympathy, advice, and assistance. The school-house bell calls 400 children daily to their teacher and summons hundreds of adults to the night-school; while the store is thronged with customers.

But few soldiers are now left to represent the large force which has garrisoned Yorktown since our forces took possession of it. With the Army, must have departed the means of support for the Negro. Efforts are constantly made to induce the negroes to remove from their huddling places upon government farms. Some still find work with the troops who remain and, satisfied with the present, shrink from looking for a new home, while the multitude wait patiently for the gates of Richmond to open that they may rush therein. Here and there, as we move about the country, we find many freed people longing for Richmond. All who come from its neighborhood refuse to find a home elsewhere. But I see no reason why the Yorktown community, if 2000, should be more than very transient. Today it is prosperous, firm, and full of interest. The money earned is still on hand, the garden vegetables supply the table, and the store satisfies a variety of domestic wants. But Yorktown is out of this world and, if we do not again make it a stronghold, each man must look to himself alone for the reward of his labors.

The positive influence for good that emanates from the zealous friends who have made their home in Sabletown is marked in its results upon the reverential, receptive people. It seems like a well-regulated realm there. Forty couples, over whom "The Matrimonial" had never "been read," because no state law could make it binding, were married in the church, while we were there, and were feasted at the Mission-house with huge slices of rich, frosted wedding cake, and lemonade without stint. The Superintendent of Contrabands united with one of the energetic teachers in compelling all living as man and wife to take the choice of separation or marriage. Many unwillingly assented to marriage, while others indicate a full appreciation of the necessity, propriety, and dignity of the ceremony. It was a strangely picturesque and impressive sight to see, in the twilight, the neatly dressed couples, moving from their various quarters and drawing near our doorway. Old men and women, hand in hand, coming up to their "bridal." "Take her by the hand," one old man said as he led his wife forward. Everyone had an air of serious modest reserve. Some were young enough to blush, and all seemed to say, "This is our marriage day." After the ceremonies in the church, the newly married were invited to the house, where the great cakes were cut for them and the air was sweetened by the magnolias and brilliantly illuminated by the kerosene. Our good friends anticipate immediate and wholesome results from the occasion. The colored people easily assume the responsibilities, proprieties, and graces of civilized life. As a class, their tastes are comely, though they are acquainted with filth. I fancy they see the moral significance of things quite as readily as white people. Eighty other applicants urged their claim to enter the pale too late to make preparations for them, but in a week they will promise faithfulness to each other and each will have a gift of a candle in its stick. The candle will be lighted that it may shine on their new way.

We are near the front, you know, so the soldier, as well as the slave, gets near our sympathies. On our return from Yorktown, we were obliged to pass across the deck of a hospital-boat. Nearly every man aboard had lost a leg, or an arm. The amputations were very recent for they were in the battle of the 22d of June.[1] The flies are a worrying nuisance both to sick and well, in this climate, and so I rejoiced when I saw the indications of thoughtful kindness that hung in the branches over the soldiers cots. It was late and dark when we touched the wharf. No boats were due at that time so, in place of the usual bustle, all was very still——Before us, we saw men with lanterns, and, nearby, the glare of white sheets ——We knew the dead were there. The surgeon stood by and superintended the removal of the bodies from the cots to the coffins. An attendant carelessly took a waistcoat from one body, fumbled in its pockets, and threw it to a colored man standing by, saying, "Here boy, here's a waistcoat." But the man took it not. The surgeon said to us, when pointing to one body, "That poor man has no name. We could learne neither his name nor his regiment." We came on to Norfolk and were met by a very large body of Norfolk ladies and gentlemen, bearing white flowers. A hearse stood in waiting, and a number of the stately gentlemen went on board the "City of Hudson," expecting to take from it the body of a rebel general. But they did not find it there, and she [sic] whispered, and bowed, and walked grimly away.

I must tell you what *excellent* care the colored soldiers received in the Balfour Hospital, in Portsmouth. Hundreds of them have been brought here from Bermuda Hundred and

1. Probably a reference to one of the many battles in the seige of Petersburg.

my sister found among them many of her old camp pupils. Noble men they are and I rejoice that noble men and women are in charge of them. I have seen in no hospital such *genuine,* direct, and gracious courtesy as the hired nurses in the Balfour show to their colored patients. Our hospitals are *full,* or the poor men, who touched at the Fortress, would not have gone on, in the heat, to Washington. The soldiers generally are cheerful and even those robbed of legs and arms are often very gay; but the colored soldiers excell in jollity. One man, who had lost his arm, said to me, "Oh I *should* like to *have* it, but I don't begrudge it." Another said, "Another arm robbed. Well, there's one thing, 'twas in a glorious cause, and if I'd lost my life I should have been satisfied. I knew what I was fighting for." " 'Twas my effort to take Petersburg," one said, "and I worked as hard as I could." (Next fall there will be no lack of cripples for my shoe-shop.)

We have our sympathies called out, almost every day, for the innocent children who are harshly beaten by their will-enemies [*sic*], their harsh mama's. Close by us lives a black woman who lashes her little boy with a raw-hide. We have remonstrated repeatedly, but she "Reckons I shall beat my boy just as much as I please, for all Miss Chase," and she does beat him till his cries wring the anguish from our hearts. We complained of her to the Provost Marshall and, for a few days, she has been more quiet, so we think he must have visited her. "A few licks now and then, does em good," a sweet woman said to us once in extenuation of her practice of beating. Many a father and mother have begged me to beat their children at school. "Spare the rod and spoil the child," is on every mothers tongue. "Now you whip her and make a good girl out of her," the kindest mother says when she trusts her sweetest child to us. . . .

A good old Craney Island friend of ours, wise and faithful in her home relations, and conscientious and loving in her business relations with the whites on the Isd. found her first husband, a few weeks ago, in a crowd of supposed strangers at the Rope-walk. "Twas like a stroke of death to me," she said, "We threw ourselves into each others arms and cried. His wife looked on and was jealous, but she needn't have been.

My husband is so kind, I shouldn't leave him if he hadn't had another wife, and of course I shouldn't now. Yes, my husband's very kind, but I ain't happy. No. He hasn't any enemy but himself as I knows on and perhaps I ought'nt to worry about him, but I do.'' Thinking again of her first husband from whom she was early parted, she said, with keenest feeling, ''White folk's got a heap to answer for the way they've done to colored folks! So much they wont never *pray* it away!'' ''I didn't thought 'twas written folks should sell folks,'' another Craney Island friend of ours said,—adding, ''God dont tell *me* any such thing.'' That was Aunt Nancy, the good old soul who cared for us tenderly, when we were sick on Craney Island. We asked her, a few days ago, if she sometimes attended services in a colored church close by her home. She said, ''I haven't been there since the church's been sittin there. 'Taint my way to have such long meetins. My way's the right way, and the straight way. The spirit dont stay so. It comes and goes you know.''

We thought she was right—''They begin with a meeting and end with a party, don't they?'' my sister said——And so it seems. The excitable people protract their evening meetings far into the night. It is customary with them to continue the exercises of prayer and singing after the benediction has been pronounced. Their spiritual gratifications are emotional, rather than rational, and they rock, and sing, and wail, and howl, till their own most lazy patience is exhausted. It is very common for a large congregation to accompany the preacher, or prayer, by a wailing chant, swaying their bodies all the time, and often drowning the voice of the speaker. It is usually the women alone who are so unseemly. In their prayer-meetings, one or many grow ''Happy,'' jump, and spin, throw their arms into the air, embrace those near them, shake all the hands they can reach, screech words of religious rapture, and give an occasional staccato howl,—horrible and startling. The minister has great control over these exhibitions. Some ministers *will not* countenance them, and check them easily; but most of them encourage the noisy. It is an important question how fast and how far it would be advisable for the whites to check such customs. The congregations have manifested determined opposition to settling white preachers. Few white men would have the tact gently to leave their loving spirits. The lash and the auctionblock could dictate to them, but not the preacher. They *must find out* that their way is not the best way, without being told so, or they will never change it.

The stumbling preachers sometimes say striking things. I heard one say, "The spirits of the wicked have gone to the wasted ends of creation"—(worse than the place of fire!) "Nebrecomezer was a Roman Catholic." "No eyes and couldn't see, no ears and couldn't hear, no actions and couldn't do nuthin." "I have been asked to take the pasticheer of the church." "Bless the brother who has the privilege of standing in the shoes of John, but let him stand behind the cross." "I pray that the dry bones may be enleavened." "On our sin-buckled canes, Lord, we bend to thee, Oh thou adore-double-name!" Another preacher said, "On our bended bow-canes, we bow down to thee, oh thou most gracious magazine."

The "Praises" [2] (Hymns) of the negroes, as you know, were often poetic and picturesque

> Oh happy is the child who learns to read
>> When I get over
> To read that blessed book indeed.

2. The Negro spirituals or "praise hymns" are fascinating in their variety as well as in the colorful imagery of their words and the haunting beauty of their music. The same songs were sung in all sections of the South, but there were local variations, even in the more widely known spirituals. Difficulties in transcription obviously added to the confusion and the misunderstanding. The words recorded by the Chases are not precisely reproduced in any of the standard works on the Negro spiritual. "You'd Better Run," as printed by John W. Work in *American Negro Songs*, p. 93, contains the line "God sent ol' Jonah to Nineveh lan'," but the detailed account of Jonah's adventures as Miss Chase gives it is not included. The admonition, "Mind how you walk on (or get hold of) the Cross" appears, in different form, in "Aint Gonna Grieve My Lord No More." See Howard W. Odum, "Religious Folk Songs of the Southern Negroes," *American Journal of Religious Psychology and Education*, III (July 1909), 265–365; Anna K. Odum (ed.), "Some Negro Folk-Songs from Tennessee," *Journal of American Folklore*, XXVII (September 1914), 255–265; J. B. T. Marsh, *The Story of the Jubilee Singers*, pp. 134–135; Thomas Wentworth Higginson, *Army Life in a Black Regiment*, pp. 197–222; and M. F. Armstrong and Helen W. Ludlow, *Hampton and Its Students*, p. 193. See also Howard W. Odum and Guy B. Johnson, *The Negro and His Songs*; and Newman I. White, *American Negro Folk-Songs*.

CHORUS:
When I get over, when I get over
'Twill take some time to study
When I get over.

"De Lord commanded brother Jonah one day, when I get over, when I get over, to preach the word in Nine-vay, when I get over, when I get over, etc. But Jonah he went on the contrary way, So God Alimighty stormed upon the sea. The Captain and mate were sore afraid, and dere anger fell on brother Jonah's head. Dey cast brother Jonah overboard, to appease de angry Lord. The Lord sent a whale upon the sea, which did swallow brother Jonah verily. So in his belly he did lay, Three long night and three long day. When dey cast him on de lily-white shore, Lily-white corruption (?) [sic] of Ninevah. Ah brother mind how you get hold on the cross, Lest your foot should slip and you get lost. You must learn to watch as well as pray, you must learn to do as well as say. You must bear your cross from day to day, In the straight and narrow way. Whenever I gets on the other shore, I'll argur with 'ee Father and chatter with 'ee son. I'll sit up with 'ee Father in 'ee Chariot of 'ee Son, Talk about 'ee world I've just come from." Sing this in a drawling chant and say its pretty.

"You must watch the sun and see how she run
I hope for to get up into Heaven
I'se afraid he'll catch you with your work undone
For I hope for to get up into Heaven
Says my guide, I hope for to get up into Heaven."
"If I had uh died when I was young, I shouldn't uh had this race for to run I shouldn't uh sinned as many has dun. De prettiest thing that ever I dun, was seek religion (or de Lord) when I was young." "My Lord 'liver Daniel, My Lord 'liver Daniel, My Lord, 'liver Daniel, Why not 'liver me. Daniel was a curus man: he pray three times a day My Lord histed 'ee winder, fur to hear brother Daniel pray My Lord 'liver Daniel, &c. So Jesus listen all 'ee night, Listen all 'ee day, Listen all 'ee night, Fur to hear one sinner pray."

I wish you could drive out with us upon some of the government farms. They are almost all upon the water and are approached through woodlands. A Massachusetts woman was left, by her [?] rebel husband, upon a lovely farm upon the oyster-famed Lynnhaven river. We took her farm this spring and she wailed like a woman to the manor born. "Do send me to Richmond, to save my funeral expenses," she cried. When her husbands colored sister refused to accompany her, she urged the propriety of her doing so by saying, "You are a near relation to the family." She took the guard, put in charge of the estate, to the family burying-ground, and with tears in her eyes, begged him to keep the sacred spot in order. The graves were without head-stones and the place was an overgrown waste.

One noble woman told us of the efforts made by her mistress to retain her and said, "I said to my Missis if folks owns folks, then folks owns their own children." "No, they don't," her mistress replied. "White folks owns niggers." "Well, then," the woman said, "Government owns *you* and *everything*." We asked one of Gov. Wise's slaves if he ever heard the Gov. speak of the Yankees. "No," he said, "but I often heard him speak of the Damn Yankees." Sometimes the women take our playfulness seriously——Finding some newcomers at the rope-walk, poring over their books, Sarah said to their guardian Auntie, "Put the books in the fire, Auntie, ain't that the place for them?" "Oh no, Missis," she replied, "looks better in their hands. Likes to see em *there*." "We have the consumption of being called refugees," a man said to us. "Where's your husband, Auntie," my sister said inquiring of an old woman. "Don't know, Missis, hadn't had him but a week, when Massa sold him away from me and havn't hearn of him since."

The good Craney Island woman, who found her early love the other day, said to us, once, when we told her she had a nice new dress, "New? No indeed, 'tis a sad enough dress to me. One night Massa came home and threw a package at my head so hard it knocked me down. When I opened it, it didn't make me feel glad, for I knew something was the matter, for he didn't give me such things. I sat up all night to make it, for he told me to make it before morning; and right soon in the morning he came and had me put it on, and he carried me to

Richmond prison, to be sold, for I was the best hand he had and he had to raise some money right away. He sold me away from my husband he'd just married me to and from all my friends. He asked so high for me that I had to stay there three weeks before I was bought. I put that dress away, as soon as I was sold, and I haven't had the heart to put in on since. I knew 'twas given to me (when I first saw it) to make me sell well. To make 'em think I had a kind master. Now I have my old man with me and all my children but one son whom I study about all the time, cause he hasn't good sense. I mourn for him and seek for him constantly. Oh, I feel as if I must get him and be kind to him, and give my life to him because I don see why a babe, before he's born, should suffer for things goin on in the world. Master worked me so hard, he warnt quite bright, so I feel as if I ought to do more for him than for anybody else." One Craney Islander once said, to us of the Island, "I shall always respect her, as long as I live, and, if I could, I'd go and see her once in awhile, for I've got three children buried on her."

. . . . .

Have I ever told you that, next to driving the colored people into the country, Genl. Butler desires to drive them upon their feet? He does not wish them to remain helpless paupers upon Government farms, so he gives (or allows the Superintendents to give) but $10. a month to the men laborers and $5. to the women, obliging them to pay, from their wages, for their rations. There is great demand for them, at high wages. The enterprising relieve the Government, at the first opportunity, and enrich themselves; but many refuse high wages. Timidity restrains some. (The dread of the rebels is universal with them)——Indolence restrains some. Stupidity still enslaves a few. At such low wages, you can readily see that means to purchase clothing are wanting. It would be [one word illegible] to draw, from Northern charity, clothing for those able, but unwilling, to earn the means to purchase. "I don't want to" and "I won't" are cold and naked, shall we aid them? Is it not time that long-suffering charity should draw its rule and line, let it cut off whom it may? We'll talk about all these things, "When I get over." " 'Twill take a long time

for to chatter, when I get over, when I get over," for my sister
and I intend to run North this summer, With your permission?
We are worthless vessels now and need to be remoulded. So,
when a transport goes to Boston, we shall sail in her, designing
to stay in Massachusetts till October. 'Till we meet adieu.
Love to all my friends.

Yours very sincerely,

L. CHASE.

. . . . .

Office Asst Quartermaster & Supt.
Negro Affairs
2nd District, Norfolk Va.
Aug. 27, 1864.

My Dear Sisters,

Yours is received. I am vexed at you both. A fine business
you have made of "resting," truly! Go away from your
friends. Let "Contrabands" and "big Organs" alone—find
some quiet out-of-the-way place where no one can find you—
stroll about some green wood—you and Sarah alone—don't
think. You have done enough of that the past year and a half—
in short become an oyster—forget that you have brains—
don't laugh at this now—it is as sound professional advice as
if backed by a five dollar fee.

The schools will without doubt be arranged or organized
under a regular system—but you understand that you two
are on my staff, and cannot go into any such organization.
Your services are too valuable *outside*. I mean it when I as-
sert that hundreds in the North can do as well in the school
room as either of you, but without flattery you can do the
negro more good "outside" than the hundred teachers can in
their school rooms.

Sarah must be a "good girl" and *keep still* until she is better, and Lucy must write me *just how Sarah is——*

By my door is darkened by my "constituents" and I will
say God bless you and end.

Truly yours

O BROWN

To Miss L & S Chase

Office Ass't Quartermaster & Supt of
Contrabands,
Norfolk, Va. Nov. 18th 1864

Dear Mr. May;[1]

This is the first moment I have felt it right to take hold of a pen, since my return. Now, while waiting a conveyance to a farm, I must tell you that I have not to wait till next week for *my* Thanksgiving; for *that* began a fortnight ago—the *moment* I set my foot on old Virginnia [*sic*] shore—and that it has not ended yet. I cannot tell you how happy I am to be back at my post. Until within a very short time of my return, it really seemed doubtful if I should be able to resume my labors in this harvest field; for each day found me more weary, instead of refreshed, but once again I have the happiness of proving my favorite "All earnest hearts shall have their dreams fulfilled."

Would I could run in and tell you all I have seen and heard since my return; and answer all questions, but to report in ink would be impossible, from the nature of the case. We returned to find a general confusion and folding of hands; and we took hold at once, apportioning work to new hands, reconstructing, newly organizing, and making a general review of work done in our absence so that every moment has been painfully crowded, and not one day has been half long enough for what I desired to put in it—where so much is to be done ——I feel I must stop for nothing until every hand is at work; consequently I have not obeyed the dictate of my heart, and reported at once to the sacredly dear and good people of Leicester Hill. Though diligently working, and to some purpose, the details of wrongs righted, change of officers, of school policy, ect [*sic*], would not interest outsiders, I think, enough to make it worth while to report. There are now in town ten teachers each from the Educational Commission, Am. Miss. Society, and National Freedmen's Ass. Each society having its mission house and (excepting us) a housekeeper; the schools are graded & each teacher has about fifty pupils—a

---

1. Fred W. G. May of Boston of the Committee on Clothing and Supplies of the New England Freedmen's Aid Society. *Freedmen's Record*, I (May 1865), 88.

Normal School has just been created from the most advanced in the other schools; and Miss Kennedy, lately of New Berne, a fine woman, has charge of it. Each teacher is to have a thorough knowledge of the familys of her pupils, and report cases of sickness and suffering to us for investigation—no giving orders on our stores for things needful. All things to whatever person in the Dept. are put in the common stock of our two stores in Norfolk and Portsmouth. Two ladies in each keeping thorough business accts and allowing nothing to go out without an order signed by L. or S. E. Chase. All who come to us personally are visited, and their cases carefully considered before anything is done for them. It is a cause of rejoycing [sic] that we have got the clothing so well organized —now we have only to contend with the unwillingness of the teachers to properly investigate——Another good thing for the people is the Industrial School which will soon be in operation, under Miss Smiley, and [sic] lovely Quakeress of much executive ability from Philadelphia——I am inexpressively thankful to the good Lord for sending her—for heretofore I have been unable to get cooperation in the plans I have had from the first—of teaching [?] the people to *help themselves*. I have always given much attention to mending and making and urged others to do the same.

. . . . .

In the day, I have not had time to think, but in the long silent hours of night, I have often thought of the Leicester Hill *nobles*—and my heart has ached to dictate many pages of this Southern Life for them but my Greek-ruined eyes can do nothing by night, and can rarely do duty by day; even if they are not with the body, hither, thither and yon. Thrice have I locked myself up for a half hours talk, but in vain. "Miss Sarah, the overseer of the Bradford Farm is here with his cart and wants to know if you can't go out there," ect [sic] or Rat-tat-tat on the door—as I am about to seat myself—— "Who is there?" say I. "One," feebly is answered. "Who is one?" "Me, why you nows me Miss Sarah," and as she speaks I open the door and "One" is an old blind man, a young woman with a sick child and two boys. Thus far it has been much as I feared, when I hesitated at the proposition wh[ich] was wholly unexpected to me, when at your house. I never doubted I could *work* enough; my heart is too deeply interested to attempt it if I did not feel competent—but I feared I could not satisfy my conscience and answer the demands of any society; or rather be able to do what I should earnestly desire myself to do, i.e., to write fully and freely. I should be unhappy if I left one or the other undone. I sometimes think I will limit my labor, and concentrating my effort more, be able better to systematize my time—take more comfort and time to record the day's history. Then I think it is far truer and better to take what is sent, and make the best of it rather than to seek what is most agreeable. Our reception camp—The "Rope Walk" is nearly empty—no large party having been brought in since early Summer.

. . . . .

A good man and his wife came in one day bringing a sweet faced granny with them—all enthusiastic, and eager for work, & full of cheer though the clothes they had on their back [and] in their hands were all they had in the World to start with. "Have you any children?"—said I to the old woman—— "No honey—no I hasn't—and yet missus I has; fourteen children I'se raised and hugged in dese old arms; and sometimes I tinks I feels de little hands on my cheeks—but deys all gone; —I don't know whar dey air—and if I was lyn stark dead out yonder in de corner, dere wouldnt be one to bring me a cup of water."

You desired me to tell what was needed; but as every want we have can be met in one way and another, I think it would be as well to forward what you collect and think best to make. Cooking utensils are the only things I would specify. We can not get enough. If each housekeeper could send the extra pots and pans or even stove lids (to bake the universal corn cake on) they would contribute much to the health and comfort of these people. . . . One good thing you could do with no expense, but time—relieving your houses and benefitting the refugees at the same time—That is: glean every library of books that are not wanted & send to a committee who will throw out books that never were or will be read & forwarding books of instruction, story books, and only such books as would be useful to the Refugees. These could be packed with the pans and kettles & the spaces filled with yarn or any thing else. No school books needed except for reference. One very important need of these people we have just met by establishing a Saving's Bank for them. Heretofore they have almost been forced to spend their money—having no where to keep it. Many a time have they brought money to me,—saying, "Buy me something wid dis, please ma'am." "What do you wish?" "Oh anyting you likes ma'am" or "Whatever it will get," or "something pretty" they say. One nice auntie said—"I wants you to buy something for yourself honey—it does me so much good to see you I'd like to give you a stocking full," and when I explain the importance of providing for the rainy day ect. [*sic*] they would say "but *sugar* I's no whar to keep my money—and if I ties it in de corner of my apron, I might lose it, or get it stolen from me, and I can't go myself to spend it"—or some equally good reason they give for wishing to get rid of money, if they chance to be encumbered by it:—but I have easily persuaded them to be prudent in the face of the new responsibility of their condition—and have been begging for a bank from the first.

Col. Kinsman did not go fast enough to suit the *workers* in this Dept. so Lucy was invited to petition Butler to put Maj. Carney[2] in his place, which good thing was this day effected so God and man favor the cause in this Department and it must prosper—Full of Hope—full of happiness—only asking for strength to labor I am with high consideration for your Committee and ever best wishes for you & them—your co-worker.

SARAH E. CHASE

. . . . .

2. Major George J. Carney of Massachusetts was Superintendent of Negro Affairs, Department of North Carolina. Horace James, *Annual Report of the Superintendent of Negro Affairs in North Carolina, 1864*, p. 3; Heitman, *Register*, I, 283.

My dear Miss Stevenson,

I despair of time in which to write as fully as I wish to do; so I will satisfy myself by giving a few items only. Upon Craney Island, we "cared for," (very indifferently and superficially, of course) two thousand negroes. Eighteen hundred we found there; and from three to five hundred came, at different times, later. We clothed them; helped them patch their rags; caused them to make bed-ticks for themselves; tried to teach them cleanliness; made both slates and pencils for them from slate tiles (not knowing that you would give us slates for the asking). Taught some—yes, many, to read and write, working ourselves twelve hours a day. Lived upon the Isd four months, counting the weeks we spent there in July, (at which time, in the absence of the Surgeon, we acted as Superintendents in every department of labor). The people then upon the Isd were refugees from Suffolk, driven into Norfolk by the withdrawal of our troops from S. We staid with them until the Island was depopulated, by command of Gen. Naglee, on account of its having been declared by him outside the lines. Negro troops were, later, stationed upon it.

When we left the Isd in May, we followed the fifteen hundred who had gone from it upon the main-land. Six or eight hundred went upon farms. Upon two only of twenty farms were there teachers, and Dr. Brown convinced us of the importance of going from farm to farm to look after the general welfare of the laborers. With cart and driver following us in Gov Wise's carriage we went with clothing books and slates, gathered all together, gave garments to the needy, and taught all, forming classes, and encouraging all to help themselves between our visits. Many of them really learned to read after learning on our first visit the Alphabet. So far as possible—with the constant breaking down of our confiscated carriages, and rumored nearness of guerillas, their actual presence, also, on the farms, and change of lines putting some farms beyond reach—we made this work of prime importance. Then, as on the Isd and as now, keeping track of newcomers, and giving them needful aid, helping them to their friends, if they could be found, caring for their sick, always giving them an immediate and powerful dose of Letters.

For three months, in addition to our other labors, we taught daily in Mr. Coan's large school of four hundred. After his health gave way, my sister took charge of the school, for two or three weeks, and left it, only to assist us in opening our own, which, in a few days, will be under the care of six teachers, really representing your Ass—. About one hundred scholars we now have. The number is constantly increasing. Five hours daily our school is in session. Each scholar constantly at work under some Teacher. I forgot to mention that for three months (while working on the farms) my sister and I lived on a Farm in Portsmouth, where we had seventy negroes under our care, teaching all who could come to school, and giving instruction to the farm negroes in the neighborhood.

Several hundred have been taught directly by us. I suppose more than two thousand clothed. Our work is never done. We dont know what leisure is. Papers come, and we don't open them. Books are something we used to enjoy. All this, *not because* we are really industrious, but because it chances that our early arrival here made it necessary for us to work in a multitude of ways; and our work is of all times and seasons.

Most of the teachers here, are teachers only, and are wholly justified in doing what I acknowledge we are not justified in doing, viz, taking a portion of the day for ourselves....
I did not tell you, in its place, that, at the Jail Yard, where we gradually gathered bunks, stoves are absolute necessaries for the refugees. We have been in the habit of patching, and teaching patching, causing boys, in some instances, to patch their clothing on their backs. The Friends (Orthodox in N.Y. and Orthodox and Hicksite in Phila) have sent to us far the larger part of our clothing. Surprisingly excellent it has been, *all new*, stout as heart (or body) could wish. The *only* people who seem to know what to send—shirts and chemises of very *substantial* cotton—Dresses, firm as the best home-spun—All things wanted, and all things right. Worcester Freedmen's

Soc six or eight barrels. 6 or 8

    Roxbury boxes   3
    Boston——
    N.Y. friends box & bar (15 or 20 I imagine)
    Phil   ''   both soc   15 perhaps
    Boston   several
    Salem   1
    Lynn   1
    Freedmens Relief N.Y.   several

. . . . .

I think I must have distributed at least sixty or seventy boxes and barrels of clothing, and *must* have clothed two Thousand people or more. When I came here, a year ago, the Orthodox fr'ds of Phil had spent six thousand dollars for clothing, and had made seven thousand garments. A few weeks ago, the Hicksites in Phil. had then just bought three thousand dollars worth of material, and money was constantly flowing in. I ought to state N Y frds Phil frds & Boston Ed. Com have sent me two thousand books, some slates & c.

Oh I have almost lost my breath in writing.

Yrs. truly

L. C.

Norfolk Saturday 9th Dec

Roanoke Island Jan 12th '65

Dear Sarah—

We arrived here yesterday, and are likely to spend the remainder of our days here. We delayed in Norfolk until 12, waiting for the Baltimore boat. It was the littlest of bits was the little steamboat that took us away. Capt Brown came down to see us off. As we had room neither to sit nor stand nor *breathe,* I said to him, "Oh, you sent word to me to know if you could do any-thing for me. I should like an ocean-steamer, if you please." "Oh, well," the Dr said, springing up, "I'll run right out and get you one." We sailed by the Navy Yard in Portsmouth, seeing many sunken hulks, a captured blockade runner, and many war-boats. We passed the Pointdexter farm,[1] too, and sailed on along the beautiful Elizabeth river. Stepping on a sandbar, at one time, and stopping there awhile, taking many a graceful curve and going on till we reached Curratuck Canal.[2] The house of the lock-guardian, with its neat office, its neat outbuildings, and its parlor kerosene-lamp, mounted high on a street post was, in every respect, worthy a New-England way-side. The forest through which the canal was cut, still holds its own on either side, and the stately pines were a delight to us. Wild cattle came to the banks edge and looked placidly at us, and the rain came down and wet us. We got into the life-boat which hung upon pulleys and sat there through long and pelting showers. Sat there until *we* were wet *We, ourselves,* as well as our clothing. Then, forced into the cabin, we threw ourselves upon benches and slept, fitfully, while soldiers played cards and drank, drank through the night.

Some refugees from Plymouth, who have been sheltered in Norfolk were our companions. One of the ladies asked me if I was a teacher (meaning a teacher of contrabands). "Well," she said, "in these times, people have to do almost any-thing to get an honest living, and I don't blame em fer it neither." I suppose she read in my face the story of my bad luck in taking in washing—read how hard it was for me to get the pittance promised me for the shirts that made my fingers sore, and learned, in some way, that I couldn't pass a school examination at the North. One lady made her bed upon the table, and held a long confidential talk with a friend at her side. She opened the conversation by saying, "I like to see a husband think a great deal of his wife." "So do I," said her friend. "Well," she replied, "I'll speak a good [sic] to you

1. C. Poindexter lived on a farm on the South Branch of the Elizabeth River, south of the Navy Yard. *Official Records of the Union and Confederate Armies,* Atlas, plate XXVI, no. 4.

2. The Albemarle and Chesapeake Canal, which entered Currituck Sound at Faraby Island, thus avoiding Cape Hatteras and Diamond Shoals, the "grave-yard of the Atlantic Coast." The canal began opposite the foot of Main Street in Norfolk and followed the South Branch to Deep Creek, Blackwater Creek, and Currituck Sound. See U. S. War Dept., Corps of Engineers, "Waterway from Norfolk, Va., to Beaufort Inlet, North Carolina," *House Misc. Doc.* 563, 58 Cong., 2 Sess. (Serial 4676), and "Norfolk-Beaufort Inlet Waterway, Virginia and North Carolina," *House Misc. Doc.* 84, 59 Cong., 2 Sess. (Serial 5150).

for my sister." Whereupon she enlarged upon her sister's beauty, and accomplishments.

. . . . .

There was on board a coarse rowdy Adjutant of the Mass. 20th Regiment who was accused by a man of being a thief. "What do you think of a man that will steal niggers?" the Southerner asked of a croaking fellow who had been forcing pious talk upon unwilling ears. The seemingly hypocritical man, unlettered and countryfied said, "I think if he'd steal niggers he'd steal any-thing else." The Adjutant said his soldiers never touched private property. "Niggers are property," he heard in answer.

At five o'clock the big boat Genl Beryl [3] took us on board and at eleven A.M. on Wednesday we landed on Roanoke Island. Fortunately for Martha and me no opportunity offered to go to Newbern. We went at once into Mr. Nickersons school and assisted him in teaching his morning classes. His very open school room was decorated with holly, which was hung on the occasion of the celebration of the Prest Emancipation Act. In the evening, again, we assisted Mr Nickerson. Our pupils interested us greatly. We took our quarters with a very genteel colored family from Plymouth. They gave us a carpeted room with a stove and a luxurious bed. After dinner Mr. Kimball walked with us a mile and a half to Mrs Freeman's. We walked along the sandy beach, looking out upon the water through the tall trunks of sparsely scattered trees. And called upon a good old uncle to lay a bridge for us over a high-tide pond. Mrs Freeman and an officer dashed by us on horse-back. We looked in upon Mr Streeter and his wife whom we found at roast turkey and sweet potatoes. We found Mrs Freeman, her daughter, Miss Roper of Wr Miss Williams and Miss Belnap with guests. Mrs Freeman calls her home "Sunny side." It is fine old house with outbuildings and many acres. Mrs F intends to raise both summer and winter vegetables. After a cordial reception and a pleasant call we returned to our own homes, while the sky was flaming with

3. Probably the *General Berry*, a transport and supply ship serving Federal troops in this area. *Official Records of the Union and Confederate Armies*, ser. I, vol. 33, pp. 283 and 959.

the sunset. The next day Mrs Freeman horse and all stood at our open door and cordially invited us to pass the day with her. We as cordially accepted the invitation; Indeed, we were already bonnetted for her family school-room which was beyond her house.

In whatever direction we walk upon this Isd we see negro cabins with their acre and a half (or more.) The school-house is on a broad magnificent avenue. We saw a very spirited horse at the door and found the Adjutant General and the Provost Marshal, as well as some of our fellow travellers visiting the school. We walked to the fort at the end of the Island and saw from there the sand hills called "Nags-head." Near the fort are the barracks built by the rebels, and afterward occupied by Burnside's men. They are now the receiving quarters for refugees. The only dividing partitions in the largest building are palings, running only towards the roof, giving the smoke freedom to run from room to room, and making it cold and cheerless. White refugees are scattered amongst the colored people. We tried to find Miss James in her schoolroom, but the soldiers had stolen her stove-pipe and she could have no school. Miss Freeman's school-room was asmoke in consequence of a similar loss. Miss James lives in a neat little house, by herself. Her walls are warmly coated with tents, which are painted white, and look rather superb. She is a pleasant body, and expressed great satisfaction at seeing us. We visited the hospital under the charge of Dr Frick of Penn. In his house we saw him, and his pleasant wife, who said the malaria of the Island had so strong hold on her her husband does not like to have her here. In one of the wards I saw a Yellow-fever patient. After our long walk Mrs Freeman's excellent dinner was very refreshing. Four large North Carolina grape-vines spreading their branches upon level terraces beautify Mrs Freemans door-way. She and her family are warmly attached to Roanoke Island, and I think with good reason. It is a beautiful home, the opportunity to serve the blacks is great, society is not wanting, and the Isd twelve miles long furnishes enough variety to satisfy the fancy. In the early evening we walked on with the family to a prayer meeting at Mr Nickersons. The Provost Marshal and A. A.

General have just been "Hopefully converted" Miss Roper said. They are both very young men. They spoke last night, for the first time, and with much feeling. Nearly twenty soldiers were present in Mr Nickersons small room. Several of them made prayers and spoke. Miss Belnap made a very touching prayer, and Mrs Nickerson spoke sweetly. On the third day of our stay in the Isd we early started for the battle-ground.

. . . . .

It was a walk of three and a half miles through the woods, over very wet roads. Finding we should pass several plantations, I determined to call on some of the native whites. We were very smilingly received by two old women in the first house we visited, and the fullest hospitality was extended us, even to the extent of urging us to dine. One of the women took us to her loom and wove cotton cloth for our entertainment. She raises her own cotton, spins it, and weaves it. The other dame was very socially inclined. She had a parrot the pet of one of her daughters, who sprang from his resting place, twirled about in distress, hurried across the floor, screaming all the while with anger, and tried to peck at the mother, because she whipped his young mistress. (The whipping was for our entertainment.) They were very chipper people and lived in a chipper house.

We were so thoroughly charmed with that visit we made entrance into the next home of a native white where we found a fine-looking cordial woman and a recent refugee from Plymouth. An old woman whose house was burned and who found her way here with nothing but the clothing upon her back. She told us a long story, in an old woman's way. Told us about Plymouth and about her son at sea, whom she has not seen for years, and of whom she can learn nothing. After our return from our seven hours walk we took our supper and went out to visit other white families. We found in a miserable room in a house with noisy soldiers, Mrs Everett and her children, the family of the pilot who rendered valuable assistance in the taking of Plymouth. They lost three houses and much more valuable property. She was very pretty and intelligent —a refugee. In another house we found two men, two women, and several children—natives. The man was noble looking, and really handsome. He was mending his children's shoes by the fire-light, while his wife was carefully washing the faces and hands of her children. I say the man because the other man sat with his face upon a chair-back, and showed neither interest nor courtesy in welcoming us. I encouraged the cordial fine looking man to present a claim to government for indemnity for his timber, brought low by our soldiers. We entered his yard by climbing a fence, and when we bade the family good-bye he very graciously accompanied us to the fence.

. . . . .

I did not tell you that small broken earth works are all that can be seen of the traces of battle on the battleground. The swamp is still there, and I thought of our weary soldiers who waded thro it——"If a Yankee can come through there he can go anywhere," the rebels said, "and there's no use resisting him." The earth works did not protect that access.

[Unsigned, in Lucy Chase's handwriting]

Newberne, N. C. Jany 15th '65

Dear Sarah—

I suppose Mr Kimball reported us as having left Roanoke, he going easterly, we going south. At half past one, seventh-day morning we heard a voice at our window saying, "Hurry up, hurry up, boat will be off in ten minutes." We had been cautioned by Mr Kimball on six day evening to be ready for a sudden warning and so we threw ourselves, in our day-light dress, upon the bed, and at the first call were ready to run. A young soldier boy from Boston was our escort. We met Mr. K. at the wharf, and saw him leave in the canal-boat. We found the cabin crowded with coarse men, and so went directly upon the open deck, where, upon settees, we passed the night, right under the sky, with a piercing wind blowing upon us. Our kind little artillery-boy forced his blanket and rubber-cloth upon us, pulled my hood over my head, and said, with a fatherly air, "Cover up your head, cover up your head." He came frequently to see us, and, toward morning, was persuaded to take his rubber-cloth. When day came on, we kept our eyes on the sea-gulls, who favored us, for many miles, with their *flighty* company. Bird-life never before seemed half so lovely to us. Up and down, away and near, high and low, in sunlight and shadow, burning and flashing in the distance like the most brilliant gem, and again blotting the white clouds with its blackness. While we sat smiling at one chatty bird who would make companions of us, a sweet, smiling lady, graceful slipped up to us (our only fellow lady passenger) and said a few careless words, and smilingly tripped away again. Later when we saw her below, we learned (by inquiry) from her that she was a refugee from Plymouth. She lost her house and her all at the time of our recent taking of Plymouth. The tears stood in her eyes while she talked about it; but she controlled herself sublimely. "My sister and I are not keeping house in Newberne," she said, "because we have nothing to keep house with," and the tears came again, but she looked a queen, all the while. Have I mentioned that several of our fellow passengers from Norfolk were on their way to Newbern to obtain the bodies of frds who died of the Yellow fever? All along in our journey we meet with sad traces of it, and everywhere we find refugees from Plymouth.

. . . . .

It was nearly eight oclock when we reached Newbern. A colored man into whose hands we placed ourselves took us to the wrong house, and left us. But a gallant youth led us to Miss Freson's [?] door. She greeted me with great cordiality, and expressed great regret at thy absence. At the breakfast table, this morning I met Mr. Briggs.[1] Mrs. Gould [2] the matron here is the wife of Mr Gould who died at Roanoke Isd with yellow fever, and the mother of the little boy whose leg was badly wounded by a torpedo some months ago; and whose story went the rounds of so many papers. Some of the teachers

1. Rev. William T. Briggs, Superintendent of Education under Horace James. See *Freedmen's Record*, I (May 1865), 87; and *American Missionary*, VIII (July 1864), 176. Briggs said that the "poor whites" were strongly opposed to freedmen's schools and that this prejudice "also pervades more or less our military."

2. Mrs. Caroline E. Gould, supported by the National Freedmen's Relief Association. James, *Annual Report, 1864*, p. 42.

charm us, and about them all I will tell you, after we return. We had classes in the Sunday School this morning, and went from there to the colored camp across the river. We visited several families, were courteously entertained by the officers in three forts, visited a large receiving camp for white refugees, and passed an hour with Mrs Croome[3] (the lady who was burned out by rebels on an island not far from here) who, under the Sanitary Commission is carefully guarding the miserable creatures. She has between one and two hundred under her care. We went into her nicely appointed school-room, where she gave a Christmas dinner to the whole community, and where she had a Christmas tree. She said she had enjoyed her life with the Contrabands much more than with the whites. She said they learn more readily, and are much more grateful. We tried to see some snuff-dipping. We caught one little sick child rubbing her teeth (or dipping) with soot from the chimney. Many of the people were fine looking, sprightly and courteous. At one of the forts I asked the Capt in command what he thought of Butler at Wilmington. "I think he took too much Porter," he said, adding "He'll be again."

. . . . .

Miss Pearson, a beautiful girl from Boston, was engaged to one of the gentlemen who died with the Fever. She told me that of eighteen gentlemen who used to visit the teachers last winter, ten died of the fever. Capt James and his wife are at Moorehead City. We shall try to find them there. We saw Miss Bell from New Bedford this morning. (The one who designed opening schools for the whites in Portsmouth). She is now teaching whites at Parkers Isd. She pronounces them very ungrateful, and says although she has long been working for them they will do nothing for her. She is about to give public readings here for their benefit. Miss Canedy[4] is a very lovely,

3. Mrs. Carrie E. Croome of Boston opened a school on Clumfort's Creek, a tributary of the Neuse River, soon after Federal occupation of the area. Her school was burned but she was not harmed, and her sponsoring agency, the American Missionary Association, immediately rebuilt it. *Ibid.*, pp. 20–21.

4. Betsey (or Bessie) L. Canedy of Fall River, supported by the Chicopee Falls Branch, N.E.F.A.S. She opened the first freedmen's school in North Carolina on July 23, 1863, at New Berne. *Ibid.*, 39, 41. Anne C. G. Canedy also taught at New Berne. She died at Fall River, Massachusetts, in August 1866. See *Freedmen's Record*, I (September 1866), 162.

attractive person; a very great favorite with the teachers. Miss Warren (Roxbury's adopted) and her brother are in this family. Miss Freson [?] and a few others have just opened the third teachers home, although they still "Mess" at Mrs Gould's table. There is general regret expressed at losing Mr Kimball's visit. Bare comforts are all the teachers find here. They have even been forced to live on contraband rations. Carpetless they are. I have sent Mrs Thomas a note, but have seen nothing of her. After our return from Beaufort we shall visit Fort Totten.[5]

"I'm all the family I've got," one woman said to us this morning. Just my case, I thought. A good old woman said, "Seems like you North folks would like to have us have some knowledge and some sense if you could put it into us. The North Carolina folks have kept us in the dark, but you folks want to put some light into us." We found an old man living in a very tidy little cabin (little, like all the cabins in the city of six hundred negroes) a veritable slab-town, with the size and dignity of Yorktown's Slab-town who keeps a "Pay School." He once had twenty scholars, but "Since you all came and opened free schools I've lost most of em. I taught myself," he said. "Picket it up by slant." His little grandson read with real elegance. He was a lovely looking child. Both grandfather and grandmother spoke in his praise. "Haint got no sauce about him," they said. "I've been trying to keep him away from these chere nigger children about town," the grandmother said. "My missis was English," she told us. "She gin me to my husband long before this yere come. I love her in the grave. I spec my master and missis in the grave. My missis tole me if I didn't get long here, to go to de Norf." "I was dragged up," one old man said. "Yes, it was dragged; They called it raised, but 'twasn't, 'twas dragged. I've got four children in Dixie, but I shouldn't know em if I should see em now, for my eye-sight aint good."

One woman, alluding to washing for the soldiers, said, "Sometimes the poor fellows don't get no money, and are

5. Part of the Federal defenses of New Berne about a mile north of the town. *Official Records of the Union and Confederate Armies*, Atlas, plate LXVII, no. 3.

ordered away, and cant pay, and I wouldn't blame em for nothin." Soldiers and teachers mourn Genl Butlers removal.

. . . . .

Lovingly

LUCY

I send the missletoe [*sic*] with its exquisite pearl berries.

Hd Qrs Dept Va In the field Feb 20th 1865

Hon Henry Wilson[1]

Sir. I perceive that complaints have been made to—and credited by—you that I am undoing all that Genl Butler did for the colored people in this Dept. and as an instance of such undoing, it is stated that I have refused to issue rations to the teachers of colored children, I am sorry you have allowed yourself to credit such statements without inquiry, for you would have found them untrue. I had received notice from the Commissary Department that issues of rations to teachers —not employed by Government,—were illegal and that the money value of such issues would be charged against my pay. I therefore directed the superintendent of the bureau of negro affairs—Mr Carney,—that they, the teachers, would be paid the value of the ration (which they could then buy at the Commissary at cost price) instead of receiving the ration in kind, this payment to be made in addition to their salaries. I imagine that the Superintendent forgot to make provision for this payment by calling on me for the amount necessary, and paying it out, so that the teachers were notified of the stoppage of supplies, without being informed how they could obtain them (precisely the same articles in the same quantity if they so preferred)—and the money to pay for them—hence the misunderstanding—this has been corrected since, and the commissary now issues rations to the teachers, charges me with the money value, sends me the bills—and I pay them—so that the teachers are put to no trouble, and accounts are simplified, only now the teachers have to take the ration as constituted by law, whereas they could—under my first order—have pur-

1. Senator from Massachusetts. As Chairman of the Senate Committee on Military Affairs, he did much to raise and equip the Federal armies, and in 1865 he sponsored the bill establishing the Freedmen's Bureau. *D.A.B.*, XX, 322–325.

chased such articles and in such quantities as they might have preferred to the value of each ration——I am much pleased with the plan now being successfully carried out by the benevolent people and societies of the north for educating colored children and providing for destitute and helpless of both races. General Butler will inform you that I heartily endorse his proceedings as far as they had gone into operation—in so humane a cause——But when disappointed or self-elected protectors of Africans go to you complaining that I will not let them help their suffering brothers, I hope you will remember that the poor blacks in my Department are not like unto a simple hearted youth from the country, arrived in town with his patrimony, a stranger is the youth, and cannot tell a friend from a sharper—and you will know that in cities there are some of the latter class who would insist upon their right to care and protect such strangers—hence it is when I find men insisting upon their right to protect helpless Africans and making a parade of their sympathies—I am a little apt to find in this parade a disguise to cover operations in their own favor——Should any of these complain to you of me, please do me the favor to give me the circumstances, name of the complainant and nature of complaint, and I may be able to inform you in what scheme of plunder the plaintiff has been disappointed.

And now sir I beg to assure you that the gentle and kind friends of the unfortunate Africans, who are really at work in the north and here will find me working with them regardless of praise or blame.

I am sir respectfully
Your obt servt
(Sgd) E.O.C. ORD [2]
MAJOR GENL VOLS

2. Edward O. C. Ord, a West Point graduate in 1839, became a brigadier general of volunteers in 1861 after a varied career in the West. He was promoted to major general in 1862, but after a violent disagreement with General Irvin McDowell he was transferred to the western zone. In 1864 he returned to Virginia and served under Grant during the last months of the war. In January 1865 he was placed in command of the Army of the James and the Department of North Carolina. Heitman, *Register*, I, 759; *D.A.B.*, XIV, 48-49; Bernarr Cresap, ''The Career of General Edward O. C. Ord to 1864'' (Unpublished Ph.D. Dissertation, Vanderbilt University, 1949).

Miss Chase—

I was glad to receive your letter, & have been making inquiries upon the subject suggested. We have had several calls for aid of the same kind. Just now the city is raising $2000 for White Refugees.

The New England Soc. is auxiliary to the "National Union Commission," [1] whose special object is aid for the poor whites. Our own S. School we pledged to support one laborer the present year, among the Colored.

I think the "Union Commission" would meet any special calls you might make. I inclose one of these circulars.

Perhaps we can make a special collection for your particular object, though our contributions are frequent. Would it not be well for you to write to the "Spy" & state the case under your name?

... Education, whether of whites or blacks, stands first. We are hoping for a speedy end of the war, & then the work of *education* in the South will command still more attention.

Very truly yours

M. RICHARDSON

Head Quarters   District of Eastern Virginia
Special Orders No. 59   Norfolk, Va., March 19th, 1865.

EXTRACT

II. Ample provision having been made by the benevolent Societies of the North for the education of colored children in this District, South of the James, Parents of all colored children between the ages of five and fourteen years are hereby notified, that their children, (unless employed at labor) must attend schools.

Parents or Guardians who neglect this duty or fail to obey

---

1. Apparently a reference to the American Union Commission, which was organized primarily for the relief of suffering among both whites and Negroes. In December 1865 this organization and the American Freedmen's Aid Commission joined to form the Freedmen's Aid Union Commission. See *The American Union Commission: Its Origin, Operation and Purposes,* and Brown, *Lyman Abbott.*

this order, will be punished by fine or imprisonment, upon conviction before the Provost Marshal.

By Order of Brig. Gen. Geo. H. Gordon:[1]

WICKHAM HOFFMAN[2]
ASSISTANT ADJUTANT GENERAL
LIEUT. AND ACT. AID-DE-CAMP.

Official:

[Washington, March 3, '65]

Dear Familiars:

We went to Morehead [1] and Beaufort [2] as we proposed. Went in cars to Morehead; passing through pine-groves green as spring and sunshine could make them at the North, through Newport,[3] and Newport barracks, and Carolina City,[4] howling wildernesses of vacuity. We passed many encampments of colored and white soldiers, took some with us, as we supposed, toward Fort Fisher.[5] The explosion at the Fort shook dishes

1. George H. Gordon, a graduate of West Point, served in the Mexican War. In 1861 he raised a regiment, the 2nd Massachusetts Infantry. He was active in the Shenandoah Valley and in 1865 was placed in command of the Eastern District of Virginia. He wrote several books on the Civil War. *D.A.B.*, VII, 421–422.

2. A New York lawyer who served as the adjutant general under Generals Thomas Williams, W. T. Sherman, and B. F. Butler. Butler made him assistant adjutant-general of Eastern Virginia and North Carolina in 1864. He was chief-of-staff to General E.R.S. Canby. *D.A.B.*, IX, 117–118.

1. Across the Newport River from Beaufort, northwest of Cape Lookout. *Official Records of the Union and Confederate Armies*, Atlas, plate XL, no. 4. It was the terminus of the Atlantic and North Carolina Railroad.

2. At the mouth of the Newport River, southeast of New Berne and north of Cape Lookout. *Ibid.*

3. Northwest of Beaufort on the Atlantic and North Carolina Railroad. *Ibid.*

4. Near Morehead on the Atlantic and North Carolina Railroad. *Ibid.*

5. Part of the Confederate fortifications for the defense of Wilmington. It commanded the entrance to the Cape Fear River and the port of Wilmington. It was the scene of one of the more amusing fiascoes of the war, when General Benjamin F. Butler persuaded his superior officers to authorize a combined army-navy assault on the fort, which, according to Butler's plan, would be destroyed by the explosion of a ship filled with gunpowder. The explosion did not damage the fort. Criticism of the controversial general reached such a peak that he was removed from command. See Holzman, *Butler*, pp. 147–157. Fort Fisher was taken by Admiral David D. Porter and General A. H. Terry in January, 1865. See West, *Mr. Lincoln's Navy*, pp. 288–302.

from horizontal piles in the Beaufort hospital, and the shock, as well as the preceding firing, was heard distinctly in New Berne and Beaufort. Landing at Morehead, we went directly to the General Hospital, a range of buildings once used as an academy.

· · · · ·

After a dinner with the steward, attendants, and chaplain we visited some of the wards; warmed, like all the hospitals in North Carolina, with huge wood-fires. The rooms of the ward-masters were scrupulously neat, and fancifully adorned with pictures, and paper cut table and wall hangings.

· · · · ·

Capt De Witt, Commissary, kindly gave us his row-boat to go to the railroad station wharf, where we could hire a boat for a three miles row to Beaufort. The two colored men who rowed us were very intelligent. One of them could not express, with sufficient heartiness, his admiration of the teachers, and his gratitude to them. His delight in his books made him as merry as a little boy. After reaching Beaufort we found our way to the Teacher's Home, where we passed the night. The night school was held in a large hall in the home, and we gladly attended it, and assisted at it. The schools, everywhere we go, are promising and interesting; and each one we see is a novel surprise to us. Intending, in the morning, to leave early for Schackleford beech [sic] and for fort Macon[6] which is directly opposite Beaufort, I knew I could get no idea of the town, without running out in the night for it. So, an hour or so before sunrise, I set forth with a brilliant moon as escort, and made acquaintance with the town in general. It is a fishing village, a decayed Marblehead. It's two or three principal streets run parallel to each other, crowding as near as possible to the water's edge. There are no paved foot-paths in Beaufort; and every pedestrian makes most emphatic footprints in the sandy-soil. The town was asleep, when I took a peep at it, and every moon-struck house seemed to have made its bed in the sand,

6. Shackleford Island or Banks is off the coast near Beaufort and Morehead City. Ft. Macon was a Confederate fort for the defense of Beaufort. It was on the tip of Borden's Banks across Bogue Sound from Beaufort and Morehead City. *Official Records of the Union and Confederate Armies*, Atlas, plate LXVII, no. 3.

and to have fallen hopelessly asleep, dragged down by its heavy eyebrows. Without the prevailing Southern porch or portico I saw few houses.

. . . . .

At the end of the street was a very large hotel, which until that morning, had been used during the war for a U.S.G. Hospital (The patients were removed to Morehead City.) Moving up into the little town I found myself in a little grove of the ever-green live-oaks, in the rear of a very picturesque, low-roofed, porticoed mansion. One step from town-houses gave me country indeed. Glossy-leaved evergreen shrubs hedged in the highway, and hoar-frost glistened on every twig, leaf, and grass. Up and down the short streets I passed, hunting the churches, walking among the graves in yards densely shaded by live-oaks, where the bright red berries the yucca (used in lieu of tea in N.C.) gave the only gleam to cheer, stopping in every street, to admire the universal highway pump, which inevitably kept to the very middle of the street; but which offered its flowing hospitality so generously that no one could complain of it as an intruder. The limitations of little folks were thoughtfully heeded in their construction and pitchers and pails were provided with supports. A good substantial shelf helps the little one to the pump-handle, and no uncertain hold on its own integrity has the pitcher on its ample shelf. Off in the water at hand to the town stands on a small island a turpentine still (Which we visited, later in the day, seeing there the manufacture of turpentine). I mourned that I did not have time to draw that still. I thought, then, and I thought when we visited it that I had never before seen any-thing so absolutely picturesque. Nothing could be spared from the picture; and nothing in Nature could look more "Like a picture." Every barrel, all the timber, the machinery, the wood-colored shed, and the clumps of live oak, all were wanted; and each builded *very much* better than it knew. When [I] saw it in the early morning the reflection in the water was the exact counterpart of that marvellous picture in wood.

. . . . .

We visited four schools gathered in churches, and visited a large collection of log-houses occupied by white refugees from

Washington City—Union soldiers and their families. They lived forlornly, destitute of nearly all things. Some of them mean-spirited, but most of them were frank, and somewhat enterprising. We saw one or two very interesting and pretty young wives. One, however, drew her dipper [snuff-stick] from her mouth, when we entered. They were sitting in rocking chairs, and had some home comforts about them. At 2 P.M. (on Fourth Day, the 18th of January,) we took the cars at Morehead for Newberne. We found Mr Briggs on board, and my warm friend Mrs Ohlhausen; arrived at New Berne, we went immediately to the General Hospital, which comprised a very large number of handsome buildings on three different streets—barracks connect the buildings, giving a large court-yard for the whole, which is tastefully appointed with walks. We found order and neatness everywhere, and a charm indeed was the whole. We dined sumptuously at the Home and attended evening school.

On Thursday, we visited Camp Totten,[7] the fourth fort we entered about New Berne. We met Col. Sprague,[8] just before we reached the Fort, on the beautiful black horse that has carried him through many battles, (and upon which I saw him mount for the first time.) He gave me a card for Major Amory,[9] who kindly conducted us around the Fort. We mounted the magnificent travers, the work of Gen Foster and the first travers I ever saw. The view from it was grand indeed. The junction of the Trent and Neuse was not far away. We could see Artillery and Cavalry exercises, near, as well as far away, and could realize how fearfully imperilled the rebels would be if they should undertake to approach the city across the level, unsheltered plains that stretch, with surpassing

7. About one mile west of New Berne between the Neuse Road and Trent Road. *Ibid.*

8. Probably Lieutenant Colonel Augustus B. R. Sprague of Worcester who entered the war as a captain in April 1861. He was brevetted brigadier general in 1865. Heitman, *Register*, I, 912; *Official Records of the Union and Confederate Armies*, ser. I, vol. 33, p. 1054; Worcester Society of Antiquity, *Proceedings*, I (1878), no. 5, p. 38; II (1879), no. 7, p. 20.

9. Probably Colonel Thomas J. C. Amory, 17th Massachusetts Volunteers, who was in command of the New Berne sub-district of the North Carolina district in May 1864. He was relieved of this command after a brief period. *Official Records of the Union and Confederate Armies*, ser. I, vol. 36, part 2, pp. 351, 369.

beauty, around it. A perfect gem of a planter's home is the
head-quarters of Col. Sprague (who commands five of the
seven large forts about New Berne) and Quartermaster
Thomas whom, with his wife, we knew well last winter, at
Fort Norfolk. An intensely white latticed-fence encloses the
intensely white buildings, and hospitality and comfort appear
to invite one to the beautiful porch of the low-roofed dwelling-
house. After leaving the Fort I called on Dr Page of the Sanitary Commission, who has, voluntarily, taken under his charge
the poor white refugees about N.B. From there I went across
the river in Mr Brigg's buggy, hoping to find the schools in
session, but I was too late. I visited Gen. Foster's block-house,
the first one built during the present war. Block-houses are
considered the forlorn hope of the beseiged; although they are
looked upon as impregnable. We found time, during the day
to visit many of the schools in New Bern and we were entirely
pleased with the order and discipline maintained in them. Indeed, we were charmed with all the schools we visited during
our journey. At sunset we went with Miss——— upon the
spire of a handsome church, dedicated to Union services, where
we had the finest view I ever saw from so low an elevation.
The delicate fingers of the elm-tree stretched over every house
in the beautiful city. The wide streets, the large, open squares,
and the magnificent rivers, with the flags flying from many a
fort, vied with each other in their power to attract us.

We made a new home, upon our return to New Berne with
Helen Freson and the new formed family that spilled over
from the Home into a near house. That night the new family
had a turkey graced house-warming, to which the other two
families of teachers were bidden. Our friend the Capt from
Fort Amory came, with one of his friends to see us (having
sent us and Miss Freson, previously some mistletoe and moss)
and Col Sprague came to see me. Soon after the Col. came
into the room we heard a band open its music before our door.
While Mr Briggs and the ladies, after wondering what it could
mean, were exclaiming, "Oh, its for the teachers," Col.
Sprague said, "Miss Chase what would you like to hear?"
We all went upon an upper balcony and grew very much
excited over "Departed Days" "Silver Shower" "Soldiers

Chorus" "Star Spangled Banner" "Sweet Home" and many another air. One of the ladies asked for Sweet Home, but Col Sprague hesitated, saying he had never dared to ask them to play that, since he saw, early in the war, a regiment stand in tears, around a band while it played "Home." Soon after the Col. and his band departed we heard delicious singing under our window and we found our friend the Capt. interested there. The singers came into the entry and sang us many songs. Several of them were very touching war songs.

. . . . .

The next morning we bade our friends good-bye and took the boat at ten o'clock for Norfolk. We were obliged to delay until twelve for Gen. Palmer,[10] military governor of New-Berne, who, with some of his staff officers, and other officers were on their way to the Fortress, summoned to attend the Court-Martial of Major Jamieson of Providence who was accused of appropriating to his own use the bounty-money raised for negro soldiers. (Major was formerly a Baptist minister, of most excellent reputation. He called here, once or twice, last winter, to see Martha, and took tea with us one night, and spoke admirably to the night scholars in our family school. He has been found guilty, and is sentenced to three years imprisonment.) While we sat on deck, waiting for the handsome General, we heard the target practice from all the forts and saw a wounded Col. taken on shore from a steamboat alongside of us which left New-Berne only the day before to carry provisions to the poor of Washington City. The boat got aground, and for three hours it was fired into by guerillas. Five men were killed, the Col. was wounded, and the boat was riddled.

. . . . .

Yours affectionately

LUCY

Washington March 3rd '65

10. Brigadier General Innis N. Palmer of Buffalo, New York, a graduate of West Point. He fought in the battles around Washington and on the Peninsula and served in North Carolina from December 1862 to July 1865. *D.A.B.*, XIV, 184–185; Heitman, *Register*, I, 767.

Worcester Friday April 7 [1865]

My dear Miss Chase,

We have just nailed up a barrel of articles for your white refugees. I am sorry we could not respond to your letter before but it takes a good many garments to fill up a barrel, and though we meet once a week, we find it takes time to get the requisite number. I saw Mrs Theo. Brown this afternoon and she thought our barrel could go perfectly well with one for Sarah for the Contrabands, and as it would save our money for buying more materials I was very glad to accept her offer, and she seemed to think there would be no difficulty about your claiming it for your *white children*.

As the understanding here is that we work for the white refugees of course I am anxious to have the contents of the barrel applied to that object. I wish I had a dozen to send for the benefit of all, black or white.

While I write the bells are ringing, the cannon thundering and peoples' faces looked very beaming as they read of Lee's utter ruin.

I thought the few school-books might be useful.

Yours, very truly,

F. A. HILL

(Barrel contains 129 articles, listed, but not priced)

Richmond ! ! Va.
April 18th [1865]

Richmond—

Hurray ! ! Then Peace—thank God!

Though much exhausted with my morning task of governing and teaching (oral and with the black board) my *little* school of *one thousand and* twenty-*five* children, who but a few days ago were slaves—I will try to give you a few hints of my work since I last wrote. It is useless to wait longer for leisure and freshness for writing——One of the first women of Richmond was your representative; myself, who said a year ago, on Good Friday, she hoped to thank the Lord on the next Good Friday—in Libby Prison—for Freedom: which hope has been *fulfilled*. Although the officers and newspapers say truly that no one can get to Richmond, unless ordered—and such multitudes are waiting in Washington-Norfolk and at Fortress Monroe for passes; our party (Prof Woodbury, who superintends our Norfolk schools, Hannah E. Stephenson, Lucy and myself) through intimate acquaintance with the leading officers here, got passes to come at once, to organize the work in the beginning of the new regime—and constantly and diligently have we labored through the day; and in the night I have *thought* for coming time. Government can only give us leave to *work,* but by ourselves we have got the field and labor organized in less than ten days, in a manner that gratifies and surprises us.

Never have I attended committee meeting more dignified and to the point than the many we have appointed with the leading men in the colored churches. At our first meeting a noble looking and most intelligent deacon started up suddenly saying, "I felt frightened for a moment seeing more than five colored people together"—it being the law here that more than five must never assemble without a white man was authorized to sit with them. Not long ago, the white man they employed to sit in one of their Sunday Schools stepped out on an errand and was detained a little, and the whole school with its teachers was carried to jail. White ministers were *saddled* on their churches who understood the "dutys of servants to masters" and no one was allowed to use a book even if able—the instruction in the Sabbath school was oral. I saw the first black man in a Richmond pulpit and heard from him a sermon that lifted me up to heights my spirit seldom reaches. The colored people of Richmond are far more intelligent and thrifty than any I have met with in the South—and though the laws against learning have been so strict, many can read and a large portion know their letters and spell a little, having been taught by the poor whites secretly and at exorbitant rates.

The work in this Department begins under more favorable auspices than any other, having the experience of the others, ect ect [*sic*]. In their meetings after congratulating them on this new blessing from the Almighty, I tell them of the responsibility that comes with it urging them to be constantly watchful that they show their gratitude & prove their worthiness by doing their best in all things——And I think the older ones fully comprehend this.

We have already enrolled over two thousand pupils and expect to nearly double the number before long. As soon as our teachers come up and the schools are turned over to them, I shall open employment offices and get manufactures under way—it is too soon yet—and most too soon for schools. The officers sent their wives passes to come up and had to telegraph them *not* to come. So of course the teachers cannot come for it is not yet safe. I have heard many threats, and these impetuous people are every day shooting or stabbing someone, so I want no one to come until these people are convinced they are under Govt. The delay is no disadvantage to the little ones, who can be taught to sit still & how to give attention, en masse—their brains can be roused and put in working order by general instructions and exercises, so that when they have their books and teachers they can make a better beginning and I feel that these mental gymnastics I give them will always make study easier for them. I have talked with them in all the churches and met them outside where they weep over me, call down blessings on my head, shake my poor hands so they keep lame so I can hardly hold my pen—as I pass some caressingly take hold of my raiment while some push back the crowd——All this I well know is not for me but for "de good Norf people." And how much I wish these same good North people who have prayed and worked for the people here [?] could join with them in their songs of joy and thanksgiving, as it has been my privilege in this, their day of jubilee. I have opened books in the different churches with headings of occupations where I register names—and soon expect to find very advantageous in getting work.

. . . . .

The colored people will need little help except in helping themselves. We are not going to make beggars of them. Will you please consult with your Society in regard to getting a box of straw & materials for braiding—and yarn & needles & other materials for manufacture. If you can learn through correspondence from what place & most advantageously these & other materials can be procured & send to the Society in

Boston at my desire they will pay, if you will attend to it. I shall be most grateful if you can give a contract for work of any kind or send any plans or materials. You will forgive the writing in consideration of my tired, *shaken* hand, and also inasmuch as I am using the pen and holder that Grant used just before he left his headquarters at City Point for Richmond. One Monday I was in our Capital, the next Monday was in Jeff Davis's—in [one word illegible] Thursday—the slave pens and Libby. I have thanked God for this day. Oh I am so happy I know not what to do——God help me to work as I wish—faithfully & effectively. Full of hope and most affectionately, Farewell, s.e.c.

Richmond April 20th '65

My dear Miss Lowell;

Miss Stevenson has already told you that we gathered the children in different churches on the 15th of April, and opened schools informally at that time. Yesterday, the 19th of April, my sister and I formally opened school in the 1st African Church (the largest church in the city—the one in which the somewhat recent peace conference, where Campbell, Hunter, and others made their notorious unsuccessful galvanic experiments.[1]) We had more than one thousand (1000) children, and seventy-five adults; and found time, after disciplining them, to hear the readers, to instruct the writers, and to teach the multitude from the black-board. Again, today, we had a huge school of nine hundred. We divided the school into classes, and made assistant teachers of the advanced children. On Friday, we shall go to Petersburg, in accordance with an urgent request from its Col'd citizens to open schools. Dont you want to be a teacher there, without delay? There are very few teachers at command, and the number of scholars is very

1. In January 1865 Jefferson Davis appointed a committee composed of Alexander H. Stephens, R. M. T. Hunter, and J. A. Campbell to confer with Lincoln. They reported to the citizens of Richmond on February 7 at the First African Church. See W. Asbury Christian, *Richmond; her Past and Present*, p. 257. Within two weeks after the occupation of Richmond, over 1,000 Negroes were attending a school at this church. Alderson, "Influence of Military Rule," p. 101.

The Mainland, Virginia   157

large. Four churches are in use here, and fifteen hundred children are already in attendance. . . .

The rebel prisoners and citizens are fattening upon our choice stores of food, some of them drawing from Government and the Christian Commission at the same time. The rebel Drs take delicacies and wines from the Sanitary rooms to their patients (?) and inquire of Northerners what concessions the North is ready to make to the South. Genl Lee draws rations! He is absolutely a beggar. He cannot lay aside his uniform because he has nothing to substitute for it. His officers are ludicrously proud of the arms they are allowed to wear about the streets!

Yours very truly

LUCY CHASE

April 20/65

Petersburg May 17th [1865]

We have seen more parallels today than can be paralled [sic] by the fortifications of all preceding war history. I want every one of you to see them. All about Petersburg, the earth is thrown up into forts, parallels, concealed batteries, and bomb-proofs. A well raised crop they look, so close and crowded they are. One can't help saying——They are very thick. The rebel works crowd upon our own, and cannot, without examination, be made to seem an opposing line. In our very renowned Forts, Stedman, & Sedgwick[1] all the quarters are bomb-proof, and the marks of defensive preparation are upon everything. Fort Stedman was built under fire. Fort Sedgwick (or Fort Hell) is of immense size, and is very formidable. Its walls are of basket-work. Both forts are protected by cheavaux [sic] de frise and abbatis [sic]. We walked through the crater[2] into which Burnsides unfortunate men were sent, and we walked upon the trench in which five thousand of the poor fellows were buried.

1. See map in Military Historical Society of Massachusetts, *Papers*, V: "Petersburg, Chancellorsville, Gettysburg."

2. Detailed accounts of the explosion of "The Crater" are in *ibid.*, pp. 207–239, and *Battles and Leaders*, IV, 545–567.

Over the field of the last battles and the field of the battles of last July we walked, where caps, bayonets, canteens, cartridge boxes, belts, coats, and shoes were very thickly strewed. In some of the earth-works, caps, coats, and boots are very thickly imbedded. We saw many, very man[y] obtruding feet of the dead, some heads were uncovered, and, in many instances the whole figure was easily traced under a thin covering of earth. We saw the leg bones with fragments of pantaloons adhering to them still standing in stocks and shoes. The rebels undertook to blow up Fort Stedman, and made a very long thoroughly constructed mine for the purpose. With candle in hand we went several hundred feet into the mine which was well-braced on every side. We also went a few steps into either end of Burnsides mine, but water prevented us from going into it.   [No signature; in Lucy's hand.]

Norfolk, May 25th 1865

Dear Mrs. May;

You see we are Home again once more. The Richmond schools are flourishing finely; but Negro affairs are miserably conducted now; but very soon *Col.* Brown will take all Virginia into his part of the "Bureau" and then things will go as nearly right as possible:—yet I am confident that the Negro will suffer more the coming year of Peace, than he has during the War:—and no organization can shield him from all the injustice he will be exposed to from the vengeful Southrons. It is surprising how many ways the F.F.Vs have of venting their spite on the Freedmen; we saw much of it while in Richmond. But the fetters are broken *forever!* Thank God;——And we must be patient in the necessary confusion of the change. I had the satisfaction of lowering rents, restoring property, and adjusting difficultys [*sic*] in several cases, but many colored people have bought property without having taken any papers— and there is no way of getting it back from the whites who have taken it.

Bold robberies were of daily occurrence. In broad day light I saw a well dressed Confederate snatch a watch from a colored man, in passing; and in getting it away, the white man cut the black man's head with something, so that the blood ran freely, and the man was partially stunned—the high-wayman ran, and *our* soldiers wouldn't run after him——Several of our men have been shot on guard; and three were killed—and they have reason to fear the Rebs. Our soldiers as well as the Johnnies plunder the houses of the poor blacks continually—so the colored people feel it is neither safe to go out or remain at home. The cry of "murder!" often came up from the hollow below where we lived where are congregated most of the poor of the city—and looking out, we could see the people running from their houses, & the soldiers running down the hillsides in many directions, after the thief who would soon get lost to sight among the houses or hollows.

In one house I went where a woman lived miserably with her large flock of little ones, and "no one to do for em but me missis, an I finds work very hard to get—an I wont beg of Uncle Sam—as long as I can get work." Her house had been most thoroughly searched—even the beds were ripped for greenback—finding nothing of value but a half dollar that was laid away for rent—and many poor women flocked around with tales of their frights and robberies.

The Richmond people colored [*sic*] are far superior to any I have yet encountered, and a very little help of the right kind will advance them in a short time to an independent position. Work and justice is all they ask—and if societies would or-ganize *work;* they would benefit the race more than any other kind of help.

One early morning I was much surprised by the appearance of Aggie Peters a nice old Auntie from Norfolk—who kissed my hands and wept for joy. "Why Auntie, how did you find me?" said I. "Find you, honey—why there aint a corner of the Earth where you could hide so I couldn't find you dare if I want to look. Ses I to myself one day—I wonder if now Babalons fallen (i.e. Richmond) I can ever get any of my property back to give my children—for 'taint long before I shall go up yonder, (die) an I went up to tell you all about it, and they said they were in Richmond, so I comes right up"—and then she told her story in wonderful language speak-ing of her wrongs so touchingly—and dwelling on the injustice to the race, as if her moral sense was more aggrieved than herself; and her eloquence was most touching and remarkable, as with streaming, uplifted eyes & clasped hands she pictured the relations of her race to the North & South—the Lord's purpose in the War—what the North had done for them and what they owed the North.

Though 65 years old Aggie has the best figure in the city, a most dignified bearing and step as elastic as a young girl—with fine manners. "I allers shows my manners and never once forgot." Her perfect faith and love of her Creator kept her cheerful and courageous through everything. A free woman:—she was allowed to do business for herself—owning a house—grocery—"hack and span" & donkeys & two keerts (carts) hiring negroes and taking pains to get those who wished to buy their freedom—giving them a part over what they paid their master. She bought her husband and a man who was anxious to get his freedom sooner than he could pay his master & let him work to repay her:—after a visit to the North she was thrown into prison immediately on her return and was examined and cross examined before some "sharp hard looking judges" who wished to know all she saw or heard of the North & her views thereon (I have seen many who had the same experience). She was banished with the threat that [she] would be taken to the whipping post if she returned & kept in jail until sold. The colored man was so faithful in the charge of her property she gave him all he made in the two years after he paid for himself—& with this money he had bought himself a little place and he had a great name for being a steady, good man with white & black. Without any warning he was taken of off [sic] the hack while driving & put into jail, with an order that no man white or black should see him; and carried away in irons the same night for the Southern market; and no one can tell where he is. One of the leading citizens, though pro-slavery, knows the partys and testifys the truthfulness—he tried to see this man knowing him to be so honest and good—and wished to get him out of jail, but the wicked white man who stole him was artful enough to secure his prey by forbidding *any mortal* to see him; and hurrying him off.

All of Aggie's property was stolen from her and she is very anxious for justice sake it shall be got back—"give it to the Union when you get it if I am gone—I've got plenty for my small wants—the Lord has been so good to me giving me plenty of work & strength and I've raised my children to do for themselves. When they first threw me in prison I was all down discouraged—thinking whats the use, if a person works hard and always shows their manners & behavior; and does as clearly as they ken what they ought—and comes to this the same as them that does bad; but presently the Lord shone in the room; and I felt as happy and easy as a baby; & I prayed and sang all night: they come and tried to stop me; I felt I ought to sing praises—but in the morning they tied me to the whipping post to take it out of me: but when I got rested I began again."

I know not what I have written from Richmond to you and what to Miss Stephenson. I sent to "Mrs Denny N.E.F.A. Soc. Leicester" in one of Jeff. Davis's envelopes about twenty bills of sale, I captured in a Negro auction room; and wrote some incidentals on the back of each—for distribution in your society; and one letter to Mrs. May and one to Mr. May from R.

. . . . .

Forgive my poor eyes for such scrawls. With love to Wde [?] and high regard to Mr May and yourself.—s.e.c.

I have a quantity of Confed. money I wish to convert into a flag for the R. schools. Can you suggest a fair or a firm who would buy it—or a curiosity broker? How I wish I could have been at the last A. S. meeting. Shan't you band together for the elevation of the Negro? An Employment Society or something of that nature. Could you get some one to learn where at best advantage could be bought a box of material for straw braiding—and could you suggest some manufacture we could undertake on a small scale in Richmond this Summer or Fall. We shall probably remove to R. ere long. I cannot say when. I would be glad if you could form some scheme of work to suggest to me to undertake in Richmond.

Beverly, Mass.
June 3/65.

Dear Miss Chase—

My absence from town prevented my receiving until very recently your letter. I recall with pleasure our acquaintance at Princeton & am glad to have the opportunity to renew it, if only by letter, & I have read with much interest your account of the condition of the women you speak of in Richmond.

The Secr'y of our Society The Rev. D. H.A. Miles has spent some time in R. & his opinion coincides with yours that the best mode of relief would be by an industrial organization or undertaking—& we are anxiously awaiting his return to see what action we can take about it.

As to the purchase of articles to be resold to curiosity-hunters, I should be very doubtful of its success. A curiosity hunter would buy a thing on the spot, from an ex-rebel which he would not look at in Boston offered at second hand.

What should you think of establishing a depot in Richmond at which materials could be given out to be made up into garments, by women destitute or nearly so—the articles to be sold at cost to the same class—or at less than cost—or in extreme cases given away? The greatest suffering & that which it is most important to relieve must be among the women. It is suggested that the best mode of aiding the men is by agricultural implements sold cheap or given to them.

I remain
Very truly yours,
MARTIN BRIMMER[1]

If any other suggestions occur to you on this subject, please address me to the care of Hamilton A. Hill Esq, Boston, in order that if I am away—as I am liable to be—the letter may be opened by our committee.
To Miss Lucy Chase

1. Brimmer was a prominent Boston philanthropist, educator, and author. He was a director of the Emigrant Aid Society, and in 1855–56 he visited Kansas to examine the situation there. He served several terms in the Massachusetts legislature. He traveled widely and published several volumes on travel and history.

Eureka!
        Eureka!
Dear Mr. May:

I am happy to say—that safe to its hum—the barrel has come! . . . It is not to be opened at present; but will probably be taken to Richmond soon—to give employment to some needy ones—whom I shall pay in money; giving the articles where they are essential and there is inability to pay.

I go to Point of Rocks[1] on the James tomorrow to see if it is a suitable place to establish Homes for the Aged-indigent and orphans——There are about fifty log barracks there—(Butler's Hospitals) and it is a very pleasant—and for the neighborhood—a healthy locality. As soon as it is abandoned by the Army, I propose to take charge, in which case I cannot get home this Summer. But as yet no ones plans can be definite in this Dept. Genl. Howard[2] is very popular, and all have faith in Capt. Brown's fitness as Commissioner for the State of Virginia. I should like to be able to give [up?] our work in Richmond as soon as possible. I do not want the North to do any thing for these people that we can make the South do for them——So I shall do my best to get them to put the colored people into the charitable Institutions already established

---

He was a member of the Committee on Finance of the N.E.F.A.S. Samuel Eliot, ''Memoir of Martin Brimmer,'' *Proceedings*, Massachusetts Historical Society, Series II, Vol. X (1895–96), 586–595; Herringshaw (ed.), *Encyclopedia of American Biography*, p. 149; *Freedmen's Record*, I (1865), 88.

1. About three miles up the James from City Point and the mouth of the Appomattox. *Official Records of the Union and Confederate Armies*, Atlas, plate CLXXVII, no. 3.

2. Oliver Otis Howard, Commissioner of the Bureau of Refugees, Freedmen, and Abandoned Lands. Howard was a native of Maine and a graduate of West Point. He was Colonel of the 3d Maine Regiment in 1861; he was immediately brevetted brigadier general and by the end of the war held that rank in the regular army. He was president of Howard University, 1869–1874, and was one of the directors of the ill-fated Freedmen's Bank. Although Howard was a controversial figure, both as a soldier and as Commissioner of the Bureau, he undoubtedly was deeply interested in the welfare of the Negro. The task set for the Bureau was an impossible one, and Howard's failure to discipline his subordinates complicated a problem which was beyond administrative solution at best. See Howard's reports in Manuscripts of Refugees, Freedmen, and Abandoned Lands; Bentley, *Freedmen's Bureau;* Howard, *Autobiography;* Carpenter, *Sword and Olive Branch.*

now while our army is here, trusting the habit once established will be kept up. They of course would not do so themselves, for years to come—ect, ect, [sic] reasons self evident.

I wish you could have seen the bright little boy who has just left me, and heard his glowing account of "our garden you helped us to, Miss Sarah" and "how much we sell from it—— Oh Miss Sarah—wes so happy to be livin in the country, whar theres plenty to do for all hands and is so much pleasanter & healthier than the dirty city." I bought some nice fresh berries which he picked, "right smart soon" in the morning and engaged soft & hard crab for tomorrow dinner. . . .

S.E.C.

THE REIGN OF TERROR IN NORFOLK.

Norfolk, Va., June 25, 1865.[1]

"The days of bayonets are passed!" is the bullying street-cry of the returned rebel soldiers in Norfolk and Portsmouth, as they fearlessly assume the once-familiar knife and pistol. At the corners, and in the market-place, many have been heard to say, "We'll kill every nigger, or drive 'em all out of town." Civil power is established here, and the military command is restricted. But Gen. Howard, commandant of the small military force retained here, has said, "There is one thing I *will* do; I *will* protect the colored people."

On Thursday last, two or three Southern gentlemen succeeded in infusing Southern sentiments into the hearts of some of the New York 13th Artillery by dosing them with drugged whiskey; and, leading themselves, they encouraged the soldiers to destroy the wares on the stand of a colored man. On from the stand, cry-

1. Clipping from unidentified newspaper, apparently written by Lucy Chase. See Wertenbaker, *Norfolk*, pp. 256–257.

ing, "Clear out all the niggers," they passed to a ball-room, through which they dashed, driving all before them, and destroying whatever came in their way. On Friday night, a body of colored men, wishing to see a circus performance, deemed it prudent to go in a body, and, protecting themselves with canes, they went forth quietly, but were fired upon as they drew near the circus. Two or three were shot; and all withdrew without offering resistance. Colored men were attacked, that night, in various parts of the city. One man was hung upon a lamp-post. Another, going home from a mission house with a letter which had been written for him there, was seized and put into prison, where he remained until the next day, when his kind amanuensis obtained his release. A worthy exhorter was knocked down, and severely injured, on his way home from church. Another was woefully bruised, while crossing the street from the house of a sick sister to his own home. On Saturday night, the wood-wharf men were attacked, and the stores of two Union white men were broken into, and much of the property destroyed. Finding the declaration, "I am a Union man," no defence against the attack of New York soldiers, one man resorted to his pistol, and, after wounding two of his assailants, succeeded in making his escape. Last night many shots were fired in Portsmouth. The demonstrations there are more violent than here.

On Sunday, two colored men were found hanging dead upon trees, this side of Suffolk. And a young man leaving a church in this city, was shot through the side, and robbed. He still lies, a panting sufferer, on an attic floor; bare of every comfort, save the inestimable one of a devoted mother, who leaves him neither night nor day. "He might have gone to the hospital," his mother said; "but I want him where I can be with him, and do for him all the time." My sister and I well remember when the mother and son came from their master to Norfolk. "We won't stay upon government one moment," the mother said. "Uncle Sam is very good, but he has too much to do; and we don't want to trouble any one. I'll get a little room, and I reckon we can scrub along." And from that little room, for months, they have gone out to their little work, coming back at night to peace and independence; never dreaming of one to molest or make them afraid.

I have just come from the bedsides of two wounded men. One of them was quietly passing to his home, when three soldiers run after him and fired three shots, neither of which took effect. They then cried "Halt!" but, as the man knew their order was not to be respected, he walked on. Another shot fired, and the ball passed through his mouth. "Finish him, finish him," some one cried. Two men overtook him, and each pointed a revolver at his breast; he turned their hands aside, and said, "You don't shoot me again." "Very well," they said, "come into the guardhouse." There he was received without investigation. In the morning, when the officer of the guard came, he inquired what brought him there, and after hearing the man's story, he said: "Pity they did not kill you." The other man is badly wounded in the leg. He was hobbling home from his day's work at the government commissary when he was overtaken by a howling crowd. His co-laborers were with him, and eleven shots were fired at them. Only one took effect. "You must fight it out, I can do nothing for you," the Mayor of Norfolk said to a committee of colored men who sought his protection. The rioters are taking advantage of the divided, and somewhat obscurely defined, responsibilities resting upon the associated military and civil authorities; responsibilites which the civil authorities shirk, when the interests of the colored man or of Union citizens are at stake. The Mayor of Portsmouth, whose city is more disturbed than our own, requests Col. Howard to "relieve Portsmouth of its military guard!" Col. Howard is abroad, with the will of an army in his breast, and we are confident he will speedily restore quiet again. The disturbance is maintained through the daytime.

A man who just passed my window told me this story:—"Two New York soldiers came up to me, fifteen minutes ago, rolling up their shirt-sleeves, and saying, 'We are going to kill every one of you.' 'You'll have a heap to do, then,' I said. 'But I shan't run away from you. I'll meet you, but I shan't run.' Then one of the soldiers drew back, and begged the other off." I heard one of the soldiers say, yesterday, in the presence of several citizens, "The citizens got us to do this. They told us to clean out all the men, and then they could take care of the women and children. I've painted here for twenty-five years, and everybody has thought a heap of me; and I've never been beaten and bruised about in this manner, and I ain't going to stand it, either. I'm one that's always quiet, and ain't meddling with nobody, and I don't want nobody to meddle with me. They think they've got all out of us they can, and now they want to get rid of us. I've always been ready to do anything for the soldiers. Many a time they've asked me for a quid of tobacco, and I have not had any, and I've gone into a store and spent the last cent I had for some, and gladly given it to them." One man said to me, "I heard some soldiers say, this whole thing was got up on New York, and was to run all through the Southern cities."

Day and night, men, boys and soldiers cry "Nig!" "Nig!" at sight of a colored man, and hasten to molest him. Several have said to me, "We're having again what we suffered when the Union forces first came into Norfolk." One man said:—"We rejoiced to see the Northern soldiers; there was nothing we would not do for them; and they knew it, too. We were humble, grateful and respectful. But the New York 99th destroyed our property, shot us down, and injured us in every possible way. They got men from their beds at night, saying, 'The general has important work for you to do,' and then took the men so willing to work for the government, and sent them over the lines, and sold them as slaves. It seems, now, as if we had no one to protect us, and there's nothing left us but to protect ourselves."

The colored people are grieved, but not cowed. "We are a nation that loves the white people," one man said, "and we would never attack them, but if we are driven to exasperation we know our duty."

CONTRABAND.

Richmond, July 17th, 1865

My good friend,
    Mr. May:—
Your letter of the 6th is just received,—and with much pleasure. You may believe all the statements that have appeared in the Northern papers (up to date) about the abuses of the colored people——The Tribune of the 15th copys [sic] a letter (from Lucy) from the Commonwealth:—making complaints thereupon——The men who were hung on lamp posts

were rescued from the mob. It was necessary to put Norfolk under Martial Law again:—and with Col. Brown and Genl. Terry at Richmond—affairs appear well on the surface in both cities——But for the Bureau; I dread to think where we should be now. . . . If I take the Chimberaso Hosp.[1] barracks —on a table land—above the boat landing—at Richmond— I shall hope to carry on many trades, for men and women. I do not wish to leave until my Fall work is mapped out—for I wish to start things; and put some one in charge, while I renew my strength in the blessed North; but finding it impossible to do so, and the hot weather depriving me of strength to do much that I would like to—I shall turn my face homeward the last of the month:—and when sufficiently rested should most gladly spend a day with you.

. . . . .

I am only here for a day—on business for the people:— and a fine spectacle I witnessed yesterday——As we lay at the wharf a transport of Colored Troops landed close by, making as fine an appearance as they marched into town as any troops I have ever seen:—and for the three hours they waited on shore they were as orderly as any group of gentlemen could be. "'Tis as much as we can bear to have the Yankees here:—but we'd rather die than have the nigger troops here" is the language of the people:—so the feelings of the citizens who met these troops as they were returning from Church —can better be imagined than expressed. Col Brown ordered them in to do guard duty.

With ever best wishes:—and a feeling that the hardest struggle is yet to be:—but full of hope——

Yours truly

S.E.C.

---

1. Chimborozo Hospital, "the largest military hospital in the history of this continent." H. H. Cunningham, *Doctors in Gray; The Confederate Medical Service*, p. 51.

Milton, Mass.
Aug. 29, 1865

Dear Lucy;

The enclosed represents an organization, chiefly of ladies, representing a good deal of pluck and a fair share of money, who do not like to give up their Sanitary work,—and propose to hold on for all the Charities of Reconstruction. They have already a "Memorial Teacher,"—among the "Educational Commission" force.

But the Society wants a general range among the wider work of Reconstruction. Can you not suggest in Richmond some special work,—outside that of teaching the Negroes,— which it could take right into its own hand? Have you wanted an Orphan Asylum there,—or a free Hospital,—or to rebuild a School-house—or in short anything good, that the Freedmen's Association has not had money for? Do not make a charity because I want one, but from time to time, as anything dawns on you let me know.

I am finishing an article for the North American on the Education of the Freedmen, knowing, alas, little enough about it. Have you any pet theory which you would like to have ventilated & put forward there? Is there anything you cannot make Government understand,—nor the Teacher's Committee, nor even Capt. Brown,—nor General Butler,—which perhaps by 8 or 10 pages of note paper you could make me understand? If so, will you try by a note written two or three days to Beverly, Mass.

I address you at Worcester because you ought to be there— and I hope are. If you are tired of Virginia shall we commission you as Superintendent of Education in our new colony in Florida?

Remember me to Sarah—and your brother Charles and anybody who seems like to forget me.

Truly yrs
EDWARD E. HALE[1]

1. Edward Everett Hale, a son of Nathan and Sarah Preston Everett Hale, was a prominent Boston clergyman, author, and reformer. He supported the Kansas emigrant aid movement and during the war worked with the Sanitary Commission. A prolific author, he is perhaps best known as the author of *The Man Without a Country*. *D.A.B.*, VIII, 99–100.

THE DEEP SOUTH

Savannah Wharf on "a stack" of boxes barrels & trunks

Dec. 1st 1865

*D*ear Mrs. May;

Since I saw you, I have been almost like a bag of the wind; at no time sufficiently settled to report on "Winter plans."

The last six weeks of our vacation were to have been given to pleasant recreation, and farewell glances into beloved households in the northern cities, but a crying need for someone who knew the lay of the land, to found a family in Norfolk made us turn our steps that way, instead; where we took a large empty old house (but two doors from the one we occupied last season) and fitted it up for the teachers. The day after we arrived, we reopened all the schools belonging to our family, and held them in a large church three weeks till other members came, teaching regularly and faithfully all who were ready to come to school. The schools are never full till Winter—all working, who are able, as long as they can get "jobs"; many selling cakes and candies about the streets. Each day the stragglers came in—and all took hold, with a good will, to learn. Mr. Banfield [1] was the young man sent out by the society to be gentleman of the house, and we three worked together in converting the dismal, deserted old place, into a pleasant home.

As soon as the family came, we gave over the schools, and opened two large schools at the Rope Walk, (the Refugee Camp)—of which we had general supervision. I wish you could have seen our grotesque, wild, lawless menagerie of a school, the first few days, when it seemed as if the little "fliberty gibbets" had arms and legs by the dozens; and all seemed to have more than the lawful number of tongues— the third day, saw an orderly and most interesting school;

1. J. Stuart Banfield of Dover, New Hampshire. He was supported by the Brookline Freedmen's Aid Society. He taught at Alexandria, Virginia, before going to Columbus, Georgia. *Freedmen's Record*, I, (May 1865), 75, 86.

and I could hardly believe it had any relationship to the first days gathering. These schools we held while we remained; taking care of the old women's home, in addition;—and fitting them up for Winter—visiting the familys of the sick and needy; and attending to the wants of all old & extremely destitute people, in the time not given to the school. The enthusiastic welcomings of the people on our return, were most touching as well as gratifying. They told us they knew we were coming back; though we had told them we certainly should not—when we left. "Wese been a praying for yer,—and prayin you might come back to us; for you knowd our ways and trials as if you was of us, always; and peared like we could tell you, and you could understand & do for us, as no one else could" said they.

"Teachers are wanted in Georgia—only men—it not being agreeable, proper, or safe for ladies——Who'll go?" We reported ourselves as ready to start any time at a days notice & Nov. 20th Mr. Banfield, Miss Ellen B. Haven (of Portsmouth N. H. one of our family and a particular friend of ours) Lucy & I took the overland route for Savannah. Nine toilsome tedious days of tortuous terrible travelling brought us to this lovely (all but the dirt) city.

I marvel much that we are here alive—travelling as we did, day and night—the wheels getting on fire—axles breaking, frequent fording and occasional collisions—the roads, engines and cars, so much out of order. Most grateful too am I to be thus far on the road. Our final destination I know not, the agent of the State being in the interior and not answering our telegram (wh. probably do not reach [him?]) The negroes here are quite enterprising, there being eight thousand in the place. They have formed an Educational Ass. and support several schools. It is refreshing to find *only* blacks in this state instead of the many shades one sees in Va. Though there are many poor of course, there will not probably be much suffering in the city, the climate is so warm; and I think they will make out full as well for food as the poor class in most citys—this Winter. In the interior there is supposed to be much suffering though particulars arent yet known.

. . . . .

In our journey we had a fine opportunity to learn the feelings of the people of the South. Always travelling at a very slow rate, we overheard many instructive conversations. The Negro is the universal subject of conversation; the better class accept the result of the war, as inevitable; and seem determined to make the best of it—only the lower classes grumble about the spilt milk, fretting and fuming like thoughtless children.

Savannah is ravishingly lovely: all the streets are very wide—running entirely across the city, dividing it in squares, like Phila. a broad strip of green, with trees on both sides, runs through the centre of the streets—which also have shade trees over the sidewalk. High in the gardens hang the golden oranges, sending their sweet perfume afar, and drooping over the full blooming Camilla [sic], which gladdens the eyes through the Winter. Our journey hither was over Sherman's track but it chanced that we passed or stop [sic] at the principal points in the darkness of night. "Eberyting is disregular dese times"——Though some things are higher than ever, most things are lower: Our travelling expenses were tremendous, but this place & Charleston are over stocked [?] with goods; so many things are cheaper & most are quite as low as in the North. Our soldiers & officers are reaping golden harvests in the shops & hotels for awhile in these two citys. Food is more reasonable than could be expected & meats are particularly low—chickens .75 pr. pair & mutton 10 cents a pound. Oranges are five cents a piece, a severe winter a few years ago having killed the trees—though others were immediately planted—there are only enough for home consumption, those in market are brought here, except the wild sour oranges wh. are only fit for preserving—these are a cent a piece.

We loaded ourselves down with shot at Ft. Sumpter [sic] for the benefit of our nieces and nephews. We are toting them round with some difficulty hoping some day to deliver them. I write now—not knowing where or when I shall be settled. With heart's best wishes for the friends of Leicester Hill——

Goodbye

S.E.C.

[clipping, no date]
WORCESTER EVENING GAZETTE

A JOURNEY THROUGH THE SOUTH.

(We take the liberty to print the following extracts from a private letter, from a lady of this city, who has transferred the scene of her labors from Norfolk, Va., to Columbus, Ga.)

SAVANNAH, GA., DEC., 1865.

We arrived in Savannah, a week ago today and shall leave tomorrow for Columbus,[1] on the borders of Alabama. We supposed until today that we should remain in this beautiful city, but the Superintendent desire[d] us to go farther, which we do willingly. We have but two Northern mails a week here, so what will it be when we get far into the interior, with broken railroad communications? Take your maps and travel with us. If we go by land to Augusta we shall have thirty miles staging. From Augusta, we must go to Atlanta, and then take a turn in Alabama before we reach Columbus. The children will be pleased to know that we sailed upon Cape Fear river, in among the rushes and trees of a semi-tropical character, draped with southern moss. Gen. Joe Johnson [sic] destroyed the railroad bridges, in the Carolinas and Georgia, so we were obliged to leave the trains four times before reaching Charleston. The children will like to know also that we forded the great Pedee, the Santee and Roanoke rivers, beautiful streams with shores of surpassing loveliness. At every fording place we had long walks and long delays.

---

1. From Augusta the sisters took the Georgia Railroad to Atlanta, then the Atlanta and West Point to West Point, Georgia, the Montgomery and West Point to Opelika, Alabama, and the Columbus Railroad from Opelika to Columbus.

In Charleston we were detained four days, waiting for transportation to Savannah. We visited the teachers living in Barnwell Rhett's[2] house; visited Gen. Devens[3] in Beauregard's Headquarters; saw Gen. Saxton and his wife and Gen. Hartwell,[4] and were introduced to Commodore Inman,[5] Chief of the Atlantic Squadron. Gen. Devens gave us the command of a boat for a day's sail in the harbor so we anticipated visiting all the forts, but the captain said that the quartermaster had furnished him with an insufficient quantity of fuel, so we were obliged to limit our trip to Fort Sumter. Yet we passed Fort Ripley and Castle Pinckney, while Sullivan Island, with Fort Moultrie and Morris Island with Forts Green, Shaw and Wagner [6] were plainly seen. The walls upon the exposed sides of the fort are thickly embedded with shot and shell; and around its base is seen a wealthy waste of ammunition, all hurled with deadly intent. The fort, you know, occupied the whole of an artificial island. The rebels encircled it with mines, supported by posts and railroad iron, making it impossible for our men to have effected a landing even if they should have succeeded in getting under the guns

2. Prominent South Carolina planter and politician. He was a member of Congress from 1837 to 1849. A strong supporter of Calhoun, he was active in nullification and secession. *D.A.B.*, XV, 526–528.

3. Charles Devens, Massachusetts lawyer and legislator. Served in the Civil War as colonel of a Massachusetts regiment, became brevet major general, and was second in command to General Sickles in the Southeastern Department. He was attorney general under President Rutherford B. Hayes. *D.A.B.*, V, 260–262.

4. Alfred S. Hartwell, a lieutenant in the 44th Massachusetts Infantry in 1863, became Colonel of the 55th Massachusetts in December 1863, and brevet brigadier general, volunteers, in December 1864. Heitman, *Register*, I, 508; *Official Records of the Union and Confederate Armies*, ser. I, vol. 28, part 2, p. 138.

5. William Inman, a veteran naval officer. He entered the Navy in 1812 and later commanded a squadron on the slave patrol. *Appleton's*, III, 352.

6. All parts of the forts and batteries engaged in the seige and defense of Charleston. John Johnson, *The Defense of Charleston Harbor, Including Fort Sumter and the Adjacent Islands: 1863–1865.*

of the fort. The paving stones of the streets of Charleston were dropped into the harbor to make a little island for Fort Ripley to stand upon, and those of Savannah were placed as obstructions in the Savannah river (leaving the walking execrable). Fort Sumpter [*sic*] must have looked not unlike Jack the Giant's well-curb, but its basket walls are torn down to the very base upon the exposed sides, and look now like purposeless earth heaps. Under the walls were light and spacious bomb proof quarters, to which officers and men confined themselves when we shelled the fort. The new flag has been torn away in the shrouds, and the flag staff is bare. Capt. Bragg [7] of Gen. Gilmore's[8] staff, the young man who hoisted the flag, on the memorable Beecher day, is dying of hasty consumption.

We visited the race course in the city where our men were murdered, and looked into the numberless holes they dug for shelter against sun and storm. We also went into the tasteful burying ground over whose entrance are the words ''The Martyrs of the Race Course.'' Mock graves are there, but one mound tells of many graves, for there, as elsewhere in the confederate states, uncoffined bodies were piled deep in trenches. Beyond that cemetery we found Magnolia Cemetery, a very pretty, deeply shaded spot. Some of the lots have quite the air of private gardens. They are very large, and enclosed by high hedges, and suggest nothing beyond. An in-and-out and round-about pond, a live oak, worth coming to Charleston to see,

7. Henry M. Bragg, aide to General Gillmore. *Official Records of the Union and Confederate Armies,* ser. I, vol. 36, part 2, p. 473.

8. Quincy Adams Gillmore of Ohio, a graduate of West Point. He served in the expeditions against Port Royal, Fort Pulaski, and Charleston. He was in command of the X Army Corps in 1863. He was a major general in 1865. Heitman, *Register,* I, 457–458.

with strange far out-stretching limb, drooping moss, and a little high pointed chapel, that would charm Vaux;[9] all do their part to make the place attractive.

The airy grace and dainty polish of the Charleston negro is really exquisite. Now and then upon the street one meets a majestic, white-haired dame in a sweeping black cloak and white turban, who has as much power of presence as the proudest white man, in whose veins flows the blood of the Huguenot. Grace and courtesy, in both Charleston and Savannah, are characteristic of black and white alike; although the Charlestonians bear the palm supremely. Every one in the street touches his hat on being addressed, and seems proud of an opportunity of doing a small service. Our army found both cities very filthy; it sweetened Charleston, but Savannah is loathsome with filth.

The Charleston market, presided over by sweet smiling, eye-snapping "Aunties" is scrupulously neat. The stalls are small and independent. Each has back and side counters, upon which are arranged with taste, the vegetables of the season. Radishes and tomatoes keep their place still; the former are taken from the ground throughout the winter. Every stall offers entertainment to man and beast alike. I really wished to take as a bouquet, a bunch of the green oats that stand on every counter, that a horse may have for ten cents. Upon every stand are bunches of cut vegetables, prepared for soups. Slices of golden pumpkins, shooting out from a quarter of a cabbage, with perhaps a few turnips and carrots, look promising as

9. Calvert Vaux, landscape architect. He worked with Andrew J. Downing and assisted Frederick L. Olmsted in planning Central Park in New York City. *D.A.B.*, XIX, 237–238.

you may suppose, but prettier than you can think. Gold and silver, sun and snow, and the beauty of gems, are tied up in these bunches. But the great beauty of the market place lies in the fruit pyramids. These large round bunches of tasteful proportions are filled with oranges, large and small, sweet and sour, green and yellow and orange, and with many-tinted apples, as fair as ever fell, golden and red, and green, sure to be polished till they shine as if glazed; potatoes perhaps, and turnips, find a place in the pyramid, making a feast indeed to the eye.

In spite of the mass of ruins left by the destructive fire of '61; in spite of our persistent bombarding, which riddled nearly every house within a circle of two miles in the best (the lower) portion of the city; in spite of the universal broken window pane; Charleston looks sunny, peaceful and lively. A delicious straw color is the prevailing tint of the houses, many of which are disfigured by peeling stucco. All the buildings are beautified by discolorations. No glaring white disfigures the poor houses, whose gray is in harmony with the stains which spread their charms everywhere.

We were detained four days in Charleston for want of transportation to Savannah. We had a strange journey through the piney Carolinas, seeing little but pine woods and turpentine stills; reaching the towns invariably in the dark night time. We travelled all one night, and spent the most part of another on the floor of the hotel at Florence[10] (one of the worst slaughter pens of our soldiers). We tried to

10. Florence, South Carolina, on the Wilmington and Manchester Railroad at its junction with the Northeastern Railroad from Charleston. *Official Records of the Union and Confederate Armies*, Atlas, plate CXXXIX.

study out the architecture of Goldsboro,[11] but could see almost nothing there. We had an opportunity to stop for most of our meals—some of which were execrable—but at one little station a very amiable woman gave us as delicate and rich a treat as we ever ate. The hominy we see daily, everywhere. It is very delicious, made of Southern *white* corn. 'Twas more delicate and luscious (to my taste) than our Northern cracked wheat. Those who cook it choicely use a boiler somewhat like a farina boiler in which it cannot burn, and where it is cooked a good while.

Most of our travelling companions were haughty secessionists. In Petersburg, some of the leading citizens called on some southerners at our hotel who had "succeeded in finding a school that was purely southern." "I was educated in New York, I am ashamed to say," said one lady. A large body of our fellow travellers expressed the conviction that the horrors of Jamaica will be re-enacted here, unless the negroes are colonized, "they are so vindictive and cruel." A gentleman said at the hotel in Charleston, in reply to the inquiry, "How are the niggers doing with you?" "Very bad, very bad! They won't work." He did not say whether they are tempted to labor like [t]he mule, which has always before its nose, the constant prospect of a dinner of turnips; or whether they are restrained by a timid faith, unnurtured by experience.

I am afraid that many of the negroes are as unfortunately situated as the servants at the hotel in Weldon,[12] where the host apolo-

11. Goldsboro, North Carolina, on the Atlantic and North Carolina Railroad between New Berne and Raleigh. The Wilmington and Weldon crossed the A. and N.C. at Goldsboro. *Ibid.*, plate CXXXVIII.

12. Weldon, a rail junction on the Dan River north of Goldsboro. *Ibid.*, plate CXXXVIII.

gized for our cold dinner by saying, "They freed all our niggers, and now we can't get anything out of 'em; *the money's the trouble.*" That "a nigger won't work," that "they are lazy and spiled," we hear from all quarters, but few of the complaints are so honest as our landlord's. "There are a great many yankees on board, but we'll treat 'em with scorn," a certain lady said. I thought of the vanquished treating the victor with scorn! ! ! A gentleman said, "We know we must take things as they are and make the best of 'em, but our women are unconquerable; like Hannibal's mother, they teach the brats at their knees undying hatred." I heard of a lady who said recently, "We want the yankees to come here; they'll develop the resources of the country, but we'll teach our children to hate 'em." "They are lazy and we shall have them to support," is the universal cry. In the hotels and on the boat we hear that the slaves voluntarily remain with cruel master, and run away from the hired ones. "Bill Mason's slaves won't leave him, though they ca'nt tell Sunday from any other day—nor night from day neither." I think it possible that Bill Mason may think the laborer worthy of his hire; while those who seek to entice by fair words and kind manner find themselves suddenly left alone. The ladies of the South are indignant at the presence of the military force, but the gentlemen frequently express a desire that it may be retained here. They are evidently afraid that they shall get their deserts at the hands of those whom they have so grievously wronged.

General Saxton told us that some Hilton Head planters who visited him not long ago, said that they would accept any terms he might offer, if he would restore their land to them.

The General replied, "If you will set apart a very small portion for the negroes now cultivating them, making provision with them for some return, I will restore them to you." But the planters "would rather give them up entirely, than have niggers upon them," they said.

The *"Fannie"* that took us to Savannah was what might truly be called a sweet little boat.

. . . . .

We were entertained at the wharf, watching the unloading of a cotton steamer. The white driver, though seemingly kind in the main, lashed the negroes with his tongue without cresing [ceasing?], spurring them with impatient orders, to the labor from which they showed no inclination to desist; calling out frequently after this fashion, "Come on Washington, come on, come on, old hoss. Hurry up, Shanghai, hurry up, hurry up." Occasionally raising his hands threateningly as of old perhaps forgetting that the Bureau had taken the lash from his grasp! Every negro held in his hand a small iron hook; the hooks were brought into concerted play in raising the ponderous bales upon wheel-barrows, preparatory to their being wheeled ashore. A young Georgian, serving in one of the near wharf stores, brought us chairs and made himself social. He said, "Georgia can never be represented in Congress unless the form of oath is made much less rigid; because no man can say he has in no way aided the rebellion. I know for instance a strong Union man who had two sons in the Confederate service; he aided his sons, so of course he cannot say he did not aid the rebellion." Gen. Grant visited Savannah while we were there, and we visited him.

L.

(To be continued.)

A JOURNEY THROUGH THE SOUTH.
(*Concluded.*)

SAVANNAH, GA. DEC. 1865.
The city lies some feet above the river.
Wagons drive up inclined planes, and pedestrians mount stone steps to reach it. One is reminded of the quay in Montreal, by the stone-strengthened embankments. The terraces are wide grass plats and now are white with cotton, which is daily spread upon them. The women employed in picking it receive twenty-five cents a day, and the men have ten dollars a week. They are picking cotton that is damaged by water. Canvass is first spread upon the grass, and the good cotton is pulled loose and spread upon it, while the water-stained is thrown aside, to be sold for paper manufacture. At night-fall the cotton is swept into win[d]rows. "There you see our blood," said an old woman pointing to the cotton. "Three hundred weight when the sun went down or three hundred lashes sure!" said another. "They said we had no souls, that we were animals; but you north folks knew we were first cousins, and so you came down and burst the bonds of wickedness." "We are first cousins, aren't we? Didn't Adam and Eve have two sons?" "Gen. Grant is in town today, God bless him! He's next of kin to Uncle Abraham who took the wings of morning and went straight up to Glory! ! ! He took the wings of morning if 'twas morning when he died. He took wings any-how, the wings of the time, and went clean home, without any delay, or going any out of the way." "Ah! you couldn't get here by land, you had to come by water! How was it you couldn't come by land? They said you couldn't." "Two hours before Sherman

came marching across the country into our city, Mr.——said he'd lay his head on the block, if Sherman got here by land! I'd always thought about this, and wanted this day to come, and prayed for it and knew God meant it should be here sometime, but I didn't believe I should ever see it, and it is so great and good a thing, I cannot believe it has come now; and I don't believe I ever shall realize it, but I know it has though, and I bless the Lord for it,''—said an old woman.

Savannah is a very beautiful city. There are more than forty little parks in its very heart, and nearly all the streets are finely shaded. I suppose it is very natural that rural habits should become established in rural cities. We saw cows tethered in the most central parks, and cows and goats are dwellers at large in the city. *The Park,* par excellence, is on the outskirts of the city, but is easily reached by everybody. There the showily dressed ladies of Savannah, and our own officers and men, can be seen every afternoon. In the park is, I imagine, the finest fountain in the United States. Four lifesize (?) dolphins spout in the lower basin; a crane among the rushes, rises from the upper one, and jets of various forms shoot out in many directions. Tall beautiful pines shade the park, which in itself, is a lovely grove. The birds sing in Savannah; the air is sweet with many odors, the jassamine, the japan plum now in full bloom, and the delicious olive. Japonicas, of every variety, are blooming in every yard and the orange trees are heavy with fruits. A heavy snow storm, six years ago, destroyed nearly all the orange trees, in and around Savannah; still we saw many bowing under the weight of fruits. Lemon trees also, we saw, and many fruit-bearing bananas.

We became very much interested in what we could learn of the negroes upon the rice plantations near the city. An intelligent colored man, an agent of the Boston "E.C." has schools upon two or three. We proposed, if we remained in Savannah, to run back and forth daily, to some near plantations, and have a night school in the city which should be our headquarters. But Mr. E. sent for us to go to Columbia, [Columbus] and so we left at a moment's notice, closing a school which we had already opened in Savannah. Dr. Augustus,[13] a colored man, of whom you may have heard, a surgeon in the U.S. army and an elegant intelligent man, is now in charge of the "bureau" Hospital, having both black and white patients, under his care. Mrs. Child's "Linda"[14] is aiding him; and her very beautiful daughter has a school in the hospital.

We proposed running down to Florida during the Christmas holidays, and picking oranges from the river banks, as we sailed along the St. John.—Though Florida is close at hand, and though cartloads of oranges are seen in the streets, Savannah asks northern prices for single oranges. The sour oranges are but a penny a piece in Charleston and in Savannah.

13. Undoubtedly Dr. A. T. Augusta, a native of Norfolk, who received his M.D. from Toronto Medical College. He became a surgeon in the United States Army and rose to lieutenant colonel, the highest rank attained by any Negro in the Union forces. He was in charge of a hospital at Savannah and later of Freedmen's Hospital in Washington. He was a member of the medical faculty at Howard University. James H. Whyte, *The Uncivil War: Washington During the Reconstruction, 1867–1878*, p. 293.

14. "Linda" was Mrs. Harriet Brent Jacobs, author of *Incidents in the Life of a Slave Girl, written by Herself*, which was edited by Mrs. Lydia Maria Child and published in Boston in 1861. Mrs. Jacobs was a nurse during the war. In 1866 she and her daughter bought first-class steamship tickets from Savannah to New York but were put off the boat when some passengers discovered that they were part Negro, despite the fact that they were "almost white." *Freedmen's Record*, II (1866), 161.

The aroma and luscious richness of a fresh picked orange cannot be imagined.

The ladies in both Charleston and Savannah, walk through the streets, and into the churches in simple house costume; except that at the threshold like gentlemen the world over, they assume a hat. Muslin dresses and lace shawls are still worn, the grates are dark and the windows are open.

S. rebuked an old cotton-picking "auntie" for calling her fellows *niggers.* "We *are* niggers," she said. "We always was niggers, and we always shall be; nigger here, and nigger there, nigger do this, and nigger do that. We've got no souls, we are animals. We are black and so is the evil one." "That you don't know," said S. "Yes I do," she replied. "The Bible does not say the devil is black," said S. "Well, white folks say so, and we'se bound to believe 'em, cause we'se nothing but animals and niggers. Yes, we'se niggers! niggers! niggers!"

We heard most excellent music in a fine colored church. The colored churches in Charleston and Savannah are still in black for the man the negro loved so well. During service the pews look like blooming tulip gardens, so gay are they with picturesque turbans and neat white neckerchiefs. I obtained from Col. Sickles (cousin of Gen. Sickles) [15] rations for some needy old women, and requested Mrs. Jackobs ("Linda") to obtain them for an old blind woman, whom I found living very forlornly, with no one to care for her. She said to me, "My sweet beloved darling, sometimes some of 'em

15. Daniel Edgar Sickles of New York. He organized a regiment at the outset of the war and had a distinguished and controversial career. He was brevetted brigadier general for gallantry at Fredericksburg, commanded the III Army Corps, and lost a leg at Gettysburg. His maneuvers there aroused a bitter and long-continuing dispute. He was military commander of South Carolina from 1866 to 1867. W. A. Swanberg, *Sickles the Incredible.*

brings me in something to eat, and more times they don't; and 'twas just so before the Yankees came here. My folks said: 'Can't do nothing for the children, and of course shan't do for you,—you good-for-nothing.'" S. asked a smiling colored woman whose house we were passing one day, if selling children was not the principal business of the city. "It has been," she said, "but that's done away with by the goodness of God." "Why did you let the Yankees come in here?" I asked. "I wish they'd come before I was born," she replied.—— "Couldn't help it missis" is the usual reply to S.'s favorite inquiry. I suppose the poor things, —questioning our principles, keep on the safe *"don't know"* side. At "Nichols' Station," a little village in Carolina, I asked a colored boy, "What is the name of this place?" "Don't know, missis." "What is the name of the town where you live?" "Don't know." "What is the name of this place to the right here?" "Station, ma'am." He persevered and I persevered, and little came of it.

Immediately after the arrival of Sherman in Savannah, the colored people formed an educational association. They support many teachers, and maintain free schools. The principal teacher is admirably qualified; for ten years he had given lessons on the piano and organ, to black and white. All the while he has had a secret school of [one word missing] scholars, as well as many private pupils, who have kept their secret with their studies; at home. We are charmed with our Savannah cousins. They *"would* have schools, under the old regime, whether or no, in spite of the laws!" as they say, with enthusiasm.

ON THE WAY TO COLUMBUS

Last Thursday we took an early breakfast and went with our baggage to the railroad station, for Augusta, knowing before we started that we should have forty or fifty miles of staging, but having heard that the Savannah was so low that boats were sinking, we thought we would take the rails. Fifteen dollars in specie we gave for our tickets, and were told just before time for the train to start that we must pay *fifty-three dollars* for the transportation of our baggage, so we turned back to our boarding house, and set sail the next day on the "Fanny Leier" (once the General Burnside). This was at twelve o'clock last Friday, and we are still sailing (Tuesday afternoon). When we reach Columbus we shall have sailed or travelled 1861 miles since we left Boston. This river is 250 miles long, and is curiously crooked.

The river is narrow, and throughout our journey we have South Carolina close at hand on our right, and Georgia on our left. At an old fording-place between the two States, we saw a number of earth batteries and a little higher up a formidable pile of obstructions placed by the rebels in what they supposed would be Sherman's way.

For a few miles above Savannah we saw many floodgates and canals, on rice plantations. The negro houses upon the plantations were always clustered and white-washed, and looked like little villages. We passed many beautiful groves of massive live oaks, hung with Spanish moss. Forty or fifty miles above the city we saw them no more, but in their stead we saw the beautiful water oak, with narrow pointed leaves like those of the live oak, gay with maple colored tints; the gum tree, gay also; the sycamore with yellow leaves; the pines; and many vines. Tall reeds skirted the river for the first hundred miles, and they are seen occasionally elsewhere. The "landings" are innumerable; though but few could be recognized. A narrow path, and sometimes an obscured road, is all that can be seen in the wilderness. The inland dwellers sometimes come down to the shore, and wait many days for a passage. It has always been customary to accommodate single passengers.

As we approach Augusta the banks of the river are often cleared, exposing cornfields and warehouses for cotton, standing upon hills, with now and then a very comfortless looking dwelling-house, with equally cheerless inmates. Two deer swam before our boat, and wild ducks abound in the river. We have seen many high stacks of rice (like hay stacks). The boilers of the rice-mills use no full [fuel] but the chaff of the rice they grind. Rice birds (bob-o-links) sometimes settle upon acres of rice, and destroy a whole crop. When they fly away their wings make a sound like the discharge of heavy artillery. I forgot to tell you that on board the "Fannie" we met a Southern abolitionist of the noblest stamp. His mother and brother oppose him, but he has one sister on his side. A Florida gentleman asked this question, answering it himself: "Do you want to know why no Southern State has changed, or will change its laws recognizing slavery?" He replied, "It is because she will not take upon herself the responsibility of a step which promises to be so disastrous to the niggers!" Nearly every person we meet in conversation and personal treatment studiously places the negro with the brute.

L[UCY]

Columbus, Georgia
Feb. 5th 1866

Dear Mrs. May;

When I last wrote we had just opened a school at Savannah.
There were already several schools opened there and Col.
Sickles was administering the affairs of the Bureau in a
most admirable manner, so it did not seem right to tarry in
that charming city, though we could have found enough important work to fill every moment. Wishing to work where
there was the most need (there being so many places where
nothing has been done for the Freedmen, and where they
are sorely persecuted), we came here, where a school house,
built by the soldiers, had just been destroyed by the citizens
and the feeling is intensely bitter against *anything* Northern.
The affairs of the Bureau have been [f]rightfully mismanaged
here; and our Govt has been disgraced by the troops who
were stationed here. Now the troops are withdrawn, and the
people are chafing at the presence of the Bureau and "a few
pious and enthusiastic N.E. school marms:" "both must be
cleared out of the place," says the daily press.

We have never seen any discourtesy in any of the citizens,
but we know that we are generally *discussed* in circles; and
many plans are proposed for "getting rid" of us.——We have
glorious schools in full blast——And I am so satisfied with
the work here that nothing in the world could make me wish
to be in another place, or doing anything else. In my own day
school and night school, I have 140 pupils, who have made
truly wonderful progress, in the five weeks I have been teaching.

How much I wish you could see my school! A more earnest,
fine looking set of scholars could not be found—than I could
show. Wouldn't I like to grace your Academy Halls with their
presence, giving the good people a chance to talk with them
and hear their varied experiences. I find the people here more
tidy and thrifty than in any place I am acquainted with—
though many are intensely poor—and there has been nothing
given them from the North, they are always tidy, cheerful
and hopeful, ever anxious to *improve*. "How I wish I were
rich!" For the first time in my life I say it, for I have so

much need of money here. We are too far from the North to make it worth while to send any boxes here—the expense is so great—but I ought to have a purse to get an occasional flannel, or drug or splint for a broken limb or piece of bedding for some good old soul, who has "raised eight children for missus, as if they were my own; and nussed master so well, the Dr. said I saved his life;—and now I'm too old to work— I'se turned out to die like a dog." Though I have a liberal allowance from home—the expense of living is very great; and no individual purse is long enough for the absolute needs—— One dollar note is worth more to me, than a bbl which cost many dollars and much time; for with it I can get the one thing needful for the moment,—which perchance might save a life;—and forty bbls might not furnish. Accounts of the use made of monies sent would be returned.

There are a number of colored people in this place who are very well off—and they cheerfully bear their burden of the new dispensation, but in a population of about 8 thousand they can do little. I shall organize mutual relief societies in the Negro churches (Baptist and Methodist) as soon as possible. Large numbers are working for their food alone; and the white people tell them that they are not free yet. Across the river, in Alabama, several Negroes have been shot *because* they were free!

Union! I can more easily conceive of the Lion and Lambs lying down together, than of a union of the North and South. In all the counties around here, the Union familys are suffering shameful persecution, and the people do not hesitate to say that those who favor the North, shall not live in their communities. We have now with us a family who fled for their lives from their plantation—fourteen miles out——They have never owned slaves & always been loyal; and consequently the neighbors have been killing their cattle and taking their farming utensils and doing many things to make them leave their place. A few nights ago, a regular armed force from the county [country?] round threw out guards around their house, and surrounded it for the purpose of killing the whole family—but finding one of the sons absent, withdrew to decide whether to postpone it for another time or not—in the delay a part of the family escaped to the woods.

Such things are occurring the whole time; but it does not do to write North about them; for if they get in print, it gives encouragement to many communities who are ready to go and do likewise. Now the military courts are withdrawn I see no alternative for Southern Unionists, in many parts of the South, between constant persecution, and going North.

. . . . .

With ever best wishes—singing at the plough.

S.E.C.

19 W. Vernon St. Boston
Feb. 18. '66

My dear good Friends
and sometime faithful co-workers,

How refreshing it is to get your letters, one from each, of the early part of the month, seeming so like your earnest selves. We have waited long to hear from you, certain all the while that you were an inspiration, a strength and a balm to many a poor oppressed wanderer, who would bless the North for sending you to pour oil on their wounds. If you are not in the heart of rebeldom now, I don't know who is; I wish Genl. Terry [1] were there with his ready incisiveness, which brooks no such utterances as your Columbus newspaper favors you with. But you two are able to dignify your position, & look down from your serene height upon the snarling demonstrations of the whipped malcontents. Your hearts are consecrated to the service of the oppressed, & the favor of the oppressor is beneath your desire. If they cannot apprehend

1. Alfred H. Terry, a Connecticut lawyer who began his active military career at Bull Run. He served in the campaigns against Port Royal, Ft. Pulaski, and Ft. Wagner, and in 1865 Grant sent him to carry out the task which Benjamin F. Butler had failed to accomplish—the reduction of Ft. Fisher, N. C. Soon after this action Terry was promoted to major general, volunteers. He succeeded Orlando Brown as Assistant Commissioner of the Freedmen's Bureau for Virginia, serving between April and August, 1866. He supported the Radicals rather than Andrew Johnson. *D.A.B.*, XVIII, 378–379; Alderson, "Influence of Military Rule," pp. 18–19.

the consecration of soul which impels the refined & intelligent women & men of the North to go to those forbidding places & devote their talents, time & strength for the benefit of the Freedmen, at least such men as Thomas Hughes[2] can; who in a recent meeting in London, where the Duke of Argyll[3] presided, paid most enthusiastic tribute of admiration & respect to the teachers. I should be delighted to have some such Englishman come here & call on the N.E. apostles in their school-rooms, & see what fine and beautiful spirits find their chosen work in these lowly places.

. . . . .

Do you know that I am your Ma'am no longer? that all my connection with the desk at 8 Studio Bldg. has ceased? that no longer I write you thence, over the title "Sec. Com. Teac." wielding that arbitrary rule over your fates? but only from my home, as friend to friend, who for years have worked heartily together in a holy cause, & cannot separate now when one link is broken? I will tell you the story & then you will see how it is.

Last winter early, the Phila Soc. & ours joined with the new-formed Balt. Soc. that we might render them most efficient help in their early struggles to introduce educ. for the colored people into Md. This was a definite object to accomplish, & did not interfere with the individuality of either Soc. Afterward N.Y. joined. Then in Sept at a meeting of the Exec. Com. of this Union, a plan was made of a consolidation of all the Freedmen's Soc. with Bishop Simpson[4] as Pres., Frederic Law

2. Thomas Hughes, author of *Tom Brown's Schooldays* and other works, was an active and eloquent advocate of immediate emancipation of the American slaves. He was a member of the London Emancipation Society and a strong supporter of the Union cause during the war. Edward C. Mack and W. H. G. Armytage, *Thomas Hughes: the Life of the Author of Tom Brown's Schooldays.*

3. George Douglas Campbell, 8th Duke of Argyll. He and his wife, a daughter of the Duke of Sutherland, were active in various humanitarian reforms, especially abolition. They were close friends of Charles Sumner. Edward L. Pierce, *Memoirs and Letters of Charles Sumner*, III, 544–548; Argyll, Duke of, "Letters of the Duke and Duchess of Argyll to Charles Sumner [1861–1865]," Massachusetts Historical Society, *Proceedings*, Series III, XLVII (1913–14), 66–107.

4. Bishop Matthew Simpson, sometimes called "Lincoln's War Bishop." As editor of the *Western Christian Advocate*, 1848–1862, and as one of Methodism's most forceful leaders, Simpson was very influential. During the war he was on cordial terms with President Lincoln and various members of the cabinet. In

Olmstead [5] [*sic*] as Sec (who, by the way had never been consulted, & refused at once), Shipherd [6] of Chicago, the manager of the whole scheme, as Asst. Sec. & then two more Secs. E. & W. all with big salaries. With wonderful haste this thing was rushed through, & our Soc. fell in though most of its oldest members & real workers protested against such consolidation. It has been found that the support of the Office at Washington costs $1000 a month while it has done nothing for 6 months but issue useless circulars; so at the Executive meeting in N.Y. a fortnight since, it was voted to give up that part of it as useless. We who opposed it say, "We told you so before trying the foolish & costly experiment." Mr. Shipherd a smart, arbitrary lobbyist, is retained for 3 months longer to save his feelings. Now you see how this departs from the economies which have reigned in 8 Studio, where no money has been wasted that was meant for the Freemen; not a superfluous

---

1862 Secretary Stanton asked Simpson to serve as chairman of a commission which would investigate the conditions among the freedmen at Fortress Monroe, Port Royal, and New Orleans, but he declined. After the war Simpson was an aggressive leader in the effort of the Methodist Episcopal Church to take jurisdiction over the churches of the Methodist Episcopal Church, South, and assisted Bishop Edward R. Ames in persuading Secretary Stanton to issue the famous order of 1863. Robert D. Clark, *The Life of Matthew Simpson*, pp. 226, 231, 245 ff.; and *D.A.B.*, I, 242–243.

5. Olmsted's reputation as the author of books on the antebellum South has somewhat obscured other important aspects of his varied life. He was a pioneer American landscape architect, and he was chief administrative officer of the United States Sanitary Commission. He thought that the freedmen must be cared for as wards of the national government and strongly criticized the "New England belief that only the boon of freedom was necessary to render the slave industrious and provident." Broadus Mitchell, *Frederick Law Olmsted: A Critic of the Old South*, pp. 53, 58–60, and footnote 38; *D.A.B.*, XIV, 24–28. See also Laura Wood Roper, "Frederick Law Olmsted and the Port Royal Experiment," *Journal of Southern History*, XXXI (August, 1965), 272–284. Incidentally, in 1857 Olmsted became Superintendent of Central Park, New York, of which Colonel Egbert L. Viele was chief engineer.

6. Jacob R. Shipherd, a veteran abolitionist. He was a nephew of John J. Shipherd, founder of Oberlin College, and was one of the "Wellington Rescuers." He was corresponding secretary of the Northwestern Freedmen's Aid Commission of Chicago and in 1864 became district secretary of the American Missionary Association. In 1865 he went to Washington as one of Olmsted's associates; from 1866 to 1868 he was corresponding secretary of the American Missionary Association, and in 1868 he became head of the Western Department of the A.M.A. Beard, *A Crusade of Brotherhood*, pp. 134, 316; Robert S. Fletcher, *A History of Oberlin College*, II, 720, 910.

chair, or ink-stand; almost all the labor volunteer & unpaid.

But worse yet. You may have encountered the Union Commission in some of your wanderings; a Soc. to help the loyal people of the South; those contributing to it who would scorn to give of their wealth to the negro. It has professed of late to help both white and colored; I saw its work in Richmond, & know it helped 10 whites at least to one black, & it established a large number of schools there & elsewhere, to which no negro has ever been admitted. Suddenly they are smitten with such an intense love of the Freedmen that they cannot resist joining their Soc. to the great assoc. of Freedmen's Soc. The Am. Fr. Aid Com. listens blandly to the pathetic appeals. The Union Com. says "give up your name of *Freedmen,* & take ours." Mr Shipherd & some others say, aye; but that was a *little too much;* the Am. Fr. A. Com. becomes the Am. Fr. & Un. Com; & the whole thing is rushed through with indecent haste; & the N. E. Soc. informed that if they agree to it, or not, it will be done. Now when I say that Messrs Endicott, Manning, Lowe, & Pierce, Mrs Cheney, Mr & Mrs Rogers & Mrs Cabot as well as myself were wholly opposed to a Union, which should use our funds for the teaching of Southern whites as well as blacks, you will perceive there was a respectable opposition. But it was done nevertheless. I opposed the whole strenuously from the beginning, both the Unions, besides being false to our grand principle & to all our past, & to the hopes we have encouraged, I maintained that we have no right to do it, without consulting our Branch Soc. We should be false to the trust they reposed in us. But in a small meeting it was carried; the N.E.F.A. Soc. no longer exists, but is now known as the N.E. *Branch* of the Amer. Fr. & Un. Com. & the constitution is amended (?) [*sic*] by introducing "& other needy persons." "Schools without distinction of race or color."

All this drops glibly off the tongue of Cambridge Professors, amiable divines &c. Magnaminity to the South may be very good in its place—but I regard it as clear bosh; and we will see how many of the Union white schools admit black children. "Oh," says one, "they will certainly not be excluded by the force of public opinion." "And does not public opinion exclude the whites from the public schools?" rejoins Mr Brimmer. "Not the public opinion of the colored people," I reply. And the saddened letters of dear Martha Chase & Bessie Canedy, who see the work in full blast in Richmond, is the best confirmation of my opinion. I said from the first that I would not give my services to the Southern whites. I could find enough of that hue to work for in N. E., & so, with a heavy heart at what I thought so wrong, I left the Soc. that night. We have so heartily enjoyed each other on the Com. on Teachers, & worked so harmoniously, that we do not easily part; & unless I go to the Office 3 or 4 days [?] a week, summons come to me. Then I must still read all the letters of the Teachers who seem to me as my children; but I have no further responsibility, or tie to the Soc. You will see the other side in the Record, where Mr. Parkman enlightens the public on the excellent change of base. Still the work is dear to me as ever; and in occasional letters to my dear friends in their schools, I shall still enjoy something of the past. Please remember me with most cordial regard to Mr Banfield & to Miss Haven. May your work be sweet to you, as the fragrance of your 4 daily lives blesses the barbarous town of Columbus.

Aff'ly yrs

HANNAH E. STEVENSON

Columbus, Ga.
March 9th '66

My good friend,
Mr. May:

Your February letter is just received.

Letters come to hand now, to my full name; Columbus, *Georgia. Policy,* for a while, protects us from practical demonstrations of the bitter hatred that is felt for us. A leading Secessionist has probably stopped the "plots" against us, by demonstrating the injury it would be to the place, if the citizens killed or mobbed us. Many individuals have sworn to shoot us, when they get a good chance.

I am just recovering from a serious attack of inflammation of the lungs, which was the result of parting with some underclothing which I thought some one needed more that I—and that immediately.——So I have not much strength for writing. ——While sick, I would sew & write for and advise with my friends most of the time. Oh! I must tell you how useful that Leicester woolen bbl. has been. Having promised to attend to it myself & having had so much trouble in its first coming (it arriving too late for the season it had to put away for this Winter) I attempted to bring it with me but I shant tell of the expense or trouble it was in getting here—it had to stop in Savannah and was not able to reach here till last month. The moment it arrived, I cut many garments; & the next night many poor, old and extremely worthy people, blessed "Leicester hill" for the comfort they had in their flannels. Under one blanket is a pleasant faced man, without any legs, who has "no kin in the World." I shall set him up, with a street corner stand, next week:—where he can sell bonnets & cakes, which poor colored people will make who cannot leave their home dutys to sell. Another blanket is over a very much afflicted young woman and child, who was brought in from the far country, and dropt in the street, with "Now go to your friends—the Yanks—I cant be feedin you no longer." Two are over a very old couple, who had to sleep in their day clothes, with only a piece of tenting over them. I have made some sacks of the flannel, for the sick and aged to wear when they sit up in bed—in our cold hospital——

Many thanks to Mrs. May for her letter—any news is so welcome——If I was not too busy to worry—our new President's course would torment me exceedingly. If I have not lost the use of my lungs for public speaking, I fear I cannot keep from it, when the heat drives me from the South——I often find myself lecturing here, and my subject so absorbs me I do not think of myself at all, or of the audience, "sub rosa." I see by your letters that you have never received a very long letter I wrote soon after we got here. Lucy is killing herself with work—as usual—and is highly satisfied with her field. The moment our "amicable" relations to these whites is made public—our usefulness here ceases——So we do not let any statement be published——Those know who ought to know about it——The exProvisional Gov.[1] of his own accord—never having met any of us, told the citizens we were "real ladys—and however they felt, any indignity offered to us would harm the city unspeakably." The flannel and blanket are not all gone. Have confidence in my simple address. I know it will be safer than any other.

With you I will trust that a Fr. Bill [Freedmen's Bureau] will yet pass. I always talk *self dependence* to the people, and strive to show them how to "go alone," & help each other. The Bureau we *found,* made cruel contracts, and was *only* useful to the whites—no redress could the blacks find—enough that an investigation was requested; which resulted in the appointment of a new officer—a young and good man who *means* well. I can only say I know there will be no intentional wrong doing on his part. The Pulpit and Press are the only partys who openly insult us—giving the citizens leave, as it were, to do anything they please to rid themselves of our pestiferous presence. Never mind, never mind! No one more contented or happy than I——Health is all I ask—that I may carry out my plans——Our grand night schools are closed by the Govt. on account of small pox——I can't feel reconciled to it—though I shall keep all my men at work— the women [?] in their homes and shops—coming to me occasionally to give lessons ——We tell our scholars to report all cases of sickness ect [*sic*] & then we investigate. Last week I got a woman out of the woods who was living with her child—her feet frost bitten & she having nowhere to go. Today we find shelter for an infirm old man who had scooped a hole in the hill side to crawl in at night—when well he tried hard to get *"some* kind of work Missus—but everybody says *no!* you're too old to do anything—and wont let me show em what I *can* do." Trials are perplexing on every hand—but

God reigns——

With ever best wishes—
Farewell [Sarah]

1. In June 1865, President Andrew Johnson appointed James Johnson, former member of Congress from Georgia, as Provisional Governor of the state. He held the office until December 1865 when he was succeeded by C. J. Jenkins. Isaac W. Avery, *The History of the State of Georgia from 1850 to 1881*, pp. 341, 352, 354; E. Merton Coulter, *A Short History of Georgia*, pp. 340–341.

Dear Mr. May

Your welcome letter, *and* the money, came duly to hand.
Lucy paid for the bbl. with other "contraband" freight we
brought, with money she had for the purpose. In regard to
"mixed schools," I regret that I am obliged to say, not what I
think, but what I *know;* id est, they are an impossibility. I
feel confident they would be of no benefit to the blacks in Md.
Va. N.C. S.C. Ga. and Ala., consequently I cannot see how
they will work well, in any part of the South.

No one is more anxious than I that the Southern whites
should be elevated; but my life is consecrated to the blacks.

Since all are friendly to the whites, there is a certainty that
their cause will not suffer. If the few friends of the Freedmen
continue in their special field, I think they will be far better
satisfied, in the end. Enough will be done for the whites, *without* the combination, and *far less* for the blacks, will be accomplished *through* it than is now. I think no one who has been
in the field could differ from me. How long it took the enlight-
ened North to make the experiment of mixed schools a success! I am not sure that they could yet be pronounced successful except in a few districts. Think how much the South is behind the North in civilization, and how much worse the feeling
is between the whites and the blacks! Wishing well to *all* mankind, I have much desired to see a movement for the elevation
of the Southern whites: (though I feel it no duty to take part
in the work, their [*sic*] being plenty of people for it) and
have had this matter on my mind throughout my Southern life
and have talked Education and Industry to them whenever I
have met them; and on my own responsibility urged them to
go to the "Yankee Schools," knowing what a benefit it would
be to the *blacks,* to be thus associated with the whites they are
to have dealings with in future. But though the parents were
"wishing their children had the advantages the Niggers were
enjoying" they usually "would rather they'd die than go to
school with the Niggers" or they said: "I never will get so low
as to have my children learnin with nigs."

No matter how strict the rules, and wise and kind the teachers plans, for the comfort, and rights of the black scholar; the *feeling* of the whites expressed or not—*will* keep the sensitive African away; though he would willingly bear cold, hunger, and whippings if need be—to "get a little larnin." I know L. agrees with me, for she made no dissent, when I was talking on the subject last eve.

We spent yesterday on a Plantation in Ala. assembling the 75 "hands" and teaching and talking to them, giving them books and slates and showing them how to help themselves and each other. The overseer on the adjoining plantation shot a slave for saying, "Please massa, do not whip my son so—he is a man—and will work better without it." The Overseer escaped punishment because "the nigger gave him sarse."

. . . . .

There are so many I want to send to their kin. Georgia is the state where I suppose more than in any other you find large numbers of persons who are far from any kin.

Schools—most flourishing—Fine weather for all—particularly the poor. Small Pox continues to rage. L & I went to the hospital to see if the patients were properly attended to but surgeon would not admit us. We have ordered a colored person to report any thing out of the way & what is needed—sure that in some way we can meet any demand. We banded the colored people to take care of their hospital—but they are so fearful of small pox the committee will not work "until the scare is ober." I shall have a meeting this week to talk with them on Health Economy ect [sic] and will make them [?] take hold

With best wishes

S.E.C.

[Fragment of letter in Sarah's hand, with marginal note: (Sarah E. Chase, Columbus, Geo May 21, 1866. The paper cut off was Miss Chases's Receipt of our Treasurers of Ten dollars—she goes on to show how it was spent.) This is initialled, but initials are illegible.]

The money met absolute need of people who had nowhere to look for money. 1. A worn, weary woman with 11 children, and another, with three, came in one night from ten days in the woods; coming away from the plantation. "We was driv off, Misses, kase wese no account with our childer."

$1. made a nourishing soup for the party for one day & a good meat dinner for the next. 2. Carried a woman with her children & "pack" to the hospital. 3. enabled an old rheumatic man, to "get about a little to pick up jobs to earn a little to keep his old body alive—" he *could* not step on the ground without shoes, & was wholly dependent on others—while with them he takes care of himself. 4 & 5 purifications after Small Pox, for a very old woman & a blind man. 6 sent an old man, who could do nothing for himself, to his friends who will take care of him as long as he lives. 7 furnished three loaves to a sick woman with young children—whose husband finds himself free to run away from home and its duties. 8 sent a Dr. to an intense sufferer and to an old man who thought he could "knock about and get his food for the chores he could do when he got about." Both should have had attention long before, but could not affoard [*sic*] it. 9 Poor Ben is released from his suffering, which has confined him for three yrs. to his bed. Always gentle and patient, never blaming his hard master for over straining him as a dray man: after having been told by the Dr., "You'd better not let your smart little dray man lift so much alone—or you'll lose him." 10th has relieved many violent attacks among the old and poor people—curing some cases where "Missus allers use to give me whisky when I was so"—(I can give no spirits).

. . . . .

I know not if you fully understand my "white" position— though I think you do. I may not have made one point as clear as I meant to. My objection was to organizing for the whites and then taking in the blacks. I have always attempted to get whites into our schools: We have 7 now—they are the minority & harmonize well with the blacks——The same no. of blacks could not go to a white school.

We are so much engaged and interested——I cannot bear to think of having to leave and wish heartily that it was Fall instead of Summer. I would stay through the Summer were it not that the climate deprives a Northerner of strength and its no use being here if I cannot *do* anything. I believe we are to go home the 1st of July. The Drs. here say we ought not to risk staying later than June & would not dare assume the responsibility of allowing it. Lucy is just recovering from a Georgia fever, wh. brought her very low but our life is so temperate and interesting we quickly recover.

I must tell you again how wonderfully useful your woolen bbl has been. Many times a week I exclaim—"Nothing could be more pat." I cut every garment myself, that the clothing may not be wasted: & I am sure every yard will tell in lasting comfort—improved health & I have no doubt—in saving life also. With ever best wishes I must leave you for the throng at the door & at my elbow.

S.E.C.

A friend has sent my sister a very large check so we shall need no more money. I speak of Alabama—because across the river within 1/3 mile there are many people exceedingly poor— who have no friends white or black, are worse off than the people on this side & we do what we can for them.

Grafton, Aug. 30, 1866

Dear friends;

We may not meet for some time yet, as a plan I had for getting over to Worcester again to see you has failed. So I will talk with you a bit on paper. You mention Florida, Charleston & Washington. We do not include Florida in our work. In Charleston we have one school only under Arthur Sumner,[1] in which are 14 native assts. & 3 northern; two of those before there will return, perhaps three. Miss Perkins does not return to Washington; but a very able successor has had her place for many months, as Head of the school, and in a few days it will be re-opened as a thoroughly graded

---

1. Arthur S. Sumner, a native of Cambridge, Massachusetts, was a member of the Port Royal group. He became superintendent of schools in Charleston. Pearson, *Letters, passim;* Towne, *Letters,* pp. 69, 103; Rose, *Rehearsal, passim;* Johnson, *Social History,* p. 174; *Freedmen's Record,* IV (April 1868), 63–64; *American Freedman,* I (September 1866), 92.

school under Miss Smith, with 3 of the same Teachers who were there last year.

Now let me tell you just the state of our society. Owing to the immense exertions of such a thorough organization as the Am. Miss. Assoc. calling, in the name of "Orthodoxy," upon the people in every town & village to give funds to them for the Freedmen, our prospects are poorer than they ever have been before. In some cases already, where our Branch Soc. have been composed of all sects, the Unitarians alone are left to pay all which comes to our Treasury; the Calvinists and Baptists withdrawing on the circular appeals from their own sectarian leaders, to support the work of the Miss. Assoc. From the commencement of this work, we have tried to confine it as nearly as possible to teaching, instead of charity work; every year, by the agreement between the Com on Supplies & the Com on Teachers, & by the expressed desire of the Soc. we have curtailed the expenses of the former and increased those of the Com. on Teachers. The N.Y. Soc., the Phila. Soc., & the Friends everywhere have devoted themselves more to charity work. Our plan is to have none of it, that we can prevent. An appeal for it, in cases of emergency, always meets with ready response; but we do not wish to organize for our Society any such work.

. . . . .

Now the special work of you two dear laborers, is not working in the departments of a graded school, which we propose this year to make all our schools in large towns. It would be Pegasus in harness over again; but yours is, & always has been, & may it always be, to be a general blessing & inspiration by word & deed & loving presence to all the suffering Freed people within your reach. I have been running over, since your note, all availabilities for you within the scope of our work. We cannot send you, as I see, on your special mission of love & mercy to any of those cities, because that work is wholly aside from our plan. We must husband our resources for [?] up to chance for suffrage as speedily as possible, & expend all we can raise for that. On the first of July our Treasury was not only empty, but many thousands minus. An appeal was then made, & half the needed sum was raised, all of it from a few in & about Boston who have been its friends from the beginning. I see by this A.M. paper an earnest appeal for $20,000 before the 1st of Nov. as absolutely necessary

[Incomplete; evidently from Miss Stevenson]

"Burning at Sea of the Steamer *Wagner*—Letter from a Lady Passenger." [1]

The following is a private letter from a lady of Springfield, Mass., who was a passenger on board the steamer *Theo. D. Wagner*, lately burnt at sea:

My Dear——: We live to thank God for His goodness and for His Excellent kindness, though the *Theo. D. Wagner* has gone in ashes to the bottom of the sea, and has taken with it our accumulated treasure of a life-time.

On Saturday [Oct. 20, 1866], at 5 P.M., a dense smoke was seen to issue from around the smoke-pipe, and the alarm of fire created universal panic. Most of the ladies, in spite of the remonstrances of the officers, worked at one of the pumps and assisted in passing buckets of water. The fire gained rapid headway, and we were unable to get to the state rooms for life-preservers. We were absolutely calm, though we had no hope of preservation. Two sails, eight or ten miles ahead, seemed wings of promise, but the man at the wheel said: "They can see the fire, but this dead calm will keep them from us; we must try to hold together till we can get to them."

Soon after 6 o'clock they were within hailing distance, and we heard from both brig and schooner a hearty "Aye, aye, Sir," in response to the Captain's cry of "We are all afire; will you lay by and lend us a helping hand, and be ready to take our passengers, if we must leave the ship?"

At 6:30 o'clock we were ordered to take to the small boats, unburdened with the smallest parcels. We felt richer then in the sweet promise of life; but I can but wish that the nutshell, which can hold all my present material possessions, was lost, and my three colossal trunks, which I shall see no more, were in its place.

1. New York *Times,* October 28, 1866.

I walked the deck of the brigantine all the night long, not closing my eyes until 9 o'clock on Sunday morning—unwilling to take them from the majestic spectacle of our burning ship. I wanted BRADFORD [2] to share the watch with me. Two days before, I looked with awe on the grand truth-telling picture of the "Sealers Crushed by Ice." This will be a picture in my memory forever, I said to him, when I turned from it to go to our steamboat. Now my life has given me a picture—all my own—solemn and grand enough to keep that company.

This is the close of our second day on the Brigantine, and hope to reach New-York at 10 to-night. We are weak and worn —exhausted first by incessant sea sickness during our two days on the *Wagner*, and feel now great pain and prostration from our heavy work.

As I stood with the two captains watching the fire when the morning was breaking, and listening to their mutual talk of life on the sea, I was struck with their expressions of awe and horror. A timid woman's lips would have trembled no more than his (the captain's) did when he said, with his eyes on the flames, "Oh, a dreadful thing is a fire at sea!"

At 6 P. M. we spied a steamer southward bound. Our flag of distress was hoisted, and our hearts leaped with confident anticipations of being helped on our way; but the steamer passed us by, drawing near the burning wreck, but passing on without looking for floating lifeboats. We felt less regret when we saw them sail on than we should have done if we had been dependent on their mercy.

In peace and satisfaction we send you this greeting. Yours truly,

LUCY CHASE.

AT SEA. Oct. 22, 1866

2. William Bradford, a Massachusetts marine painter. His paintings of sea scenes were realistic in detail, and his work was popular in England as well as in the United States. *D.A.B.*, II, 566–567.

Dear Mr May

Through flame and flood and shipwreck I come to report. Our baggage (valued at a thousand dollars and uninsured) and the vessel which took us from Boston are a cloud in the horizon. I need not tell how this all happened, as the papers have probably told you that "Theo D. Wagner was destroyed by fire & no lives lost"——I have not reported for a long time; for there has been nothing definite to say—and now I can only tell that we *hope* to work in Charleston this Winter Deo Volente. I came home, all worn out from last years (untold) hardships;—and have had a season of agony in my chambers, from which I have made two or three attempts to be among people, but always regretted it. I kept waiting to see or hear from some of you, or to be well enough to go up to call though determined to get out if I got well enough—of course I had to wait until the way was plain.

I accepted a call to Charleston hoping to be ready when the time came—and *most* well, I started on Saturday for my field of labor—with a happy heart grateful that the good Lord was permitting me to go to my people again—forgetting my summer of pain & confinement in my joy at the prospect of being again at my work. I spent the morning before we sailed, enjoying Bradford's Iceberg—and it seemed indeed a reality as I gazed. How soon we realized the near wreck, and the far-blazing ship! I was never more calm—happy and useful—and I am as thankful for this sublime experience as of any in my lifetime. It is such a satisfaction to find that one can do just as one would wish and to feel that your calmness and control may have been instrumental in saving lives. What pleasant thoughts and visions came to me as I took the last drop into— uncertainty——The women behaved perfectly well & worked with the buckets till taken off except four ignorant women & the children who were frantic—together with one of the mates who kept up a volley of panic exciting cries, "We're all lost!!! Bilers will burst in a minute, and not a sail in sight" ect! [sic] At the first cry, I rushed to the buckets, and cast water to the last. The women formed a line and passed buckets constantly. Not till after we knew we could not save the ship did the welcome sails appear; but they had not a breeze, & our only hope was in the possibility of our boiler holding out till we could reach them. We put on full steam & rushed our flaming bark upon them——When we had been put off in the small boats, and reached the bark, the sailors said, "You've come to a poor place; we're a wreck ourselves; and out of provisions." (She had lost her galley, cabin, provisions & some rigging, in coming from Cuba, in the recent gale.) On deck, songs of thanksgiving welled from our hearts—and only our *good* fortunes presented themselves to my mind. Then I thought— how little the loved ones at home were thinking of our surroundings, or how cold, wet, hungry & tired the absent ones are! The only moment of anxiety was when I was helping a little child down the side of the boat to a young mother—with a babe in her arms——

Now the cold morning reminds me—I have nothing to make myself warmer—That *this* time we had *all* our wardrobe with us, except one good dress apiece & some common small articles, all contained in one drawer at home——Any other time we have been out we should not miss what we had with us. "We never had our wardrobe so complete & in such order, and how nice it is to have so many garments that will serve us our life time!" we said, as we were packing. This tough climax recalls the many pecuniary losses that have attended our whole Southern campaign—which we had till this ignored (together with the loss of health, risk of life & atmosphere of hate & contempt) in the entire satisfaction of our work. The last time we went South I had a carpet bag containing our united valuables & money stolen on the journey; this time there [they're?] in the trunk (what we have left) for safe keeping.

Thank God—all right! Deo Volente we take the next *chance* for Charleston, & when we get there though we can borrow linen and shoulder covering until our familys help reaches us——*If* I live, I must work *among* my people again—this Winter, for I fear the Southern people will soon have some effectual way of keeping us out of their country.

With heart's best wishes to the Leicester friends——Hoping all is well with them.

Adieu [Sarah]

My dear Lizzie

So far on our way. Sarah is not particularly fresh, and the rest is essential to her. Tomorrow we shall move on. Genl Brown has frequent interviews with Fitzhue [*sic*] Lee, Genl Joe Johnson, and Gov. Wise. The Gov. said to him, one day, "Give me my choice between the oath and arsenic and I'll take the aaarrr-ssse-nic, *Sir*." He asked if it was true that John Brown's daughter was teaching in his house, adding, "John Brown was one of the greatest men who ever lived in this country or in any other but it was my duty to hang him." He said, "I never fought under the Confederate flag. The Stars and Stripes were always my flag. I fought under the flag of Vir. and I never wore any buttons but the buttons of my own State." This afternoon we shall call on Sarah Smiley, and the teachers are coming to take tea with us. But we shall not move about much here.

. . . . .

We called at the Friends Community in Washington & at the Bureau. We only saw Genl Howard in the distance. In the cars we had our usual experience in being entertained by secessionists; who boasted of being rebels, crowed because they were going to Dixie, and one lady spent the night in singing and loud talking. . . .

Affly

LUCY

Charleston, S. C.
December 29th '66

A happy New Year! to My good friends of Leicester Hill— Hoping your Christmas has been merry; I trust the New Year will bring you God's richest blessing.

December's work is almost done; the time has been mostly occupied with school, and its duties; and I think I now understand my ground pretty well. I had been anticipating the "Holidays" as a time for mastering my position, by acquainting myself with the home life of my children; and had refused several tempting plans, that I might do so, but—sickness prevents, and I must plan, pray and hope for the New Year—in my chamber. A few of my scholars I have visited and helped to find work:—and have helped and visited a few old people. Charleston abounds in the latter; in the street you see a great many sawing wood or selling at corners:—and I have learned, by inquiry, of a great number past work: I have a long list, to visit when I can, of people near and over a hundred: Many of these will be turned into the street on New Years Day, as the white people "can not have them in their yards." Genl Scott [1] (in command; and also, head of the Bureau) is very efficient in his dutys, and will rent a house, as soon as found, for these and will build a permanent Home as soon as land suitable is found.

．　．　．　．　．

In the cold, leaking, tottering quarters of a handsome house near us, I found two women crouching and shivering over a few chips smoking in the fire place, each wrapped in a piece of Yankee blanket to which they were mostly indebted for the little comfort they had; their clothing underneath being extremely worn and thin. They were 95 and 103! years old; had worked hard all their days; and had "plenty of children in the World—some whar! If they only knew whar they'd take good care of de mudders. De folks in de big house has got only de house to eat and drink and war except what sewin de ladys kin git." From a woman who came in I learned the people in the house let them stay there and gave them weekly rations of meal; and the poor neighbors give them now and then a bit. Govt. gives no rations now (Tis right, I think) and if it did, such feeble old souls could not go for them or cook them—and the *Home* will be the place for them. I shall speak in the different colored churches about it, helping them organize committees to sustain it. I changed their bed to the warmest corner away from the "leakings"—engaged a woman to stop up the

1. Robert K. Scott, Assistant Commissioner of the Freedmen's Bureau for South Carolina, 1866–1868, and Radical governor of the state, 1868–1872. A native of Ohio, Scott was a brigadier general in 1865. *D.A.B.*, XVI, 498–499. See also Francis B. Simkins and Robert H. Woody, *South Carolina During Reconstruction*, *passim*.

chinks, and after doing a few other things for their comfort, left them, wondering how many old people there were more blest than these in temporal things, and *as* blest in spiritual. Both loved the Good Father and were sure of His loving kindness: and their faces glowed with happiness while they spake of Jesus and Death.

I wish you could visit the "Orphan's Home" and adopt a goodly number of the little ones. They could save so many steps, make such capital waiters, are such inexpensive luxuries. It seems such an easy way of doing good—and the benefit would be mutual——They are of all sizes, ages, and descriptions. I think you would *wish* you could take *several* instead of *wondering* if you *could* take one. Please consider this matter for yourselves and others. Please think if you know some one who needs a pair of little feet to run, and recommend them to send to Mrs. Pillsbury for them. Govt will forward them. Couldn't some member of the Society draw up a convincing encyclical letter, for the use of a Comm. who shall get all the "orders" they can—and will send for a number at one time?

Another chance to make one's heart warm—by giving toward a land site for the Orphanage to Mr. Tomlinson, Supt. of Edc. for S.C.[2]—a life long practical Abolitionist and a fine man. If we can get the land while the Bureau lives—Govt will build the house—and then the Charlestonians will maintain it.

Mrs. Pillsbury is the right person in the right place. I wish there were more mothers as faithful to the little ones God has given them—as she is—to these human waifs.

I have been greatly blessed in my four years of Southern life and anxiously and prayerfully anticipate the fifth. Hope

2. Reuben Tomlinson was one of the first agents sent south by the Port Royal Relief Association. He also was an officer of the American Freedmen's Union Commission. He soon became prominent in South Carolina politics. He served on General Rufus Saxton's staff, represented Charleston in the General Assembly of 1868, was State Auditor, and was a member of the state Board of Education. He was Commissioner of Education from 1865 to 1868 and was Republican candidate for governor in 1872. See Simkins and Woody, *South Carolina,* *passim;* John S. Reynolds, *Reconstruction in South Carolina,* pp. 107, 123, 225, 446-467; Rose, *Rehearsal, passim;* and Forten, *Journal,* pp. 126, 163, 184.

with me—that I may see right, act well, and accomplish *much* in this rich field of labor.

With best wishes

Farewell

S.E.C.

I am well but my sister is very ill—with something like Lung Fever.

. . . . .

[Charleston, S.C., 1866?]

[No salutation]

My sister and I have, now, afternoon and evening classes for the benefit of persons who are unable to leave work for the morning school. We have a very interesting class of young men in our evening class. "We are *moral* young men, Miss Chase," one of them said to my sister, when she expressed a hope that they made no use of tobacco or intoxicating drink. They then told us that they are all members of a "Moral improvement Assond [*sic*]." bound to good behavior, by strict rules. Ready to visit the sick, bury the dead, & to "assist" young men or young ladies. We are teaching them book keeping. We have several young men in our afternoon class who are studying book keeping.

I must tell you what I have just learned. That Gov. Orr[1] telegraphed to the Col'd political committee, asking leave to address them at their field-meeting, and they replied that he might do so, if he would first publicly endorse their platform, which is laid on strong-timbered, broadly radical resolutions. Trenholm[2] and Wagner[3] have also had permission granted them on the same terms. To Gov Orr the Commte have sent

1. James Lawrence Orr. Although he was a member of the Confederate Senate, he supported Johnson's reconstruction policies. He was elected governor in 1865. Politically able and shrewd, he attempted to persuade South Carolina whites to accept reconstruction. He supported Grant in 1872. *D.A.B.*, XIV, 59–60.

2. George A. Trenholm, Charleston merchant who served as Secretary of the Confederate Treasury. *Ibid.*, XXI, 689–690.

3. Probably John A. Wagener, commissioner of immigration for the state and mayor of Charleston. See Simkins and Woody, *South Carolina During Reconstruction*, pp. 244–246, 281.

an invitation to preside at their meeting if he will promise to endorse their platform. White men, the peers of this land, asking leave of Col'd men speak a word to them! The Gov. of the state asking leave of colored men to speak on Citadel Green! I have been told that the Citadel, which, is of course, a fortification, was built by the shoe-shaking slave-holders for a retreat in case of a slave insurrection.

I dropped my pen to attend a col'd meeting this evening. The principal speaker was a colored preacher of considerable general intelligence, a great talker, a crowd collector, a truly eloquent man, who thinks the war is over; does not believe in being ruled by the North, is for the whole country, has a right to think and speak what he pleases. Advises his people to trust no one, to join no party because it says its principles are true, to keep one eye open while they pray. Commends Congress for its reconstruction policy, but says the protection provided by Congress for the Southern states is for the benefit of the rebels, as well as of Union men. He talks long and loud of his love for his race, and great fears are entertained that through his influence a serious division may be made in the ranks of the Republican Party of the state. Yet a mighty pressure has the way to declare that he endorses, fully, the principles set forth in the platform of the U.R.P. of S.C. and that he will vote for no man for any office who does not fully endorse that platform.

Tuesday March 26th. Thousands of colored people, in one solid mass, stood, this afternoon, with upturned faces to listen to Republican speakers on Citadel Green. ''The platform'' was unanimously adopted by the crowd, who gave a hearty ''Yes'' when they were asked if they would stand upon it, if it must go down. Charleston has two other colored ministers, as intelligent as Mr Kane, and far more gifted in moral perceptions, who lift up their people with their eloquence and feeling. They both spoke on the Green, the pure white light of truth shining in their faces, God's truth on their lips, and his handwritings on their foreheads. Solon Robinson,[4] with his

---

4. Solon Robinson was agricultural editor of the New York *Tribune*. A prolific writer on agricultural subjects, Robinson was familiar with slavery and the plantation system but was not an ardent abolitionist. See Herbert Kellar's excellent introduction to *Solon Robinson: Pioneer and Agriculturist*.

silver beard and hair, raised his hands to bless an enfranchised people, and poured on that vast crowd a flood of fraternal feeling. ''Where am I!'' he exclaimed. ''I am dreaming! Will some one *pinch* me, pull my *hair,* knock me on the head. Can this be Charleston? When last I stood on this green it was to attend a great slave auction. Are you here to be sold? Well, I will sell you. I never separate families. I will not take a husband from his wife. I will not tear a child from its mother's arms; but I will put you all up together. Going—going——'' Then raising his eyes and pausing a moment, he added, ''Look above for the bidder. *It is the spirit of Abraham Lincoln!* Oh bless God that he died for you—he has bought you all! and given you to yourselves! That I should have lived to see this day! It is the happiest day of my long life! That a man from the Tribune office should be able to stand up in Charleston, and tell ten thousand colored people that they are free! Oh, Lord, now lettest thou thy servant depart in peace, for mine eyes have seen thy salvation!'' Thus said the old man, in a voice tremulous with feeling. Like a prophet he stood, giving glory to God for the fulfilment of his prophecies. Then the sun went down, and the people went to their homes. When darkness settled, they gathered again, with lighted torches, lanterns, and transparencies, and went, with bands of music, and with songs of liberty, to the houses of their prominent political men, and to those of the U.S. officers on duty here. Drinking in at every point, words of encouragement and hope, and returning thanks, in hearty cheers, for words most fitly spoken to them. Mr Cardozo[5] was called to his window, and we had the pleasure of hearing his eloquent speech, and of looking down upon the multitude. Men of intellectual force, of determined persistent effort are not wanting, here and else-

5. Francis Louis Cardozo was one of the most able and best educated Negroes in the Radical government of South Carolina. He was a free mulatto, a graduate of the University of Glasgow, and a Presbyterian minister in New Haven. At the close of the war he returned to Charleston, became active in freedmen's education, and then entered politics. He was head of the Union League in the state and served as Secretary of State and as Treasurer. After the collapse of the Radical government he became a clerk in the Treasury Department in Washington and later principal of a high school. *American Missionary*, X (April 1866), 79–80; Simkins and Woody, *South Carolina During Reconstruction*, 116–117, 546.

where, in the Southern states, to hold firmly what Congress grants them, and to lead their people from the pitfalls the Southern whites may dig for them.

[No sig., Lucy's hand]

[Charleston, S.C., 1866?]

Dear Mr. May—

Another month of hard and not unsuccessful labor is accomplished.

In that time, I have entered the hearts—of all—and the homes—of many of my children.

With few exceptions, I find the parents hardworking; very poor, and exceedingly "anxious that the children should get lernin," and willing to make any sacrifice to that end.

When I began visiting children, my escorts failed me, day after day, with remarkable forgetfulness, as I thought: but it afterwards transpired that they could not conceive of anything that should bring the teacher home, but a complaint which would bring them a "good strappin." But I found my way alone, to the—first—dismay and—final—delight of the little ones; who reported to others the "nice visit," and how glad "de mammy was to see" me;—so that a great eagerness, sprang up, for a visit; and escorts are only too ready. The children as well as parents are anxious through the first call, for the expected complaint, (!) or the request for money, (!) and it is truly amusing to see their relief, when it dawns upon them, that 'tis because I am interested in their welfare, that I have sought them out.

Most ardent and grateful letters come to me from my Georgia friends. Some write for me to find their lost ones—and I trace them, to "a gang was taken away de firs year of de war—missus; and dey wouldn't let nobody know whar to"— or to the Grave; or to their *homes;*—as was my good fortune to do, last week;—when I found the aged parents and the brother and sisters of a nice, smart woman, who wrote us from Columbus, that she knew not where one of her kin lived; and felt little hope; but wanted the satisfaction of trying to hear of them.

There are seven congregations of colored people in this city; most of them,—large and flourishing——And, to most of the people, going to Church is their highest pleasure. One church, built and paid for by freedmen, is as pretty, and home like, as I have ever seen. It is crowded three times on the Sabbath, and three times in the week with the most orderly well dressed people; who give surprising amounts of money in the constant collections that are taken there. This church has 5000 members and a fine Sunday school of 800.

I had written this far, when your letter came; and I have been waiting to report the arrival of your "goods" which have just arrived—the evening of the 14th. Just what *I want, and in perfect order.*

. . . . .

The orphanage (cold.) is not to buy a place. It is thought best to concentrate efforts towards buying a site for a permanent school for colored people. Anyone sending contributions will receive a receipt from Mr. Tomlinson, Supt of Education of S.C. Returning from school, I met a colored woman, with a bucket of oysters on her head, walking rapidly, and gesticulating drolly, as she exclaimed—"Never mind! Never mind! Bucra tief de pint from me—and dough Ise poor enough he hurt his self de most——Never mind! he tief from me—I pray for him——No! I wont put de police on em & I wont trouble em myself——I just give em to God—Poor Buckra. Live honest! Die right!" She exclaimed impressively. After I got her to tell how the white folks stole her measure—I asked her if her feeling was not vengeful. "I don't tink so, missus. Ise provoked to see em do so mean, but ever since my mammy died I'm resolved to meet her in glory——I promised her I would & I makes myself comfortable tryin to do right."

I met a very feeble old colored woman, miserably clad, in a drenching rain, a few days ago and asked her where she was going ect [*sic*]. "To de shop, missus, to buy half a pint of lasses & half a pound of flour, to make cakes to sell—to get something to keep me and my little grandchild. Wese alone in de world, with no friend but God." The poor people pay unreasonable rent for miserable quarters—and have chills & fever much—from stagnant water about their places; I show them how to drain and put things to rights about their homes.

Last week I heard three colored boys examined in Latin, who have gone this week to "Oberlin." It was very interesting to see them,—and find how thoroughly they understood what they had learned:—they were truly promising boys—leaving out their hue. Many hundred people have sailed from here to Florida—the past month——I longed to go with the poor people—I fear they must suffer much—they are going in too great numbers & without sufficient arranged plans——If I live another season—I mean to join them——I am truly glad to have *opportunitys* for colonization, for those who desire it;— but the needful wisdom for *management* is *so* rare—I can't but feel much anxiety——But the right man will appear at the right time:—he always does. And though there are many clouds around, here there rays of light break through——The day after "Nasby" [?] shows that the North ain't education up to its principles—Philadelphia street cars admit blacks— in faith that all things work together for good——

Yours truly

S.E.C.

Boston June 8, 1867.

Dear Miss Chase,

I was very glad to get your note. Indeed I did think you sincere in your inquiries after my health, & I think you were very kind to make them. I have been better, thank you, since warmer weather has come. I am always better when it is warm. All the spring I suffered dreadfully with my head. I cannot tell you what a luxury it was, for a few days of the week, not to be conscious of a head. The weather is delightfully warm,— others complained of the heat,—I *luxuriated* in it. But to-day there is a horrible east wind, & it is almost cold. So we plunge from one latitude into another in this capricious climate. I dread unspeakably spending another winter here, & if I am well enough to teach, I think I shall try to go to Florida, next year. I long to enter into the work again, & although for some reasons it would be very hard for me to leave Boston, yet I feel that I ought to go South, if I am able to teach. But the last year of my experience there taught me that it would be folly for me to attempt teaching again, anywhere, until my head should be better. Often, I was haunted by the fear of insanity, & indeed, I think I should have become insane had I continued to teach. Oh, if one could only be well! I am disgusted with myself. I feel as if my life were a failure. Not one of its long-cherished aspirations has yet been fulfilled. But enough. I fear I have rather too fully complied with your request to write about myself. Pardon me if I have wearied you.

I need not tell you, I am sure, how deeply I sympathize with you in your self-sacrificing labors, & in the discouragements, too, with which you have to contend. I know so well how manifold they are. But, dear friend, you have the noblest of compensations—the knowledge that you are giving your life to the highest ends—the regeneration of a down-trodden & long suffering people. I envy you; I who find it so hard to believe. "They also serve who only stand & wait." But do not wear yourself out. Remember that you "need the lower life to stand upon," & be prudent.—advice far easier to give, than to take—I know full well. But when one has been lectured on independence all one's life, you know, doubtless, what a luxury it is to lecture others.

I wish I could write something worth your reading, but I have been very busy this week, & am so tired that I have reached the depths of stupidity. Accept my sincere thanks for your kindness.

With kindest regards to your sister & yourself.

Very truly your friend

CHARLOTTE L. FORTEN

P. S. I forgot to say anything about the Festival. You ask if the teachers generally complain of its being too early. I have not heard the complaint made though I can understand that many have hardly time to rest! but I suppose they can be more readily gathered together then than later.

[Fragment of letter from Lucy Chase to unknown, no address.]

You probably saw the story in the papers. Genl Sickles[1] learned that the U.S. Flag was not floating over the engines, and ordered the procession not to move without it. Furthermore, he forced every man to lift his hat and pass before it after it was fixed in its place. Many men left their ranks. Some engines lacked enough men to move them, others were dragged with difficulty, and the flag received few honors. That day, and for many days, the order of Sickles was spoken of well and ill. "Pretty way to reconstruct us, to hurt our feelings in every possible way." " 'Twas a civil procession, no occasion for the U.S. Flag." "We have never been accustomed to take it in Firemen's Parade." " 'Twas merely done to humble us." As the procession passed a store in whose door way Sarah stood, she heard the storekeeper say, "See how they hang their heads. When they passed this morning they looked proud and happy; now they are ashamed to look up to their ladies." An exasperated young man in the procession tore from the Flag four stars, and as a compensation therefore was kept at public expense, for several weeks, in Castle Pinckney.

You can hardly imagine the elegant repose which filled the public mind, when the street rail-cars were forced to admit Col'd people. Sarah chanced to ride the day of the change. She was the only white person in a car filled with colored people. At every stopping place white people looked in with curiosity, but no one entered, and the conductor did not stand upon the platform to secure passengers. All the Col'd people sat quiet, seemed somewhat embarrassed; but gave no sign of thinking themselves out of place. Just after Genl Sickles welcomed Prest Johnson and party to the Carolinas,[2] and said

1. In April the fire companies of Charleston held their annual parade on Citadel Green. Sickles ordered them to carry the United States flag with a color guard. Each fireman was to salute by lifting his cap as he passed in review. The firemen protested, but Sickles was adamant, and "a storm of protest arose." Swanberg, *Sickles*, p. 287.

2. President Andrew Johnson visited North Carolina early in June 1867. He spoke at the dedication of a monument to his father at Raleigh. See Leroy P. Graf and Ralph W. Haskins, " 'This Clangor of Belated Mourning': James

in his speech, "No people could do better than the Carolinians are now doing"—some of the citizens provoked with one of the Genls new orders, said, "What does it mean? He says he is pleased with us, and yet he issues these orders." "Did you ever know a Puritan to be satisfied? I suppose they'll make a row in heaven," said the one addressed. . . .

We visited the charming ladies of the Penn F. A. Sy at Mt. Pleasant, Miss Hancock,[3] cousin of Mrs Henderson, and the Misses Taylor, nieces of Bayard Taylor.[4] Some weeks later we hired a boat to visit Fort Wagner on Morris Island, as we had promised Miss Russell, whom we met at Cousin Marcus Springs[5] that we would take to her some thing from the spot where her brother fell with Col Shaw.[6] The Island is long, bare

Russell Lowell on Andrew Johnson's Father," *South Atlantic Quarterly*, LXII (Summer 1963), 423–434. I am indebted to Professor Graf for this information.

3. Cornelia Hancock of New Jersey, an Army nurse and a teacher in freedmen's schools. She began her work as a nurse at Gettysburg and served until the end of the war. In 1866 she organized Laing School at Mount Pleasant, S. C. She died in 1929 at the age of 87. See Cornelia Hancock, *South After Gettysburg: Letters, 1863–1864*, p. 275. Miss Hancock's comments on the Misses Chase may be revealing. While visiting Reuben Tomlinson, she found at his home "Martha Schofield, the two Miss Chases, most inveterate talkers, Miss Patrick, a Hopedale enthusiast . . . all talking at full speed and I can hardly hear myself think. It is quite a pleasant change from the monotony of our home, but preserve me from it for a permanence."

4. Bayard Taylor was a popular lecturer, traveler, and author. During the war he was a Washington correspondent of the New York *Times*. Cornelia Hancock says that two of her assistants at Laing School were cousins of Bayard Taylor. Hancock, *Ibid.*, p. 221; Marie Hansen Taylor, *On Two Continents; D.A.B.*, XVIII, 314–316; and Russell H. Conwell, *Life of Bayard Taylor*.

5. Marcus Spring, a wealthy Brooklyn merchant and philanthropist, was a friend of Theodore Weld, Lydia M. Child, and other abolitionists. He, the Welds, and others founded a "radical" colony at Perth Amboy, New Jersey. The town was surveyed by Henry David Thoreau. The Springs took Margaret Fuller on her tragic journey to Europe. See Madeleine B. Stern, *The Life of Margaret Fuller*, *passim;* Mason Wade, *Margaret Fuller*, pp. 139, 170, 172; Van W. Brooks, *The Flowering of New England*, p. 440; and Benjamin P. Thomas, *Theodore Weld*, pp. 225 ff.

6. Robert Gould Shaw, a son of Francis G. Shaw and a brother-in-law of George William Curtis, Francis G. Barlow, Charles Russell Lowell, and Robert B. Minturn. He entered the Army in 1861 and was a captain in a Massachusetts infantry regiment when Governor John A. Andrew asked him to take command of the 54th Massachusetts, the famous Negro regiment which Andrew had organized. He was killed as he led his regiment in the assault on Ft. Wagner on July 18, 1863. Many prominent citizens of Massachusetts came to consider Shaw a symbol of the Union cause. Indeed, probably he "came as close to canonization as a

of trees, sandy, and ocean-washed. Many of the bodies have been taken up and reburied three or four miles from where they fell. Just before we landed a colored man was torn to pieces by the bursting of a shell from which he was trying to extract the fuse. We went also to Fort Sumter and passed the whole underground circuit of the fort. We had [sunset?] glories as a home-bound feast, and a pretty picture as we passed the Battery—a grand promenade with two water-sides.

Every Seventh-day the national band play most excellent airs on the Battery, and all the officers and their ladies —Northern people by the multitude, and Southerners in equal *profusion* gather to listen to it. The show is always fine. But want of time has made it impossible for us to see [it] but once.

A week ago we went to John's Island, where the Bureau built, a few weeks ago, a very fine house and a school-house for the Penn F.A. Society. The A.M. Society has recently bought the land upon which the houses stand, and they will probably occupy the houses. We saw a large mud cabin upon the Isd and children unclothed, though in their right minds. One large boy, with whom we had a good deal to do, wore hanging from his neck one or two black-white strings of cloth. They were given to the winds, along with his fears, most of the time. But it was very ludicrous to see him now and then lay the bits in place, only to let them fly at once again. The men— even those with books in their ha[n]ds exposed their persons very freely. We sailed through Wappo Creek and Crooked Stone river which remind us of the serpentine James—after long sailing we came so often to points already passed. Through several cuts we went, one made by "Pompey" and bearing his name, another made by the English at the time of the Revolutionary War. On the Island we visited a plantation owned by a certain Dr who lifted his hat to us, said a few courteous words—"Don't stay over night Ma'am, on account

New England Puritan can," and in 1897 an impressive monument in his honor, done by the illustrious Augustus St. Gaudens, was unveiled in Boston. *National Cyclopedia of American Biography*, VIII, 142–143; Dudley T. Cornish, *The Sable Arm: Negro Troops in the Union Army: 1861–1865*, pp. 106, 155.

of the fever. Go twelve miles to the ocean-side where it is always healthy.'' There we saw a very magnificent old live oak grove from whose far-reaching limbs the Southern moss swung in the breeze. The colored people having the new school-house always before them, fancied, of course, seeing kind-feeling written in our faces that on that occasion they saw, for the time, the N-T's before them, and so one said, ''Are you the teachers?'' ''Yes,'' I said. ''Oh, I'm so glad,'' he said. And he sparkled all over with delight.

At almost every cabin door, we had kind eager words. Of a woman in the field Sarah asked some questions, and she left her work to serve her. ''Oh, no,'' Sarah said. ''Yes, indeed,'' said the woman, ''the Yankees have done too much for me. I can't do enough for them. I shall never lose a chance to serve them.'' On board the Mt Pleasant boat a lady in black eyed us all very rudely. ''I wonder who they all are,'' she said. ''Oh I know, they are Marms. I guess those who are talking with them are Southerners. I'm glad I haven't any Northern friends. I hate the Yankees more and more, every day. *Coming down here and filling up all the places.''*

Sarah one day heard two policemen beneath our windows settling vexed ethnological problems. ''How did they happen to be black, anyway?'' one asked the other. ''Don't you know? There was two brothers, Cain and Abel. Cain killed Abel because the Lord loved Abel best, and the Lord turned him black for it, and told him he must serve all his days.'' One said to the other, at the opening of the conversation, ''We are all animals, and we are different colored just like horses. There's red horses, those are the Indians, and there's gray horses, I don't know what they stand for.——'' ''They have a right to enjoy themselves as long as they behave. I do like to sit here nights and hear them sing in church.''

On a boat again we heard a lady alluding to the recent removal of a Bureau officer, saying, ''I suppose one of the Yankee Marms got him removed because they could not bear to see white people treated as well as niggers. All the white people thought everything of him, but that did not please the marms. Every-thing was quiet and orderly while he was there; and that was not the state of things they wanted. They wanted the whites and blacks having messes all the time, so as to make a fuss, that they might raise the blacks above the whites.'' Under her breath, she added, ''I've just been in Charleston, and they do say the colored people there are going to ride in the street cars! and there's a Col'd regiment on Citadel Green; and they say we are to have a Col'd Major in Mt Pleasant.''

Want of work is a cry here. One day Sarah looked out the window and saw two colored men ride by in a cart. ''One has a job and another has a ride. . . .''

Ever affectionately

LUCY CHASE

Charleston June 25th 1867

Fairmount,[1]
July 28, '67

My dear Miss Chase—

Your very welcome letter of May 28, found me whelmed under the pressures of our anniversary week at Lexington, and tho ever since busily at work clearing up [?] old scores, and in equipping for the next campaign, still, divers unanswered letters, and much unfinished work, look reproachfully at me from stuffed pigeon-holes.

We rejoice that your five [?] year experience of the myriad trials and perils of your [illegible] have only served to quicken your earnestness, strengthen your faith, and gird you anew for your great good work.

I see that the exhausting labor & experiences of these intense years, have left their deep traces on your health, and strength, as well as on those of the thousands of our officers and soldiers.

I can well appreciate your misfortune in being unable to use your eyes without pain. At seventeen, when fitting for college, I had to exchange my books for a dark room, and thus ended my ''education'' for three years thereafter, I could not use them except in snatches. From what you say of them and of your other ailments it seems plain that they are due to the

---

1. The Weld home on the Neponset River near Boston. Benjamin Thomas, *Theodore Weld*, p. 253.

incessant over-drafts upon your reservoir of nervous power, for which perfect relaxation, rest, abundant sleep, & nutriment, (simple) cheerful society, and untaxed brain, much open air, and the sweet quiet that comes to the spirit, through that uniform trust [?] that sayeth "My Father's at the helm" are the [illegible] prescription which, doubtless, your own experience has suggested and which I trust are now doing their good work with you.

You speak of the wife of Robert Mott. Angelina and Sarah keep up communication with her through their relatives in Charleston, who, tho rampant slave holders till emancipation and still more unrepentant *rebels,* yet faithfully transmit whatever we send. The dear old soul had laid up in bank twelve hundred dollars when the rebellion broke out. The whole was swept away! With what a storm [?] of destruction has the whole South been swept, and what a cup of trembling [?] has been pressed to all our lips! God grant that these "terrible things in righteousness," may do upon us all their own work.

Angelina & Sarah write with me in earnest love and gratitude to you and your sister for your works of faith and abundant labor of love for those who have had no helper and we heartily invite you to visit us before you return to C. With cordial regards to your home circle.

Faithfully—THEO. D. WELD [2]

[1867]

My Friends trusty & good,

In Charleston we have a school very flourishing & very interesting. Arthur Sumner of Cambridge is its principal; he has eighteen assts. Of these 15 are natives, colored & white. We were to send to him in Oct. (about the 2d week) 3 skilful teachers from here, each to have charge of a floor; and had selected those who should fill that place. Two of them were in S.C. last year; Ellen Patrick, a sweet girl from Milford, and

2. Weld, the leader of the western wing of abolitionism, undoubtedly was one of the most influential of the nineteenth-century reformers. Thomas, *Weld;* Gilbert H. Barnes, *The Antislavery Impulse: 1830–1844.*

an excellent Teacher, whom Mr Sumner & Mr Tomlinson both begged to have again; & Miss Buttrick from Concord, "a whole team." Instead of sending the third, the Com. has decided, since your last letter, to send both you dear souls there to this Morris St. School, whose welfare we have much at heart.

We could not of course, separate you, & we believe you can so share the work in the Dept. of the school which will be assigned by Mr Sumner to you, that you will be *as one.* Teaching will pretty much demand & task all your energies; for it is very important in our programme that the Charleston School should be a superior one.

Our reputation has rather suffered in Charleston & we look to the Teachers whom we shall send there this year to retrieve it. We were so unfortunate, both last winter & the Spring before, as to send there some teachers, who while faithful in school, were more earnest for their own amusement at other times than for the Treasurer's good; Misses Patrick & Buttrick are not of that stamp; and we well know that the dignity of the good cause is safe intrusted to you. The N.E.& A S. must become respected in that hostile city, spite of the past.

The Bureau furnished us a house & our Teachers live together in it. Thus your family this year will be five. After consultations with Teachers & others, we have fixed the salary of the Charleston Teachers this year at forty dollars per month; & to each Teacher *returning* to work, wherever it may be, $30 is presented on leaving here.

We shall probably send the Charleston Teachers by the Boston & Chs. [?] steamer in the middle of Oct.

Are our plans agreeable to you?

Afftly yours
HANNAH E. STEVENSON

Miss Chase,

The subject of enquiry in your note is one so broad that I fear I cannot give satisfaction both from my imperfect understanding of the matter & from want of time——

When you ask "if any laws exist in any state prejudicial to the colored man?," I suppose southern states are intended—— Of course all former slave codes are prejudicial to his interests & if they have not been abolished or modified since the war, they still exist, but of course only as a *dead letter:* for such civil laws would come in direct contact with Bureau & Military requirements——South Carolina, during the past year, giving to the Negro civil rights in common with the white men——

Alabama I think has recently passed a bill establishing a system of common schools for black and white, with the proviso of a *separate attendance*——

If the black race were in possession of pecuniary means, I have no doubt they could establish as many schools as they might choose—for whatever might be the malignant desires & designs of the whites, they must give way to *Southern interests* & to the inflexible demands of the North in favor of present Justice——

As to the "usual temper & relation existing between the Freedmen & their old masters" it is growing better just as fast as want & starvation stare the masters in the face, for want of productive labor!——This one thing has brought S. Carolina to her knees! Some of her legislators advocate now, instead of the "whipping post" of former times, the building [of] school houses & churches for Freedmen, a greater leniency of feeling towards them, a forebearance with their faults, & various other *Christian virtues*—never before found in the Slaveholder's calendar!——This is ostensibly their *Creed,* but how much unfair dealing, exploitation &c— is covertly practiced, God only knows.——

You know people vary in opinions of "laws prejudicial" to the colored.——*I* think N. York state has laws prejudicial to the race—in the *property qualification* for *suffrage*——I think Pennsylvania has "laws prejudicial" when Philadelphia turns a colored man or woman from her street cars, with *violence & hate*.

I will return all flannel, unused—& beg you to receive my thanks for your kind forethought in our behalf.

Very truly

A. Y. PILLSBURY

[Matron of Shaw Orphan Asylum, Charleston]

Fort Howard

Sept 4th [1867?]

My dear Miss Chase;

I was very glad to hear from you—for, somehow, I seemed many months ago when we met to have found in you a deep and rare sympathy, one so seldom met that I cannot forget the little time we saw each other in. But the fates have kept us apart. I have heard of your pioneer work in the South, and, Mr Chase, a few days ago told me you were going to Pensacola next year. Why so far? Isn't Virginia difficult enough for you—you and your noble sister put to shame the timid manhood of the North.

The spirit expressed in Tennyson's "Ulysses" is the finest of earthy aspirations. This planting seeds of and patiently watching the slow growth of ideas among our curly headed brothers is in the long run wearisome, isn't it? But you haven't fainted yet & may you never grow weary.

Sinc yours

S. C. ARMSTRONG[1]

---

1. Samuel Chapman Armstrong, founder of Hampton Institute, was born in Hawaii of a missionary family. In 1866 he was appointed to the Freedmen's Bureau and assigned to duty at Hampton. Armstrong believed in the desirability of manual labor schools, which he had seen in Hawaii, and in 1867 he obtained the support of the American Missionary Association in establishing such a school at Hampton. *D.A.B.*, I, 359–360; Edith Armstrong Talbot, *Samuel Chapman Armstrong: a Biographical Study, passim.*

American Missionary Association, No 53 John St.,
New York, Sept 10, 1867

Miss Sarah E. Chase,
Worcester, Mass.,
Dear Madam:

Your favor of Aug. 7. did not reach us until yesterday.

You probably misunderstood Mr. Whipple[1] respecting the education of Freedmen free of expense to them. We can select fifty students for Oberlin who shall receive *free tuition*.

We are intending to open a Normal School at Hampton Va., on the Labor plan. When we know how much we are going to do there, perhaps some of these you name can be admitted. Keep them in mind and in a few months we will see what can be done for them.

I regret to hear of your illness. Yours Truly

EDWD. P. SMITH[2]

S.A.G.

Columbus Ga J. 29 [1868]

To Miss Sarah & Lucy Chase
My Dear Teacher

I take the present opportunity to write to you and you all informing you that we are all Well at this time present and doing well   I go to school to Miss Gayle and am learning quite fast   I study 3d Geography, 3d Reader 2 Arithmetic Websters Dictionary Elementary Spelling Book   Miss Gayle has 33 scholars   I live in Beall Wood, two miles north of Columbus on a large farm   the time has expired again for our Northerned Teacher to leave us   I suppose you heard of

---

1. George Whipple, professor of mathematics at Oberlin College. He held various offices in the American Missionary Association and after 1868 was virtually in charge of its work among the freedmen. Beard, *Crusade*, pp. 31, 128, 207, 316; Fletcher, *Oberlin, passim; Letters of Theodore Dwight Weld, Angelina Grimké Weld and Sarah Grimké, 1822–1844*, eds. Gilbert H. Barnes and Dwight L. Dumond, pp. 51n, 47–58.

2. Smith was in charge of all American Missionary Association work in the South immediately after the war. He was one of the founders of Fisk University. He was chosen president of Howard University in 1875. He died before taking office while inspecting A.M.A. mission points in Africa. Beard, *Crusade*, pp. 68, 134, 205; Fletcher, *Oberlin*, pp. 912, 916.

the death of Mr Ashburn   there is one good thing the Military
has taken that Case in hand another good thing our City is
now under Military law   I dont think our City has ever been
in such condition before   We have not forgotten 2 times 1 are
2 and 5 times 5 are 25   We are going to A Singing School and
Miss Gayle our Teacher also   Mr Thornton our Teacher is
going to give concerts and I wish that you and Miss Lucy
could attend   the Colored people are very anxious for you all
to come back

Miss G received A letter from you and was very glad to
hear from you   Nor have I forgot that pretty little Speller
that you gave me before you went away   Miss Gayle say that
she will write to you soon   Miss Gayle say she would like to
see you   so would I

Yours truly—DAVID BARR

Howard Grove Hospital
Richmond, Va. June. '68

My dear Miss Lowell:

I have run away from home, desperate to get where I can
reach you; and now I will talk right on, saying whatever comes
to my mind. On my way here, I walked through the streets
where black-smith's shops and stables centre, and urged the
laborers to abstinence from liquor and tobacco. Here one can
seldom urge the expense as an argument against its use, because it costs nothing to the thousands of colored-people who
are employed in the tobacco warehouses; and tobacco-lovers
outside of the warehouses find many ways of keeping up the
weed, without dropping coin in change. Yet there are many
who leave their money in cigar-shops and never learn the way
to the Freedmen's Bank.

I embrace every opportunity to suggest building up dollars
by saving pennies, and investing them singly in bank-stock.
Of course, I say that the dollar must not represent an essential
need unmet—but I say to them it is well to put money that
may be idly spent or lost where it can be found when a real
need must be met. Not many days ago I joined a bright looking working man in his walk, and asked him if he ever went

to the Temperance meetings. He said, ''Yes,'' adding that he never drinks. In reply to my question, ''Do you ever put your money into the bank?'' he said, ''Yes, I put in $35 last year; and I don't want to touch it. I want to buy some land, sometime, but not now. I want to buy when Government sells.'' ''Why do you think the govt will sell?'' I asked. ''Uncle Sam gave it out so, during the war,'' he replied with confidence and simplicity, adding, ''I served two years and a half in the war.'' I felt, all the time that I was walking by the side of a noble man. No invitation is more welcome to an intelligent colored man than this, viz. ''Come, and let us reason.'' It is pleasant, indeed, to talk with the thoughtful and earnest; to catch the serious light of their eyes, and to take counsel with them. Paying, as one does, most justly, due reverence to crude opinions, or prejudices honestly held and honestly expressed.

At one of the temperance meetings a man said, after signing the pledge, ''I'se taken the pledge tonight, not hastily, but wisely, I hope. I had a great deal of trouble, and instead of applying at the throne of grace, as I ought to have done, I thought I would seek consolation in liquor.——Its stronger than any chain. Its the worst master you ever had in your life. It'll make you sell your soul.''

One speaker said, ''Those who have made money by the sale of liquor must be made to resort to the pickaxe and the hoe.''

One very interesting speaker said his father was president of a colored temperance society formed more than thirty years ago. He said he intoxicated himself when he was five (or seven) years old, and, in shame, he next day signed the temperance pledge, which he had always kept. For some years no colored person was allowed to join the 1st African Church without having first signed the temperance pledge. The colored men love their pipe. They often say to me, ''I can give up whiskey much easier than I can tobacco.'' But instances where the unwholesomeness of both are acknowledged, and neither are used, are by no means rare. Though Parton would say, if he should look upon our numerous and busy tobacco-houses, ''It does not pay,'' we tobacco-haters are half-reconciled to their activity, because they bring present relief into so many households.

Still, we see all around us the demoralizing influence of idleness, and the depressing influence of unsuccessful clamor for remunerative work. Not a few hardworkers are growing thin and weak by trying to live on promises to pay. Still, here—as elsewhere, people with ready money leave their washing-bills unpaid; and I visit many women stooping over their washtubs, weak in body and hopeless in mind, who say, "I keeps on washin for em, for if I leave em they'll never pay me what they owe me." So wearing care and scanty food unite with their task-masters in grinding them very small. It is astonishing what light food sustains *men hard-working*. I have seen a coal-heaver sit down to a dinner of half-baked corn-bread and coffee. I have seldom seen a greedy col'd child, and I have never seen one who would not give up his dinner for almost anything that would bring him pleasure.

Children of the poorest and most distracted mothers seem to pick up certain general all-pervading ideas of neatness. In all my schools a general cry would be raised if a child should return an undrained dipper to the water-bucket. And until taught economy by the teachers few children would pass a school-mate a dipper of water to which he had put his own lips. Anything like an oath sets a whole schoolroom on fire, and if it is heard at recess, the children rush to their teacher with Oh's! and Ah's! and staring eyeballs.

I have often told you how rare it is to find a dirty colored-house. A curiosity-hunter from the North might think the neat-houses the rare ones; but to one unfamiliar with the homes of the poor, simple barreness [*sic*] and poverty express filth.

Our brightest and most advanced scholars are leaving us for the factories, and a religious revival, which has spread its wings all over the city, has shut the eyes of many at their desks. The new spirit takes the same phase in every school. The children refuse to join in the singing, are disinclined to go out at recess, and are very unwilling to lift their heads from their desks. Sometimes a child is two or three weeks in this condition, and the teacher is perplexed to learn her duty in the premises. The children are unwilling to stay away from

School; and yet their presence is unprofitable to themselves, and distracting to the others. In the majority of instances, the children fall back into their former careless, hard ways. One of my most rebellious boys, an urchin who has the past winter been dismissed from two private schools for insubordination, has been religiously inclined for some-time; but his natural surliness and unwillingness to obey have held him back. A few days ago I sent for his father, who works near my school, and told him of some special misdemeanor. I was particularly interested in the tone of the Father's condemnation. "I thought, my son, you had experienced religion! You should show in your life that you have done so. Religion will break your self-will; it will make you humble and submissive. *You* disobedient! and speaking in church as you did last night! You shall not go into the water, young man, until you *show* that you have changed. Obey your teacher. Don't use your judgment." I find that most religious col'd people demand a change of heart, and a change of life from all who are quickened by revivals.

Mr. Forester, an intelligent colored man (at whose [house?] Miss Stevenson, my sister, and I boarded, for a while, three years ago) and a leading member of a Methodist Church in this city said, in church, a short time ago, "Our children are not taught hell either in our week-day schools, or Sunday Schools." Our (Boston) ladies, some of whom heard the statement, felt that the censure was meant for them because they teach on Sundays in Mr F's school.

One morning on my way to school, I passed two or three abandoned women, who were listening with respectful and serious attention to a tall, dignified-looking woman who was showing them the better way. I stopped near the group, and heard her say, "He says come just as you are. *Does not* he," she said, appealing to me. "Come ragged, come naked, come filthy, come just as you are. I hate nobody, I only hate their ways. And I'm bound to urge everybody to love the Lord. My soul was set free long before the fetters fell from my body. God gave me *his* freedom, *but the little children of this earth would not give me theirs.* I brought religion with me into this place. I'm so glad I did, for I could not get it here."

(She keeps a small eating house in a low neighborhood.) "I want all these women to find peace. Nothing that can happen to them will trouble them if they will seek religion, not the noises, and coming and dying away of a revival, but something deep, to live by. And then they will have peace in heaven. God will say 'Sit down, your feet are sore, and rest. You'll never have to work more for a mouthful of food, or a rag of clothing.'——You are a Yankee——God sent the Yankees to Richmond. I always knew they would come. I said they would come, and I said never a gun would be fired, and no gun was fired." . . . . .

I today attended a monster baptism of two hundred and thirty persons (colored). But few of them lost their self-control. Now and then a woman would "Thank God! thank God!" with exultant emphasis. And two or three gave way to physical excitement. The officiating minister (a colored man) and the deacons checked all such demonstrations. And the minister said, after some shouting, "We shall expect that all who shout, will fall back into the ways of the world again." Thousands crowded the church as spectators, and, at times, the buzz of tongues was heard. But the vast multitude was under the ready control of the quiet, dignified preacher, when he said, "My friends, remember that this is the house of God. We are not in a theatre. Let us have *quiet*."

Judge Underwood,[1] Chief Justice Chase, and Henry A. Wise sat in front of me this morning. It was a strange sight indeed, to see H. A. Wise walk in as the companion of Cf. Jtice Chase, ——Phillips, Greeley, Charles Burleigh, and others would, perhaps say Chase hopes to employ Wise as a paving-hand on the White-house road; but I am willing to believe that their seeming intimacy indicated that Wise is turning to the right. Not long ago he said, "I will say one thing for the North, it does not mete out to us what we, as victors, should have given it. We should have disfranchised the entire people, and they would have found no mercy at our hands."

1. Judge John C. Underwood, United States District Court. For a detailed analysis of the part which Judge Underwood and Justice Salmon P. Chase played in the protracted legal struggle over the fate of Jefferson Davis, see Robert McElroy, *Jefferson Davis: the Real and the Unreal*, vol. II, *passim*.

I saw in her home, today, a very interesting colored woman, who reads the Anti-Slavery Standard with great readiness, and with understanding. She was sold from her fathers at five years of age, and he was her sole teacher. Miss Canedy found two of her boys lying on the grass the other day—reading Wendell Phillips' and Sumner's speeches. One of them asked what Charles Sumner meant when he said, "The God of Christianity is not the God of battles." "Why," said the young man, "we *always* said after a successful battle, *God* gave us the victory."

I have some classes in the "Lincoln Primer," which has a picture of freedmen dancing in honor of liberty. One day a very black, thick-lipped, broad-nosed, savage looking boy of mine (who has gone right on, with marvellous strides, from his A.B.Cs into the Second reader) made the discovery of the picture and made merry, from his woolly crown to his shambling shoes, crying out, "*So* glad they're free, dun gone and put it in a book!"

Oh, I must decline for you the verb "Dun" as I hear it daily used.

Present	*Imperfect*
I dun it	I dun dun it
You dun it	You dun dun it
He dun it	He dun dun it
We uns dun it	We uns dun dun it
They uns dun it	They uns dun dun it
You uns dun it	You uns dun dun it

Perfect	*Pluperfect*
I gone dun dun it	I dun gone done it
You gone dun dun it	You dun gone done it
He gone dun dun it	He dun gone done it
We uns gone dun dun it	We uns dun gone done it
You uns gone dun dun it	You uns dun gone done it
They uns gone dun dun it	They uns dun gone done it

First future	*Second future*
I gwine dun it	I dun gwine dun it
You gwine dun it	You dun gwine dun it
He gwine dun it	He dun gwine dun it
We uns gwine dun it	We uns dun gwine dun it
You uns gwine dun it	They uns dun gwine dun it
They uns gwine dun it	You uns dun gwine dun it [2]

2. This letter contains a marginal note: "E. E. Hale put this in his book 'Mrs. Merriams Scholars' p. 97."

One of our teachers asked a child the meaning of forget. "When you are sent for a thing to fergit fur to git it," the child replied. I wonder if I ever told you a Norfolk child's definition of irrational——"It's rational when you have rations, and irrational when you do not." I had a little imp in my school early in the winter who was known as Moses Propkins Juice. After careful inquiry, his name was found to be, "Moses, the prophet, the King of the Jews." I had in my night school, a man who persistently read Abercrombies philosophy, until I happened to think of the "Freedmen's Book," as a most refreshing substitute. He was deep in its pages when the ladies from Roxbury accidentally found their way into my school. Let me beg you to thank them for looking there again for me; and will you also state to them that I very much regretted

[end of letter missing; in Lucy's hand and style]

Normal School Va.
Oct 4th 1868

Dear Miss Chase

I will venture to send you another letter hoping you will may get it   I have not heard a word from you for the last year wich keeps me in an anxious state   Dear Miss Chase I cannot tell you how very anxious I am to hear from you—if you get this letter I will send my picture as I promise it and would like you to have one   please if we are fortunate enough to take up our corresponds again I would like very much to have a picture of you and Miss Lucy. I will give you an account of my self. I am here in virginia at school the school you wrote to tell me about paying my own way by working   the girls work in doors and the boys on the farm   the girls all have all the domestic affairs wash for the boys sow all the scrubbing to do
    there are about 14 girls and 22 boys five from Charleston
    Mr Jefferson are one of the number   I like it very much indeed   we are very comfortably fix   our chambers are neatly furnish cottage setts and every convienientcy we have water pipes in the house a baithing room.

I will tell you the rules   the bell ring at half pass five allowing us half our to dress then it ring at six for breakfast
   tha allow five minutes   if you are not there in time you are
mark   the bell ring at eleven for the boys to stop work and
fix for dinner and school   we dine at 12 clear up our dineing
room and get in school by one   we have school from one to
five and then we recrute about a half our and the bell ring for
evening prayers   after prayers we go in to supper   at half
pass seven the bell ring for us to study   we study untill half
pass 8   the bell ring for us to get ready for bed   at nine it
ring for us to out the lights. and the best of it were have such
a very kind Matron   She tries in every way to make us happy
   each schollar love her and would not be happy without her
She is a Miss Breck from Massachusetts. I hear from home
pretty often   Sarah did not come she is at home   My sisters
did not think wise for both of us to leave home   the rebs have
taken Mr Sumners school building at the corner of Morris
and Jasper Court where we spent those delightful ours in
the afternoon trying to gain kowledge   tha have it for the
Colored Children   the picture you gave I had it very neatly
frame in a guild frame   I have sent to have it here with me
   Louissia Elliott expect to come on very soon   Louissia are
one of your schollars. dear Miss Chase I am very anxious to see
you   I often wish you were here to teach   I trust I will have
the pleausure of seeing you once more. Should we not meet
on earth may we meet in heaven where parting is no more
   give my best love to Miss Lucy   tell her I will write her
next——

Good bye with a double potion of love.

Yours truly.

JULIA A. RUTLEDGE

Lake City, Jany 14 '69.

My dear Miss Lowell.

Our Christmas tree still spreads its branches. We had one
grand festival-day; but as twenty or thirty were unable, from
different causes, to be with us then, we receive visitors daily
in our holiday room. And we intend to have a singing festival

under our sweet bay-tree. We shall send far and near for those we missed on the great day, and shall also let all the children of the neighborhood come on the last day. We early found that our children had never seen a Christmas tree, and during all the days of preparation and waiting, the wonder grew, as they queried about the tree. We asked the children to guess the nature of a Christmas tree. Nearly all of them guessed it was a big dinner. One guessed "a big toy." And one or two guessed it was a tree! Those who thought the tree was a tree, acknowledged once having seen a Christmas tree "at the Post-Mistresses." With the exception of one or two who assisted us in decorating the tree, no little eyes looked on it till its lamps were lighted. And then more than eighty children marched two by two into the large room where it was planted, and passed around it, again and again, singing as they went. Although each one took from the tree whatever article most tempted him, every one revelled in the novelty and beauty of the spectacle. It was a real pleasure to look around the room before the fruit was picked, and see the joy of possession written on every face. For one moment, at least, each little heart owned all its eyes looked upon. Our tree reached the ceiling. A flag swung from the upmost bough; popped corn and red berries festooned the branches. Your dolls, and candy toys, with apples and oranges, hung near the lighted candles. It was all a beautiful vision to my little Floridians.

As I wrote to Boston, each little one saw every-thing but the oranges (sight most welcome to a New England child) for with a Lake City child, an orange on a Christmas limb, a simple orange was to him, and it was nothing more. We found our experiment of letting each child choose his own gift in every way satisfactory. In several instances we noticed a good deal of hesitation in trying to decide between a toy and a book. "But I want the book most," two or three said, and went away, looking far more satisfied for the struggle. One girl from the country chose a sack, but laid it down again as soon as she saw a "reading book." *Everybody* wanted a picture handkerchief, but one or two boys said, "I *want* a hdk, but then I *must* have this book."

You may imagine that confusion and delay must have ensued from our course. It was not so. The children, knowing they could select, used their eyes in doing so while they marched around the tree. The dolls were real heart-warmers, and even our married women (day scholars) chose tea-setts [*sic*]. The tea setts and hdkfs won universal favor. The prettiest, most refined, and most cultivated girl in Lake City, and one of our best scholars, has Prangs[1] Two Sisters (I thank you, very much, for sending Prangs beautiful pictures. I shall rejoice in knowing that they will be in homes that need them.) One of the birds we gave to a colored teacher, a gentle, delicate natured person, whose school is somewhat connected with ours. Two of the pictures will cheer two of the noblest families here. Families whose fathers are reverent and faithful Union men. One of them keeps bread on his shelves, but he says, "The people here would starve, before they would buy bread of a Republican." The other lives in crumbs, but he lives for ideas, and worships truth and justice. His daughter is a good scholar, and a lovely girl. The candy bags took everyone's fancy captive. Many chose them as a sole gift, supposing nothing could go with them. We have kept most of them upon the tree, to be given on the last day. The children still remain satisfied with their choice.

Some of the clothing has gone to a very destitute family of small children who are fatherless.

The valuable box of sewing materials is invaluable for Sewing School. I shall give the emory berries,[2] in course of time, to the deserving. One or two we gave to the tree.

I designed saying many things, but I cannot keep this sheet waiting. Every afternoon and evening brings many people, and my time for several days has been given to callers, so I will say more anon.

Yrs ever sincerely

LUCY C

1. Louis Prang, publisher and lithographer, was a native of Germany. He came to the United States in 1850 and became a successful publisher of colored lithographs, especially reproductions of masterpieces. He introduced the Christmas card into America in 1875. *D.A.B.*, XV, 165–166; Groce and Wallace, *Dictionary of Artists*, p. 514.

2. An emery ball, or "strawberry," a small bag filled with emery powder, used for keeping sewing needles sharp and clean. Mitford M. Matthews (ed.), *Dictionary of Americanisms on Historical Principles*, I, 553.

[No salutation]   [Gordonsville.Va.?, 1869?]

Yesterday I had in my own rooms a very interesting class
of men. One of them was very earnest in wishing me to read
as much as I possibly could from "General John." (The
Epistle general of John.) I imagine he thinks the word of a
Genl is a voice of authority. The col'd people hold Genl Grant
as hardly second to Lincoln. "I shall reverence him till I die,
and every colored person ought to," Mr Hume says. "Didn't
he take the yoke off my neck? And a heavy yoke it was, too.
I can't help respecting all Northern people, whether they
are good or bad, they did so much for my color." Mr Hume
is a young stage driver; enthusiastic, anxious to learn, but
not persistent; broken by the ladies who preceded me from
using tobacco and drinking whiskey. I want to tell you some
of his outloud thinking. (It was truly simple and honest).
Mr Hume was very much charmed with my friend Miss
Whittier and he frequently speaks of her with great interest.
A few days ago he said to me, "Strange that a voice should
have such an effect! I never shall forget hearing Miss Whittier
speak so pleasantly to her white mice, and when I go driving
along, I find myself saying, as she did, '*Why* don't you come
out?' I wish I was worth one hundred thousand dollars; I certainly would court Miss Whittier, as sure as you are born.
Perhaps she would feel insulted, but why should she? Ar'n't
we all human? Didn't God make us both? Some folks wouldn't
marry a white person, but I'd just as lief as to marry a
colored one. I like em just as well, if they are allright. If they
are republican. I surely *do* love her."
A col'd man, not as sober as he should be, came to me a few
days ago, and said he wished me to teach him to read and
write. "I want to get office," he said. "I want to qualify the
county." One mother who had sent her boy to me, month after
month, without tax, said when I sent to her directly for it,
"I have not a mouthful of food in the house," and the next
morning she was seen drinking a glass of whiskey at a shop
counter. I only wonder where the money comes from for the
whiskey. The Father of two of my boys had six thousand
dollars owed to him when I came to Gordonsville, and he has

built house after house since I came, but he cannot get pay for his work.

Many families earn a scanty support by taking lunches to the train but the depot agent kicks and cuffs them unmercifully and knocks their waiters from their heads. One young consumptive, in whom I felt a great deal of interest, found his way to the cars with his waiter, one day, after weeks of close confinement. He was weak, and was really unable to work, but he had a wife and babe at home, and felt proud that his weak hands could still support them. But Mr Scott overturned his waiter, scattering his provisions and breaking his crockery. The poor man has lately died. He was an eloquent eulogizer of "the North" and it was refreshing to talk with him.

I don't know whether I have told you Laura Spicers story. She was sold from her husband some years ago, and he, hearing she was dead, married again. He has had a wavering inclination to again unite his fortunes with hers; and she has been persistent in urging him to do so. A few days ago she received a letter from him in which he said, "I read your letters over and over again. I keep them always in my pocket. If you are married I don't ever want to see you again." And yet, in some of his letters, he says, "I would much rather you would get married to some good man, for every time I gits a letter from you it tears me all to pieces. The reason why I have not written you before, in a long time, is because your letters disturbed me so very much. You know I love my children. I treats them good as a Father can treat his children; and I do a good deal of it for you. I was very sorry to hear that Lewellyn, my poor little son, have had such bad health. I would come and see you but I know you could not bear it. I want to see you and I don't want to see you. I love you just as well as I did the last day I saw you, and it will not do for you and I to meet. I am married, and my wife have two children, and if you and I meets it would make a very dissatisfied family."

Some of the children are with the mother, and the father writes, "Send me some of the children's hair in a separate paper with their names on the paper. Will you please git married, as long as I am married. My dear, you know the

Lord know both of our hearts. You know it never was our wishes to be separated from each other, and it never was our fault. Oh, I can see you so plain, at any-time, I had rather anything to had happened to me most that ever have been parted from you and the children. As I am, I do not know which I love best, you or Anna. If I was to die, today or to-morrow, I do not think I would die satisfied till you tell me you will try and marry some good, smart man that will take good care of you and the children; and do it because you love me; and not because I think more of the wife I have got than I do of you. The woman is not born that feels as near to me as you do. You feel this day like myself. Tell them they must remember they have a good father and one that cares for them and one that thinks about them every day——My very heart did ache when reading your very kind and interesting letter. Laura I do not think that I have change any at all since I saw you last.——I thinks of you and my children every day of my life. Laura I do love you the same. My love to you *never* have failed. Laura, truly, I have got another wife, and I am very sorry, that I am. You feels and seems to me as much like my dear loving wife, as you ever did Laura. You know my treatment to a wife and you know how I am about my children. You know I am one man that do love my children. You will please make a [one word illegible] of the thing."

[No signature, in Lucy's hand]

Gordonsville, Decr 14th '69

Miss Lowell,

My kind, generous frd:

Excuses are said to be "lame"; but surely mine halt not; they are indeed sure footed. I am still alone! . . .

In the meantime, although my duties are onerous, I am delighted with my school. As I am alone, of course, the school is ungraded, and my classes are many; but I keep school until half past three; and, very often until four o'clock, and so I am able to add what I will call intellectual exercises to the ordinary exercises. I oblige every class to learn the meaning of all the important words in every-days reading-lessons;

and I am daily gratified by their promptness and accuracy in defining the words, when they stand in class. I appoint, every morning, one from each class as interlocutor, and I oblige the whole school to listen to all the definitions; while all who can write, put upon their slates the words in their own lessons, with the definitions thereof. Time is demanded for that exercise, but it is indeed well spent. The children, all of them, enjoy it. Most of them comprehend it, and their wits are perceptibly quickened by it. I have one class in the Fr'dm'ns Book which offers an amazing store of valuable words. I frequently call the attention of the whole school to illustrations of the meaning of familiar words. I spend a good deal of time in teaching Arithmetic both Mental and Written. Many of the children add, almost without halting, long columns of figures which I place upon the black-board, and many of them can mentally add, subtract, multiply and divide, units tens, and even hundreds, with readiness. I spend so much time upon these exercises that I can mark the improvement, which is rapid. I have three classes in Geography, and I give, daily, lessons to the whole school on Maps. All the children can navigate the Gulfs and Bays of the Globe, and they are now journeying with pleasure through the U.S., halting at the capital cities and sailing on the pleasant rivers. In addition to the defining exercise, of which I have told you, I hear the spelling and defining of the words above the reading lessons, and I also hear the whole school spell daily from a speller. Pleasant though my task is, I have all the trials that every teacher must have, who—*empty handed,* takes charge of a school that, for three previous winters, has had a rod suspended over it.

Alone, too, I keep a night school. For awhile, I kept it five nights in the week, but generally I have but three night sessions. What little time these labors leave me is industriously seized hold of by the needy and sociable, who, having no love for the rebels about them, would fain seek help from me; and give me the reverence they love to bestow on a white skin.

. . . . .

Sincerely
LUCY CHASE

244   Dear Ones at Home

My dear Miss Lowell:

Days pass swiftly by, and find and leave me treading one round. I do not close school until four o'clock, and then, on half the nights, I have night-school. I cannot resist the inspiring habit of standing while I teach, so I have little spare strength when I leave the school-room, and literally, I am never-by day—for many minutes alone. Today, two persons came, with wants to be met, before eight o'clock in the morning. Add to this the fact that I am in the country, and so am sought after more than I should be in a city, and am *alone,* so I can never be relieved by a fellow-teacher. Country-people come to have the Bible read to them. I am often asked to read and to write letters. And then so many *"Do* love to sit with the teacher and hear her talk. For somehow I can get the right understanding from you," they say. Though they never know when to go away, I *cannot* say, "Get thee hence." And then, all times are alike to the children, and some of them are sure to be at my side when I should be at rest.

The keeping of book and tax accounts, from which a teacher under a Superintendent is relieved, is a great tax on one's time. Truly, my days should be forty-eight hours long. I have now no mate to whom to say, when I wish to write, "Attend to these people, please, I must write." But my school goes on, though I am silent; and now and then some poor soul gets a *rag* of comfort from me. Today, I have put two flannels into the hands of a long-time rheumatic woman, while three sick men are already warmer made by flannels of the same pattern. Some of your warm things went to a house-hold which was stripped by fire some-time ago.

A little girl came to me, yesterday, and said, "Santa Claus gave me some candy and gingerbread in my stocking last night. I left it by the chimney." Then she added, "What do you think Miss Chase! my mother says? Only think, she says *she* 'dun' it! She *always* says so. Now, Miss Chase, tell me, don't you think it's very wrong for her to say so?" (Miss Lowell, I wonder if you would have told the little girl that her mother *was her* Santa Klaus [*sic*]? When any of my children are particularly infuriated, and desire to annihilate a com-

panion, they say, with glaring eyes, "You are a *rebel! !*"
Some time ago a colored man was put in prison for stealing
a hog; and to this day the col'd people say, "Where are his
white friends, who promised to stand by him if he'd vote
for Walker? Not one would bail him out. We knew 'twould be
just so!" (The mail says I must cover the companion sheet
tomorrow.)

Yours very truly, LUCY CHASE
Gordonsville, Vir. Feby 28th 1870

[Gordonsville, Va.]
Sunday March 10th [1870]

My dear Miss Lowell:

If I have five uninterrupted minutes this morning I shall
be amazed; but I will do my best to say a word to you before
the hour for sewing school. Just now, I find myself singing,
"Ole sheep dun know the road: Young lambs gwine to learn
the way." I wish you could hear that chorus, and see heads,
feet, and hands giving emphasis to the beautiful sentiment!
I should think its frequent repetition would draw many to
the "anxious seat." And, again, I wish you could hear wailing
voices shout the solemn inquiry, "What make poor sinners
dont pray!!? Great God listening every day!"

I wonder if I have told you of a significant talk I had, not
long ago, with the zealous but unenlightened colored minister
of Gordonsville? Mr Tibbs, the said minister, holds in high
esteem both Northern people and Northern opinions; but
mortal cannot weaken his hold on his traditions. "Miss Chase,
is there any-thing in the Bible in favor of dancing?" he
said to me one day. "There is nothing in the Bible against it,"
I said. "Doesn't it say, 'you must become a new creature and
lay aside old things,'" he said. I told him I thought each
church organization had a right to require its members to lay
aside certain harmless practices; being careful, however,
to speak of them simply as "unbecoming," not "wicked,"
as Mr Tibbs persisted in styling dancing. After much talking
on both sides Mr Tibbs inquired, "Well, Miss Chase, do you
suppose God dances?" I could not resist setting him thinking,

by saying, "Do you suppose he eats three meals a day?" I told Mr T. (of course), the legitimate objections to dancing, and made him acknowledge that raising the feet with a light, rapid motion, is in itself no more sinful than walking. "But, then, there's the fiddle, you know," he said. "But the fiddle is not wicked," I replied. "I think it is," he said. I labored hard to make him see the amount of evil that must necessarily spring from calling unsinful practices wicked. "We hide real sins by so doing. Lying, stealing, talking evil of one's neighbor, and wasting time are wicked," I ventured to say. "And, oh, don't," I said, "take your people's attention from those, by dwelling too much in your preaching upon practices which are simply unbecoming or unwise." My Sunday School (deferred through the early winter, while waiting for a Northern assistant—but appointed several weeks ago) has been sadly annihilated by church dissentions [*sic*]. Until this week the house has, for several Sundays, been closed. My school would have been unhampered if it had been exclusively a children's school; but it was specially a *grown* persons' school and I could not refuse to comply with the request to "Wait awhile."

. . . . .

I am sorry to close abruptly.

Yrs truly

LUCY CHASE

Gordonsville   March '70

. . . . .

Gordonsville va   Apr 16th 1870

Much respected Friend

I will acknowledge the note you sent me   I was much gratified to hear from you and hope to be able to hear from you again before you start on your Journey.

Mrs Esther is getting along nicely and sends her love and best wishes to you & little Emma sends lots of love and would like to see you again. We all hope for your welfare and hope you will have a pleasant Journey and to and return safely

I did not Appreciate untill now that you was so good &

I am determined to learn all I can Certainly I think you had the most Patience of any Lady I ever saw & I regret very much that I couldn't have come to School more than I did

I now have commenced to board at Mr Manns & have a much better chance to study than I did I think of you every day and will not soon forget you

You must try and write before you go on your journey

Please to excuse so short a letter and I will try and do better next time

this from a faithful friend and well wisher

Now good bye for now and may God bless and take care of you

this from MOSES HUME

[Marginal note] Miss Forten will have the kindness to put this with papers for the Misses Chase

dear Miss Lucy Chase I send Rosanna and Willis to school to obey your orders for I certainly do feel [?] you I heard that you had mighty bad schollars at that school I want you to please send me word whether Willis and Rosanna do obey you or not if they dont obey you I want you to send me word for I promised to remember them if they dont it would please me very much if you would punish them when they dont obey you I want [you] to please send me word of them at home when the trains come

CELIA COONTS

MISCELLANY

[Undated fragment, Chase manuscripts]

I left North Carolina august be fore last and I had god by my side and he helped me a long. I traveled 65 miles and we had 52 in our number. before we crost the river we could whear the pickets soods [swords] strike the stirrup and we taught we wold be taken eny moment   the babys cried and we could whear the sound of them on the wanter   we lay all night in the woods and the next day we trabeled and we reached Suffolk that night and we lost twenty one of the Number

EMMA BYNUM (BRYUM)

Charlotte Ann Jackson

When i was liveing whith White People i was tide down hand and foot and they tide me to the Post and whip me till i Could not stand up and they tide my Close over my head and whip me much as they want and they took my Brother and sent him to Richmond to stay one year And sent my Aunt my Sister my farther away too and said if he did not go away they would kill him they said they was Goin to Put me in Prisens But the light has come the Rebles is put down and Slavry is dead God Bless the union Forever more and they was puting people in tubs and they stead me to Death and i hope slavly shall be no more and they said that the yankees had horns and said that the yankees was Goin to kill us and somthing told me not to Believe them and somthing told me not to Be afraid and when they Come hare they would not let me Come out to see them and when i was out in the Street they was Stead i would go away from them and they said I Better stay whith them for the yankees would kill me I would Better stay

CHARLOTTE ANN JACKSON

[no place, no date, no address]

[no place, no date]

Guards will please pass this boy
To the Government shop;
He's in Uncle Sam's employ
So you will not say—Stop!

s.e.c.   Uncle Sam's Employee

Dear Lucy & Sarah

I send you these scissors because none of our household claims them.

I long to hear whether you got home without such fatigue as would incommode you on the next day. If you did, I shall be proud to cite you as worthy of all praise and imitation. I wish we could have such physical developments in women as should forever put to rest the phrase "weaker vessel"

as applied to our sex. You know that well bred men do not
use the words, now a 'days, as applying to the intellect of
the sex.

A. K. FOSTER

Friday morning

[An example of teaching materials; undated]
    First stands the lofty Washington
    That noble, great, immortal one!
    The elder Adams next we see
    And Jefferson counts number three
    Then Madison is fourth you know
    The fifth one on the list's Monroe
    The sixth and Adams comes again
    And Jackson seventh in the train
    Van Buren eight upon the line
    And Harrison makes number nine
    The tenth is Taylor in his turn.
    And Polk eleventh, as we learn.
    Then comes Tyler for his term of four
    The thirteenth on the list's Fillmore.
    The fourteenth and Frank Pierce came
    A drunkard whom we blush to name
    Then came Buchanan to execute the law
    Who plunged the country into civil war
    Then Abraham Lincoln, the honored & brave
    Who passed through the Red Sea his country to save
    Then Johnson came in martyred Lincoln's place
    The promised Moses of the colored race
    [Two closing versions:]
    A traitor he, a curse to our free land
    Soon in his place brave Grant shall stand
            or
    A Pharoah [sic] he thank God his reign is over
    Now Grant will take us to the promised shore!

My dear Friend,

I thank you most heartily for your good, kind & welcome letter. I should have answered it ten days ago but for a sudden pressure of proof-reading that came upon me and made a hard week's work for me, for I have just sent my last book to the press, and the printers have rushed it out at the rate of 50 pages a day, an amount which I had to correct daily. I was greatly pleased with your letter and to know that I was so kindly remembered in your home circle, in which I enjoyed so many genial hospitalities over forty years ago, and which I shall never forget. The memory of my Worcester life is very dear and very fresh to me, and I am so glad that so many are still living there who remember me kindly. An old friend of mine, Harriet E. Henshaw, has lately written me about my surviving acquaintances in Worcester, and I was rejoiced to hear that your venerable father is still living, and I can almost hear his well-remembered voice speaking to me through your letter.

And now as to your literary object in writing: I am the last man in the world to give you any information in regard to works in different languages worthy of translation that have not already appeared in English. When I first set out with an ambition to be a writer, my first and highest thought was to translate books of other languages. But a word from Dr Young, Boston, gave me a bias in a better direction. He advised me to cultivate and exercise my own language and produce thought of my own. I have followed his advice from that time to this with a somewhat satisfactory result. I would earnestly advise you to do the same—put forth your thoughts to the world in some department of literature in which you can make your mark and a healthy impression upon a large circle of readers. You will soon find out what field is most congenial with your genius.

Now in regard to myself—I am truly an invalid, having been virtually shut up within doors for five months. Early in December last I had a second and very severe attack of hemorrhage at the lungs, which lasted several days before the doctor could check it. But in the course of a few weeks I was able to come downstairs, and have been a pretty comfortable invalid ever since. I sit in my big armchair, given me nearly thirty years ago by the "Olive Leaf Sisters" in England, and read the newspapers, and sometimes I write a letter published in the N.Y. Tribune or other papers on the stirring questions of the day. I am greatly interested in the Eastern Question, as some of the Worcester readers of the Tribune may have noticed.

I am a little tired in writing a long letter, so I must now end this with my best regards to every one of your circle, and to "all inquiring friends," if such there be.

Affectionately yours,

ELIHU BURRITT [1]

---

1. Elihu Burritt, linguist and pacifist. Without the advantages of formal education, Burritt became proficient in most ancient as well as modern languages. He was an important figure in the peace movement in the United States and Europe, an advocate of compensated emancipation, and an intimate associate of many American and British reformers. *D.A.B.*, III, 328–330; Merle Curti, *The Learned Blacksmith: The Letters and Journals of Elihu Burritt, passim.*

BIBLIOGRAPHY AND INDEX

BIBLIOGRAPHY

Abel, Annie Heloise, and Frank J. Klingberg (eds.). *A Side-light on Anglo-American Relations: 1839–1858: Furnished by the Correspondence of Lewis Tappan and Others with the British and Foreign Anti-Slavery Society.* Lancaster, Pa.: The Association for the Study of Negro Life and History, Inc., 1927.

Alderson, William Thomas. "The Freedmen's Bureau in Virginia." Unpublished M.A. Thesis, Vanderbilt University, 1949.

———. "The Influence of Military Rule and the Freedmen's Bureau on Reconstruction in Virginia, 1865–1870." Unpublished Ph.D. Dissertation, Vanderbilt University, 1952.

American Freedman, April 1866–July 1869.

American Missionary Magazine, 1846–1934.

American Union Commission. *The American Union Commission: Its Origin, Operations and Purposes. Organized to Aid in the Restoration of the Union upon the Basis of Freedom, Education, and Christian Morality . . . October 1865.* New York: Sanford, Harroun & Co., 1865.

Ames, Mary. *From a New England Woman's Diary in Dixie in 1865.* Springfield, Mass.: The Plimpton Press, 1906.

Andrews, J. Cutler. *The North Reports the Civil War.* Pittsburgh: University of Pittsburgh Press, 1955.

Appleton's Cyclopaedia of American Biography, eds. James Grant Wilson and John Fiske. 8 vols. [vol. 8 ed. James E. Homans, 1918]. New York: D. Appleton and Company, 1887–89.

Argyll, Duke of. "Letters of the Duke and Duchess of Argyll to Charles Sumner [1861–1865]," Massachusetts Historical Society, *Proceedings,* Series 3, XLVII (October 1913–June 1914), 66–107. Boston: The Society, 1914.

Armstrong, Mary Frances Morgan, and Helen W. Ludlow. *Hampton and Its Students: By Two of Its Teachers.* New York: G. P. Putnam's Sons, 1875.

Avery, Isaac Wheeler, *The History of the State of Georgia from 1850 to 1881, Embracing the Three Important Epochs: The Decade before the War of 1861–5; The War; The Period of Reconstruction.* New York: Brown & Derby, 1881.

Barnes, Gilbert Hobbs. *The Antislavery Impulse: 1830–1844.* New York, London: D. Appleton-Century Company, Inc., 1933.

Battles and Leaders of the Civil War: Being for the Most Part Contributions by Union and Confederate Officers. Based Upon "The Century War Series." Eds. Robert Underwood Johnson and Clarence Clough Buel of the Editorial Staff of "The Century Magazine." 4 vols. New York: The Century Co., 1884–1888.

Beard, Augustus Field. A Crusade of Brotherhood: A History of the American Missionary Association. Boston, New York: The Pilgrim Press, 1909.

Bentley, George R. A History of the Freedmen's Bureau. Philadelphia: University of Pennsylvania, 1955.

Brant, Irving. James Madison. 4 vols. Indianapolis, New York: Bobbs-Merrill Company, 1941-48.

Brooks, Van Wyck. The Flowering of New England: 1815–1865. New York: E. P. Dutton & Co., Inc., 1936.

Brown, Ira Vernon. Lyman Abbott: Christian Evolutionist: A Study in Religious Liberalism. Cambridge: Harvard University Press, 1953.

Butler, Benjamin Franklin. Autobiography and Personal Reminiscences of Major-General Benj. F. Butler: Butler's Book. A Review of his Legal, Political, and Military Career. Boston: A. M. Thayer & Co., 1892.

————. Private and Official Correspondence of Gen. Benjamin F. Butler, during the Period of the Civil War. 5 vols. Norwood, Mass.: The Plimpton Press, 1917.

Carlyle, Thomas. The Works of Thomas Carlyle. [Edinburgh ed.] 30 vols. New York: C. Scribner's Sons, 1903–1904.

Carpenter, John Alcott. Sword and Olive Branch: Oliver Otis Howard. Pittsburgh: University of Pittsburgh Press, 1964.

Caskey, Willie Malvin. Secession and Restoration of Louisiana. Louisiana State University Studies, No. 36. University, La.: Louisiana State University Press, 1938.

Christian, William Asbury. Richmond: Her Past and Present. Richmond, Va.: L. H. Jenkins, 1912.

Clark, Robert Donald. The Life of Matthew Simpson. New York: Macmillan, 1956.

Congregationalist, 1849–1867.

Conwell, Russell Herman. The Life, Travels, and Literary Career of Bayard Taylor. Chicago, New York: The Werner Company, 1895.

Cornish, Dudley Taylor. The Sable Arm: Negro Troops in the Union Army: 1861–1865. New York: Longmans, Green, 1956.

Coulter, Ellis Merton. A Short History of Georgia. Chapel Hill: The University of North Carolina Press, 1947.

Cresap, Bernarr. "The Career of General Edward O. C. Ord to 1864." Unpublished Ph.D. Dissertation, Vanderbilt University, 1949.

Cromwell, Otelia. Lucretia Mott. Cambridge: Harvard University Press, 1958.

Cunningham, Horace Herndon. *Doctors in Gray: The Confederate Medical Service.* Baton Rouge: Louisiana State University Press, 1958.

Curti, Merle Eugene. *The Learned Blacksmith: The Letters and Journals of Elihu Burritt.* New York: Wilson-Erickson, Inc., 1937.

Davies, John D. *Phrenology: Fad and Science: A 19th-Century American Crusade.* Yale Historical Publications, Miscellany, 62. New Haven: Yale University Press, 1955.

Dictionary of American Biography, Allen Johnson, *et al.,* eds. 22 vols. New York: C. Scribner's Sons, 1928–1958.

Dictionary of American History, James Truslow Adams, ed. 5 vols. New York: C. Scribner's Sons, 1940.

Dowdey, Clifford. *The Great Plantation: A Profile of Berkeley Hundred and Plantation Virginia from Jamestown to Appomattox.* New York: Rinehart, 1957.

Drake, Richard Bryant. "The American Missionary Association and the Southern Negro, 1861–1898." Unpublished Ph.D. Dissertation, Emory University, 1957.

Dupuy, Richard Ernest, and Trevor N. Dupuy. *The Compact History of the Civil War.* New York: Hawthorn Books, 1960.

Dyer, Frederick Henry, compiler. *A Compendium of the War of the Rebellion: Comp. and Arranged from Official Records of the Federal and Confederate Armies, Reports of the Adjutant Generals of the Several States, the Army Registers, and Other Reliable Documents and Sources.* Des Moines, Ia.: The Dyer Publishing Company, 1908.

Eaton, John. *Grant, Lincoln and the Freedmen: Reminiscences of the Civil War with Special Reference to the Work for the Contrabands and Freedmen of the Mississippi Valley.* New York: Longmans, Green, and Co., 1907.

Eliot, Samuel. "Memoir of Martin Brimmer," Massachusetts Historical Society, *Proceedings,* Series II, X (1895–1896), 586–595. Boston: The Society, 1896.

The Encyclopedia Americana. 30 vols. New York: Americana Corp., 1954.

Fielding, Mantle. *Dictionary of American Painters, Sculptors, & Engravers.* New York: P. A. Struck, 1945.

Fletcher, Robert Samuel. *A History of Oberlin College from Its Foundation Through the Civil War.* 2 vols. Oberlin, Ohio: Oberlin College, 1943.

Forten, Charlotte L. *Journal,* with introduction and notes by Ray Allen Billington. New York: Dryden Press, 1953.

Freedmen's Record, 1865–1874.

Freeman, Douglas Southall. *George Washington: A Biography.* 7 vols. New York: C. Scribner's Sons, 1948–1957.

Freeman, Douglas Southall. *R. E. Lee: A Biography.* 4 vols. New York, London: C. Scribner's Sons, 1936.

French, Mrs. A. *Slavery in South Carolina and the Ex-Slaves: or, The Port Royal Mission.* New York: W. M. French, 1862.

Goodwin, William Archer Rutherfoord. *Bruton Parish Church Restored and Its Historic Environment.* Petersburg, Va.: Franklin Press Co., 1907.

Gottschalk, Louis Moreau. *Notes of a Pianist,* ed. Jeanne Behrend. New York: Alfred A. Knopf, 1964.

Graf, Leroy P., and Ralph W. Haskins. " 'This Clangor of Belated Mourning': James Russell Lowell on Andrew Johnson's Father," *South Atlantic Quarterly,* LXII (Summer 1963), 423–434.

Groce, George Cuthbert, and David H. Wallace. The New York Historical Society's *Dictionary of Artists in America: 1564–1860.* New Haven: Yale University Press, 1957.

Hancock, Cornelia. *South after Gettysburg: Letters, 1863–1868,* ed. Henrietta Stratton Jaquette. New York: T. Y. Crowell Co., 1956.

Harrington, Fred Harvey. *Fighting Politician: Mayor General N. P. Banks.* Philadelphia: University of Pennsylvania Press, 1948.

Hatch, Charles E., Jr., and Thomas M. Pitkin (eds.). *Yorktown: Climax of the Revolution.* Source Book Series, No. 1. Washington, D. C.: U.S. Department of the Interior, National Park Service, 1941.

Heitman, Francis Bernard. *Historical Register and Dictionary of the United States Army, from Its Organization, September 29, 1789, to March 2, 1903.* 2 vols. Washington, D. C.: Government Printing Office, 1903.

Herringshaw, Thomas William (ed.). *Herringshaw's Encyclopedia of American Biography of the Nineteenth Century.* Chicago, Ill.: American Publishers' Association, 1901.

Hibben, Paxton. *Henry Ward Beecher: An American Portrait.* New York: George H. Doran Company, 1927.

Higginson, Thomas Wentworth. *Army Life in a Black Regiment.* Boston: Fields, Osgood & Co., 1870.

Holzman, Robert S. *Stormy Ben Butler.* New York: Macmillan, 1954.

Howard, Oliver Otis. *Autobiography of Oliver Otis Howard, Major General, United States Army.* 2 vols. New York: The Baker & Taylor Company, 1907.

Independent, 1848–1924.

Jackson, Luther P. "The Educational Efforts of the Freedmen's Bureau and Freedmen's Aid Societies in South Carolina, 1862–1872." *The Journal of Negro History,* VIII (January 1923), 1–40.

James, Horace. *Annual Report of the Superintendent of Negro Affairs in North Carolina, 1864, with an Appendix Containing the History and Management of the Freedmen in this Department up to June 1st, 1865.* Boston: W. F. Brown & Co., [1865].

Johnson, Guion Griffis. *A Social History of the Sea Islands, with Special Reference to St. Helena Island, South Carolina.* University of North Carolina Social Study Series. Chapel Hill: The University of North Carolina Press, 1930.

Johnson, John. *The Defense of Charleston Harbor, Including Fort Sumter and the Adjacent Islands: 1863–1865.* Charleston, S. C.: Walker, Evans, & Cogswell Co., 1890.

Kellar, Herbert Anthony (ed.). *Solon Robinson: Pioneer and Agriculturist: Selected Writings.* 2 vols. Indiana Historical Collections, XXI, XXII. Indianapolis: Indiana Historical Bureau, 1936.

Lane, Wheaton Joshua. *Commodore Vanderbilt: an Epic of the Steam Age.* New York: A. A. Knopf, 1942.

Loggins, Vernon. *Where the World Ends: The Life of Louis Moreau Gottschalk.* Baton Rouge: Louisiana State University Press, 1958.

Mack, Edward Clarence, and W. H. G. Armytage. *Thomas Hughes: The Life of The Author of Tom Brown's Schooldays.* London: Benn, 1952.

Manuscripts of Lucy and Sarah Chase, American Antiquarian Society Library, Worcester, Massachusetts.

Manuscripts of the Bureau of Refugees, Freedmen, and Abandoned Lands, The National Archives, Washington, D.C.

Marsh, J. B. T. *The Story of the Jubilee Singers with Their Songs.* Rev. ed. Boston: Houghton, Osgood and Company, 1880.

Mathews, Mitford McLeod (ed.). *A Dictionary of Americanisms on Historical Principles.* 2 vols. Chicago: University of Chicago Press, 1951.

Maxwell, William Quentin. *Lincoln's Fifth Wheel: The Political History of the United States Sanitary Commission.* New York: Longmans, Green, 1956.

McElroy, Robert McNutt. *Jefferson Davis: The Real and the Unreal.* 2 vols. New York and London: Harper & Brothers, 1937.

Military Historical Society of Massachusetts. *The Peninsular Campaign of General McClellan in 1862.* Military Historical Society of Massachusetts, *Papers,* vol. I. Boston: J. R. Osgood and Co., 1881.

———. *Petersburg, Chancellorsville, Gettysburg.* Military Historical Society of Massachusetts, *Papers,* vol. V. Boston: The Society, 1906.

Mitchell, Broadus. *Frederick Law Olmsted: A Critic of the Old South.* Johns Hopkins Studies in History and Political Science, XLII, No. 2, Baltimore: The Johns Hopkins Press, 1924.

Moore, Frank (ed.). *Anecdotes, Poetry, and Incidents of the War: North and South: 1860–1865.* New York: Privately Printed, 1866.

——— (ed.). *The Rebellion Record: A Diary of American Events with Documents, Narratives, Illustrative Incidents, Poetry, etc.* 11 vols. and supplement. New York: G. P. Putnam, 1861–63; O. Van Nostrand, 1864–68.

Moore, Thomas. *The Poetical Works of Thomas Moore.* New York:

D. Appleton & Co., 1854.

Morton, Richard L. (ed.). "A 'Yankee Teacher' in North Carolina, by Margaret Newbold Thorpe." *The North Carolina Historical Review*, XXX (October 1953), 564–582.

————. " 'Contrabands' and Quakers in the Virginia Peninsula, 1862–1869," *The Virginia Magazine of History and Biography*, LXI (October 1953), 419–429.

———— (ed.). "Life in Virginia by a 'Yankee Teacher,' Margaret Newbold Thorpe." *The Virginia Magazine of History and Biography*, LXIV (April 1956), 180–207.

Nation, 1865——.

The National Cyclopaedia of American Biography, Being the History of the United States as Illustrated in the Lives of the Founders, Builders, and Defenders of the Republic and of the Men and Women Who Are Doing the Work and Moulding the Thought of the Present Time. 54 vols. New York: James T. White & Company, 1893——.

New York *Times*, 1851——.

Nutt, Charles. *History of Worcester and Its People.* 4 vols. New York: Lewis Historical Publishing Company, 1919.

Odum, Anna Kranz (ed.). "Some Negro Folk-Songs from Tennessee." *Journal of American Folklore*, XXVII (July-September 1914), 255–265.

Odum, Howard Washington. "Religious Folk Songs of the Southern Negroes." *The American Journal of Religious Psychology and Education*, III (July 1909), 265–365.

————, and Guy B. Johnson. *The Negro and His Songs: A Study of Typical Negro Songs in the South.* Hatboro, Pa.: Folklore Associates, 1964.

Osol, Arthur, George E. Farrar, *et al. The Dispensatory of the United States.* 24th ed., Philadelphia: J. B. Lippincott Company, 1947.

Parmelee, Julius H. "Freedmen's Aid Societies, 1861–1871," *Negro Education: A Study of the Private and Higher Schools for Colored People in the United States.* United States Department of the Interior, Bureau of Education, *Bulletin*, 1916, Nos. 38, 39 (2 vols.), Washington, D. C.: Government Printing Office, 1917.

Patrick, Rembert Wallace. *Jefferson Davis and His Cabinet.* Baton Rouge: Louisiana State University Press, 1944.

Paul, Howard, and George Gebbie (eds.). *The Stage and Its Stars Past and Present: A Gallery of Dramatic Illustration and Critical Biographies of Distinguished English and American Actors from the Time of Shakespeare Till To-day.* 2 vols. Philadelphia: Gebbie & Co., 189—.

Pearson, Elizabeth Ware (ed.). *Letters from Port Royal Written at the Time of the Civil War.* Boston: W. B. Clarke Company, 1906.

Pearson, Henry Greenleaf. *The Life of John A. Andrew, Governor of*

Massachusetts, 1861–1865. 2 vols. Boston and New York: Houghton, Mifflin and Company, 1904.

Pease, William H. "Three Years Among the Freedmen: William C. Gannett and the Port Royal Experiment," *The Journal of Negro History,* XLII (April 1957), 98–117.

Peirce, Paul Skeels. *The Freedmen's Bureau: A Chapter in the History of Reconstruction.* State University of Iowa, Studies in Sociology, Economics, Politics and History, Vol. III, No. 1. Iowa City: The University, 1904.

Pierce, Edward Lillie. *Memoir and Letters of Charles Sumner.* 4 vols. Boston: Roberts Brothers, 1877–93.

[Pierce, Edward Lillie]. "The Contrabands at Fortress Monroe," *Atlantic Monthly,* VIII (November 1861), 626–640.

————. "The Freedmen at Port Royal," *Atlantic Monthly,* XII (September 1863), 291–315.

Phisterer, Frederick. *Statistical Record of the Armies of the United States.* Vol. 13 of *Campaigns of the Civil War.* New York: C. Scribner's Sons, 1884.

Port Royal Correspondence, The National Archives, Washington, D.C.

Porter, David Dixon. *The Naval History of the Civil War.* New York: The Sherman Pub. Company, 1886.

Reynolds, John Schreiner. *Reconstruction in South Carolina: 1865–1877.* Columbia, S. C.: The State Co., 1905.

Roper, Laura Wood. "Frederick Law Olmsted and the Port Royal Experiment," *The Journal of Southern History,* XXXI (August 1965), 272–284.

Rose, Willie Lee Nichols. *Rehearsal for Reconstruction: The Port Royal Experiment.* Indianapolis: Bobbs-Merrill, 1964.

Schouler, William. *A History of Massachusetts in the Civil War.* 2 vols. Boston: E. P. Dutton & Co., 1868–1871.

Schuckers, Jacob W. *The Life and Public Services of Salmon Portland Chase, United States Senator and Governor of Ohio, Secretary of the Treasury, and Chief-Justice of the United States.* New York: D. Appleton and Co., 1874.

Simkins, Francis Butler, and Robert Hilliard Woody. *South Carolina during Reconstruction.* Chapel Hill: The University of North Carolina Press, 1932.

Stern, Madeleine Bettina. *The Life of Margaret Fuller.* New York: E. P. Dutton & Co., Inc., 1942.

Swanberg, W. A. *Sickles the Incredible.* New York: Scribner, 1956.

Swint, Henry Lee. *The Northern Teacher in the South: 1862–1870.* Nashville: Vanderbilt University Press, 1941.

Taft, Lorado. *The History of American Sculpture.* New York: The Macmillan Company, 1924.

Talbot, Edith Armstrong. *Samuel Chapman Armstrong: A Biographical Study.* New York: Doubleday, Page & Company, 1904.

Taylor, Alrutheus Ambush. *The Negro in the Reconstruction of Virginia.* Washington, D. C.: The Association for the Study of Negro Life and History, 1926.

Taylor, Marie Hansen. *On Two Continents: Memories of Half a Century.* New York: Doubleday, Page & Company, 1905.

Thomas, Benjamin Platt. *Theodore Weld: Crusader for Freedom.* New Brunswick: Rutgers University Press, 1950.

Towne, Laura Matilda. *Letters and Diary of Laura M. Towne: Written from the Sea Islands of South Carolina: 1862–1884,* ed. Rupert Sargent Holland. Cambridge: Riverside Press, 1912.

Trexler, Harrison Anthony. *The Confederate Ironclad "Virginia" ("Merrimac").* Chicago, Ill.: The University of Chicago Press, 1938.

U. S. Congress. *Biographical Directory of the American Congress: 1774–1927: The Continental Congress, September 5, 1774, to October 21, 1788, and The Congress of the United States from the First to the Sixty-ninth Congress, March 4, 1789, to March 3, 1927, Inclusive.* Washington, D. C.: Government Printing Office, 1928.

U. S. Congress. *Report of the Commissioner of the Bureau of Refugees, Freedman, and Abandoned Lands, December, 1865.* House Executive Document 11; 39th Congress, 1st Session. Serial 1255. Washington, D. C.: Government Printing Office, 1865.

U. S. Navy Department. *Official Records of the Union and Confederate Navies in the War of the Rebellion.* 30 vols. Washington, D. C.: Government Printing Office, 1894–1922.

U. S. War Department. *The War of the Rebellion: A Compilation of the Official Records of the Union and Confederate Armies.* 70 vols. in 128. Washington, D. C.: Government Printing Office, 1880–1901.

U. S. War Department, Corps of Engineers. "Norfolk-Beaufort Inlet Waterway, Virginia and North Carolina." *House Miscellaneous Document* 84, 59th Congress, 2nd Session. Serial 5150. Washington, D. C.: Government Printing Office, 1907.

———. "Waterway from Norfolk, Va., to Beaufort Inlet, North Carolina." *House Miscellaneous Document* 563, 58th Congress, 2nd Session. Serial 4676. [Washington, D.C.: Government Printing Office, 1904].

Virginia. *Calendar of Virginia State Papers and Other Manuscripts . . . Preserved in the Capitol at Richmond.* 11 vols. Richmond, 1875–93. [Imprint varies].

Wade, Mason. *Margaret Fuller: Whetstone of Genius.* New York: The Viking Press, 1940.

Webb, Alexander Stewart. *The Peninsula: McClellan's Campaign of 1862.* (Vol. 3 of *Campaigns of the Civil War.*) New York: C. Scribner's Sons, 1882.

Weeks, Stephen Beauregard. *Southern Quakers and Slavery: A Study in Institutional History.* Johns Hopkins University Studies in Historical and Political Science, extra vol. XV. Baltimore: The Johns Hopkins Press, 1896.

Weisberger, Bernard A. *Reporters for the Union*. Boston: Little, Brown, and Co., 1953.

Weld, Theodore Dwight. *Letters of Theodore Dwight Weld, Angelina Grimké Weld and Sarah Grimké, 1822–1844*, eds. Gilbert H. Barnes and Dwight L. Dumond. 2 vols. New York, London: D. Appleton-Century Company, Inc., 1934.

Wertenbaker, Thomas Jefferson. *Norfolk: Historic Southern Port*. Duke University Publications. Durham, N. C.: Duke University Press, 1931.

West, Richard Sedgewick. *Mr. Lincoln's Navy*. New York: Longmans, Green, 1957.

White, Newman Ivey. *American Negro Folk-Songs*. Cambridge: Harvard University Press, 1928.

Whyte, James Huntington. *The Uncivil War: Washington during the Reconstruction: 1865–1878*. New York: Twayne Publishers, 1958.

Willard, Frances Elizabeth, and Mary A. Livermore (eds.). *American Women: Fifteen Hundred Biographies with over 1,400 Portraits: A Comprehensive Encyclopedia of the Lives and Achievements of American Women during the Nineteenth Century by a Corps of Able Editors and Contributors*. 2 vols. New York, Chicago: Mast, Crowell & Kirkpatrick, 1897.

Wise, Barton Haxall. *The Life of Henry A. Wise of Virginia: 1806–1876*. New York, London: Macmillan Co., 1899.

Wistar, Isaac Jones. *Autobiography of Isaac Jones Wistar: 1827–1905: Half a Century in War and Peace*. New York and London: Harper & Brothers, 1938.

Worcester Society of Antiquity. *Collections, I, No. 5, Proceedings, 1878*. Worcester: The Society, 1879.

Worcester Society of Antiquity. *Collections, II, No. 7, Proceedings, 1879*. Worcester: The Society, 1880.

Worcester Society of Antiquity. *Collections, XII, Nos. 42–44, Worcester Births, Marriages and Deaths*, Franklin P. Rice, comp. Worcester: The Society, 1894.

Work, John Wesley. *American Negro Songs: A Comprehensive Collection of 230 Folk Songs, Religious and Secular*. New York: Howell, Soskins & Co., 1940.

Writers' Program, Virginia. *Virginia: A Guide to the Old Dominion: Compiled by Workers of the Writers' Program of the Work Projects Administration in the State of Virginia*. ("American Guide Series.") New York: Oxford University Press, 1941.

INDEX